The Harlem Renaissance

The Harlem Renaissance

The One and the Many

MARK HELBLING

Contributions in Afro-American and African Studies, Number 195

Greenwood Press
Westport, Connecticut • London

Library of Congress Cataloging-in-Publication Data

Helbling, Mark Irving, 1938–
    The Harlem renaissance : the one and the many / Mark Helbling.
      p. cm. — (Contributions in Afro-American and African
studies, ISSN 0069–9624 ; no. 195)
    Includes bibliographical references and index.
    ISBN 0–313–31047–5 (alk. paper)
    1. American literature—Afro-American authors—History and
criticism. 2. American literature—New York (State)—New York—
History and criticism. 3. American literature—20th century—
History and criticism. 4. Harlem (New York, N.Y.)—Intellectual
life—20th century. 5. Afro-Americans—Intellectual life.
6. Harlem Renaissance. I. Title. II. Series.
PS153.N5H38   1999
810.9′896073—dc21   99–16100

British Library Cataloguing in Publication Data is available.

Library of Congress Catalog Card Number: 99–16100
ISBN: 0–313–31047–5
ISSN: 0069–9624

First published in 1999

Greenwood Press, 88 Post Road West, Westport, CT 06881
An imprint of Greenwood Publishing Group, Inc.
www.greenwood.com

Printed in the United States of America

The paper used in this book complies with the
Permanent Paper Standard issued by the National
Information Standards Organization (Z39.48–1984).

10 9 8 7 6 5 4 3 2

Copyright Acknowledgments

The author and publisher gratefully acknowledge permission to quote from the following:

Quotations from letters written by Waldo Frank, Sherwood Anderson, and Jean Toomer held by the Walter H. and Leonore Annenberg Rare Book and Manuscript Library, University of Pennsylvania.

Quotations from letters written by Waldo Frank held by Jonathan W. Frank.

Quotations from letters written by Franz Boas, Carter G. Woodson, Alain Locke, Zora Neale Hurston, and Julius Rosenwald Fund held by the William S. Willis, Jr. Papers of the American Philosophical Society.

Quotations from Houston A. Baker, Jr., *Modernism and the Harlem Renaissance* (Chicago: University of Chicago Press, 1987). Used with permission of the University of Chicago Press.

Quotations from letters written by Albert C. Barnes, Alain Locke, Walter White, and Charles S. Johnson held by the Barnes Foundation.

Quotations from letters written by Ruth Benedict and Zora Neale Hurston, held by Special Collections, Vassar College Libraries, Poughkeepsie, NY.

Quotations from letters written by Ruth Benedict held by the Institute for Intercultural Studies, Inc.

Quotations from letters written by W.E.B. Du Bois and Melville Herskovits. Reprinted with permission of David G. Du Bois.

Quotations from Mark Helbling, " 'My Soul Was with the Gods and My Body in the Village': Zora Neale Hurston, Franz Boas, Melville Herskovits and Ruth Benedict." *Prospects* 22 (1997): 285–322. Reprinted with the permission of Cambridge University Press.

Quotations from Mark Helbling, " 'Feeling Universality and Thinking Particularistically': Alain Locke, Franz Boas, Melville Herskovits and the Harlem Renaissance." *Prospects* 19 (1994): 289–314. Reprinted with the permission of Cambridge University Press.

Quotations from Mark Helbling, "African Art and the Harlem Renaissance: Alain Locke, Melville Herskovits, Roger Fry, and Albert C. Barnes," in *The Critical Pragmatism of Alain Locke*, ed. Leonard Harris (Lanham, MD: Rowman and Littlefield Publishers, 1999). Reprinted with permission of Rowman and Littlefield Publishers.

Quotations from Robert E. Hemenway, *Zora Neale Hurston: A Literary Biography* (Urbana: University of Illinois Press, 1977).

Quotations from letters and other materials written by Melville Herskovits held in the Melville Herskovits Papers, Northwestern University Archives.

Reprinted by permission of the publisher from *The Harlem Renaissance in Black and White* by George Hutchinson, Cambridge, Mass.: Harvard University Press, Copyright © 1995 by the President and Fellows of Harvard College.

Quotations from a letter written by Jean Toomer held by the Joel E. Spingarn Papers, Manuscripts and Archives Division, The New York Public Library, Astor, Lenox and Tilden Foundations.

Quotations from letters written by Langston Hughes. Reprinted by permission of Harold Ober Associates Incorporated. Copyright © 1925, 1928, 1930 by Langston Hughes.

Quotations from *Tell My Horse: Voodoo and Life in Haiti and Jamaica* (New York: Harper and Row, 1990). Copyright © 1938 by Zora Neale Hurston. Copyright renewed © 1966 by Joel Hurston and John C. Hurston. Used with permission from HarperCollins Publishers.

Quotations from letters written by Charles S. Johnson. Used with permission from Patricia Johnson Clifford.

In everything that is power, interiority and expansion can be distinguished, and so also in the cognitive, governing power of the soul. . . . This profound power requires expansion, in order that it not be consumed by itself; and it requires interiority, in order that it not dissolve into airy nothingness.

Johann Gottfried von Herder, *On Knowing and Feeling,*
the Two Principal Powers of the Human Soul (1775)

I consider [the ancient problem of the "one and the many"] the most central of all philosophic problems.

William James, "The One and the Many" (1906)

My interior life was, very early, divided between the call of the Ancestors and the call of Europe, between the requirements of Negro-African culture and the requirements of modern life. These conflicts are often expressed in my poems. They are what binds them together.

Léopold Sénghor, "Interview with Armand Guibert"
in Armand Guibert, *Léopold Sédar Senghor:*
L'Homme et l'oeuvre (1962)

Ambiguous legacies, hybrid cultures.

Cornel West, *Beyond Eurocentrism*
and Multi-Culturalism (1993)

For Joan

Contents

Acknowledgments

This book has a long history; hopefully I have not overlooked those who have been of great help and inspiration. In addition to the libraries and their staffs listed under the copyright acknowledgments, I would also like to thank the University of Hawaii, which provided sabbatical leave and travel funds for research on this project, as well as the Fulbright Commission for Senior Lectureships. As a result of this support, portions of this book have been given as papers to students and scholars in Cape Town, South Africa; Abidjan, The Ivory Coast; Frankfurt, Germany; and Giverny, France. I have profited greatly from their critical reactions.

Nearer to home, I wish to thank my colleagues and students in American Studies at the University of Hawaii who have been both supportive and stimulating company. In particular, I am especially grateful to David Bertelson and Donald Worster, whose incisive criticism and imaginative cast of mind has been especially important. Invaluable, as well, has been the help of Sandy Enoki and Gerry Uveunten.

Others who have helped in one way or another deserve mention: Dan Boylan, Alan Davies, Richard and Nancy Baldwinson, Leonard Harris, David Noble, Allan Spear, Michael and Margery Taylor, and Ahmed Triquie.

I also wish to thank Maureen Melino of Greenwood Press as well as Terri Jennings and Gary Alexsiewicz, who have helped this project to reach completion. Above all, I am indebted to Bruce Kellner, whose good cheer, wise counsel, continuing support, and encyclopedic knowledge of the 1920s have been not only invaluable but a model of scholarly friendship.

Finally, and most importantly, this book would not exist without the love and support of my wife Joan and my children Robin and Joshua. The demands I have placed upon them have been enormous; hopefully this book merits their patience, their concern, and their faith.

Chapter 1

Introduction

Harlem, the Harlem of the 1920s has never been entirely absent from our minds. But one had to know where to look to keep in touch with that remarkable generation of poets, novelists, playwrights, painters, essayists, and musicians who collectively represent what is now known as the Harlem Renaissance. It has been a difficult search at best; the individuals, let alone their works, had all but vanished from view. In the 1960s, however, the American public began to discover what only a few remembered and a few others had sought to keep alive. In Harold Cruse's, *The Crisis of the Negro Intellectual* (1967), Robert Bone's, *The Negro Novel in America* (1965), and in the explosive response to the photographic exhibit "Harlem on My Mind" held at the Metropolitan Museum of Art (1969), the renaissance centered in Harlem was reborn.

Soon, most of the literature of that time and place was reissued; scholars began to comb overlooked archives and private collections; books and dissertations appeared; conferences blossomed; and universities as well as high schools began to teach the writings of Jean Toomer, Claude McKay, Zora Neale Hurston, Countee Cullen, and Langston Hughes, among others. We stand in their debt, for this scholarship has enriched our understanding, recreating a past that was too quickly neglected and too quickly forgotten. This scholarship, however, was more than the celebration of an earlier generation, for there was also a sense that what took place was flawed in its very inception and thus predetermined to be somewhat inconclusive.

Harold Cruse was one of the first to call attention to the Harlem Renaissance ("something . . . which has not been adequately dealt with in the history books") and to link this outburst of creative energy with what he argued to be the problematic cultural identity of present-day black Americans, a people "left in the limbo of social marginality, alienated and directionless on the landscape of America." Direction should come and should have come from the black intelligentsia, but, in his opinion, there were only aimless and contradictory gestures that trace back to the truncated visions of the 1920s.

The essentially original and native creative element of the nineteen twenties was the Negro ingredient—as all the whites who were running to Harlem actually knew. But the Harlem intellectuals were so overwhelmed at being "discovered" and courted that they allowed a bona fide cultural movement . . . to degenerate into a pampered and paternalized vogue.[1]

Thus, a unique historic opportunity to forge the cultural and intellectual identity of black Americans was missed. Equally important, Cruse argues, these cultural stirrings mark "a twentieth century harbinger of the African awakening in political and cultural terms."[2] That this clarification failed to take place, however, was the movement's greatest failure and has been the burden subsequent generations have continued to bear.

Elements of Cruse's analysis inform Nathan Huggins's *Harlem Renaissance* (1971). In particular, Huggins sees reenacted on this newly constructed urban stage deeply rooted patterns dictated by those with power and wealth:

As long as the white norms remained unchallenged, no matter what the Negro's reaction to them, he always needed to return to the white judge to measure his achievement. It would have required a much more profound rejection of white values than was likely in the 1920s for Negroes to have freed themselves for creating the desired self-generating and self-confident Negro art.[3]

Rather than a bright new beginning, the renaissance was profoundly conservative, best understood as an updated minstrel show staged by whites. However, whereas Cruse challenged his readers to break with the past so as to free the present, Huggins argued that Cruse's understanding of a "bona fide cultural movement" simply perpetuated the past he sought to escape: "as one looks today, there is a similar race promotion and self-conscious search for identity which cannot help but perpetuate the ethnic province. Whatever that provincialism may contribute to identity and sociology, it will constrict the vision, limiting the possibilities of personality."[4]

Cruse had argued that although the reality of America was "a nation dominated by the social power of groups, classes, in-groups, and cliques," the intellectuals of the Harlem Renaissance had looked at their world with individualistic eyes.[5] As a consequence, they remained powerless and marginal, their art imitative and thin. Huggins, however, saw this emphasis on group identity as a form of provincialism, a provincialism that enfeebled artistic expression and marginalized those who stayed within its protective or enforced embrace. For Huggins, "artistic production [was] an extremely personal, individualistic thing, not to be turned on or off by nationalisms of any kind."[6] As a consequence, the true "Negro renaissance" awaited those with the courage to explore their deepest individual natures and the confidence to assume their rightful place in the "seamless web" of American society.

Two more recent interpretations traverse what their authors now consider to be well-traveled territory. Although Robert Bone considered the story of the Harlem Renaissance to be a twice-told tale, he offered one more interpretation, "a truly literary interpretation," to supplement the work of Cruse and Huggins. Bone's focus in *Down Home* (1975) was on "two traditional literary modes: pastoral and anti-pastoral," which, he argued, were a natural voice for black writers. With the forms themselves—"the 'deep structures' of Afro-American fiction"—he had no quarrel and found them a perfect vehicle to explore "the antagonism between the self and the objective world."[7] But when he turned to the writers of the Harlem Renaissance, Bone perceived these black writers to have been especially vulnerable to white conceptions of black identity:

The modernist writers who arose in the first three decades of the century introduced a new stereotype into American literature. They abandoned the image of the Negro as contented slave, or as ravisher of white womanhood, replacing these with subtler, if no less racist caricature. In the writings of the Lost Generation, the Negro was depicted as a primitive. This was the image, for better or worse, that was thrust upon the writers of the Harlem Renaissance. Some black authors embraced the new stereotype, others tried to fend it off, or adapt it to their own ends, but all succumbed in one way or another to its seductive power.[8]

As a consequence, true self-understanding was impossible and art inevitably foundered upon the more general failure to replace racial stereotype with human complexity.

Following in the wake of these three scholars, David Levering Lewis felt it was time to move on to other considerations, at least to ask questions that had as yet not been posed:

Whether the output of the Harlem Renaissance was unevenly outstanding or was truncated by the Depression at the very moment when truly great products would have been offered to publishers who no longer wanted "exotica," or whether, as Alfred Knopf maintains, there was little more worth publishing, is more or less well expatiated in an extensive literature, of which the works of Vernon Loggins, Saunders Redding, Robert Bone, Darwin Turner, Jean Wagner, and Arthur P. Davis, inter alia, are only some of the more distinguished sources.[9]

Successful or not, how, Lewis wondered, did it all take place? Was there, in fact, a structure of support (or control) that made possible what more breathless accounts attributed to the "spirit" of the times? Thus, Lewis provided in *When Harlem Was in Vogue* (1982) a detailed account of six principal figures—Jessie Fauset, Charles S. Johnson, Alain Locke, Walter White, Casper Holstein, and James Weldon Johnson—whose networks of influence, assistance, and ambition helped make possible the work that was achieved: "without the patient assemblage and management by [this] handful of Harlem notables of a substantial white patronage . . . the

Harlem cultural scene would have been little more than a larger version of Philadelphia or Washington, places where belle-lettres meant Saturday night adventures in tidy parlors, among mostly tidy-minded literati."[10]

Of the six principal figures Holstein was the least visible, for he controlled organized gambling in Harlem and the money he gave for literary awards had little directly to do with cultivating a white patronage. But for the others outside support was the game to play, and, Lewis argued, they played it well—some perhaps too well. Alain Locke's principal benefactor, for example, was the wealthy Mrs. Charlotte Osgood Mason. Through Locke she met and gave money to Zora Neale Hurston, Aaron Douglas, Arthur Huff Fauset, Hall Johnson, Claude McKay, Richmond Barthé, Langston Hughes, and others.[11] Support, however, did not come without a price, especially to those who did not heed her advice "to slough off white culture" and to tread lightly the "slippery pond of civilization." As Hughes later recalled, once he no longer felt "the rhythms of the primitive surging" Mrs. Mason severed all ties with "her most precious child."[12] For the next few months Hughes was physically and emotionally sick. Although Lewis shifts our attention to the men and women behind the scenes, we are still witness to actors performing roles in scripts written by others. As the title of his book suggests, we look back to a time that was soon to collapse under the weight of the depression and its own artificiality.

There is much to recommend in these several interpretations. For these various critics have sharpened our awareness of the racial dynamics of creative expression and the vulnerability of black artists in the 1920s to the demands, the constraints, and the fantasies of others. How appropriate, then, that Alain Locke himself, looking back from the wreckage of the 1930s helped set the tone for subsequent criticism: "Eleven brief years ago Harlem was full of the thrill and ferment of sudden progress and prosperity; and *Survey Graphic* sounded the tocsin of the emergence of a 'new Negro' and the onset of a 'Negro renaissance.' " Today, with that same Harlem prostate in the grip of the depression and throes of social unrest, we confront the sobering facts of a serious relapse and premature setback; indeed, find it hard to believe that the rosy enthusiasm and hopes of 1925 were more than bright illusions or a cruelly deceptive mirage."[13] Now, it seemed, Harlem stood forth for what it really was, "a mass of unemployed stranded in an over-expensive, disease and crime-ridden slum."[14] And Locke was quick to conclude, "there is no cure or saving magic in poetry and art, an emerging generation of talent, or international prestige and interracial recognition, for unemployment or precarious marginal employment."[15] One hears in Locke's disillusionment the future voices of Cruse, Huggins, and Lewis. Rather than a new beginning, as Locke had once prophesied, there was only a frustrating sameness. If Harlem was a vogue, it was a vogue long in the making.

More recently, however, a second generation of critics—Bernard Bell, Henry Louis Gates, Jr., Houston A. Baker, Jr., and Arnold Rampersad— has both drawn upon and modified the work of these pioneering interpretations. In so doing they have significantly altered our understanding of the past and the terms in which we understand that past. In *Modernism and the Harlem Renaissance* (1987), for example, Baker offers an important revision of the critical lens through which the Harlem Renaissance has been viewed. In particular, Baker singles out the interpretations of Huggins and Lewis, both of whom argued for a renaissance more problematic than achieved—"While Huggins adduces provinciality and narrowness as causes for a failed Harlem Renaissance, his contemporary and fellow Afro-American historian David Levering Lewis takes a contrary view. Lewis ascribes Harlem's failings to a tragically wide, ambitious, and delusional striving on the part of renaissance intellectuals."[16] But the real failure, Baker argued, was in the judgment of those unable to see (to hear) what, in fact, had taken place. The renaissance could only be judged to be "provincial," a "failure," a "vogue" if one assumed that "notions of British, Anglo-American, and Irish 'modernism'" were relevant to understanding the "history of Afro-American modernism, especially the discursive history of such modernism."[17] Thus, Baker directly challenged the dominant analytical trope, modernism, which had served in the critical literature to define as well as explain the failure of black writers and intellectuals in the 1920s. Ironically, then, it is not the men and women of the renaissance who failed but the "scholarly" establishment of African Americans who, having failed to transcend the "critical vocabulary and . . . assumptions of a dominating culture," have employed this vocabulary to see failure in others.

Baker not only deconstructs the critical assumptions and vocabulary of past scholarship but makes deconstruction itself what is uniquely modern about the Harlem Renaissance and the consciousness of African Americans—"I suggest that the analysis of discursive strategies that I designate 'the mastery of form' and 'the deformation of mastery' produces more accurate and culturally enriching interpretations of the sound and soundings of Afro-American modernism than do traditional methods."[18] As a consequence, we now see the past from a radically different perspective and encounter familiar individuals playing unfamiliar roles. Booker T. Washington, for example, is no longer the sycophant mouthing "accommodationist" platitudes, but the consummate trickster who had both mastered and subverted the language of the dominant culture. As a consequence, whites were lulled to sleep with the language of the day while Washington's black audience was awakened to healthy doses of ridicule, burlesque, and contempt for those who thought they understood what he had to say. Even more surprising, Washington's *Up from Slavery* now emerges, in Baker's telling, as the defining text and his address at the Negro exhibit of the Atlanta Cotton States and International Exposition the defining moment "that constitutes a primary move in Afro-American discursive modernism."[19]

In shifting the discussion away from the "familiar geography of a familiar Harlem-Renaissance" to what he calls "areas of Afro-American production," Baker situates Locke, Countee Cullen, and Claude McKay in the lengthened perspective of Washington and Washington's contemporaries Charles Chesnutt and Paul Laurence Dunbar. This larger perspective, however, is itself but a bracket of time grounded in the deeper imaginative structures of African American consciousness, the "sounding strategies" or language an enslaved and exploited people have employed to challenge power and to sustain their integrity and identity as a people. But even this voicing, "the common sense of the tribe," is rooted in the "sound and space of an African ancestral past."

In order to redefine and recenter the moral and cultural geography of the Harlem Renaissance, Baker draws upon the writings of Michel Foucault, Jacques Derrida, Roland Barthes, and Mikhail Bakhtin. However, Baker's most profound intellectual and emotional debts are to individuals, writings, and "performances" closer to home. As Baker writes in the preface,

The orientation of the reflections that follow derives from a family history and, in particular, from reminiscences of the life of my father, Houston A. Baker, Sr., who died in 1983. Reflecting the labors of generations of black men and women in the United States who have been exploited, segregated, physically and verbally abused, denied access to opportunity, and called all manner of untoward names, and who have, nonetheless, forged a mighty identity and forced the white world to stand in awe and, sometimes, to effect powerful imitations of their signal labors—thinking on such indisputable facts of our family history (and on my father as metonym for that history) I suddenly wondered who, precisely, had consigned the Harlem Renaissance to the domain of "failure" and how we, as Afro-American scholars (but more importantly as descendants of a resonant black lineage), could tolerate this consignment.[20]

Not only is Baker's vision intentionally personal, even intimate, but it is a point of view and a self-consciousness that marks a profound shift in the visions of a generation of scholars who have came of age since the climactic years of the 1960s.[21]

Baker's immediate intellectual debt is to John Blassingame whose "sensitive ear to black communal sounds" detected in Booker T. Washington levels of meaning, discursive strategies, both traditional and modern. However, it is to the fertile imagination of Henry Louis Gates, Jr. that Baker is most indebted. In *Modernism and the Harlem Renaissance* he pays special tribute to Gates, whose essay on masking and dialect in African American expression—"Dis and Dat: Dialect and the Descent"—(indeed all of his writings) helped Baker to see language itself as simultaneously the "mastery of form" and "the deformation of mastery." Gates, in turn, in his important work *The Signifying Monkey* distinguished Baker as his "ideal reader," the "critical voice that I trust and respect and to which I address my work." Thus, Baker's *Blues, Ideology, and Afro-American Literature: A Vernacular Theory* both inspired and reassured Gates in his effort to locate within the African and African American expressive traditions a genuinely "black" system of theory and criticism. Taken together, the work of Blassingame, Gates, and Baker reflects in broad outline an important turning point in literary and historical scholarship.

Central to this increasingly conscious, even self-conscious, awareness of the problematics of scholarship itself is the question of language as it functions in scholarly discourse as well as the symbolic world of those one seeks to comprehend. In *Blues, Ideology, and Afro-American Literature*, for example, Baker nicely details these various referential levels and the challenge this self-consciousness now poses:

The assumption of normative relativity, far from being a call to abandonment or retrenchment in the critical arena, constitutes an invitation to speculative explorations that are aware both of their own partiality and their heuristic transitions from suggestive (sometimes dramatic) images to inscribed concepts. The openness implied by relativity enables, say, the literary critic to re-cognize his endeavors, presupposing from the outset that such labors are not directed toward independent, observable, empirical phenomena but rather toward processes, objects, and events that he or she half-creates (and privileges as "art") through his or her own speculative, inventive energies and interests.[22]

Most important, Baker argues, this "openness" allows for a freedom to imagine the past and the present in radically new ways. Thus, we see a privileging not only of culture, but an African American culture, to contextualize historical experience. In Baker's own words, "if the investigator's efforts are sufficiently charged with blues energy, he is almost certain to remodel elements and events appearing in traditional, Anglo-American space-time in ways that make them "jump" several rings toward blackness and the vernacular."[23] With this shift in emphasis, black Americans emerge as resourceful men and women and not simply pawns in the stream of someone else's history.[24]

Thus, Baker insists, the Harlem Renaissance was not the half realized efforts of imaginative individuals, but a "complex field of sounding strategies" drawn from the collective experience and consciousness of black peoples, "the spirit house and space of black habitation." Freedom not frustration; openness not closure; ingenuity not imitation; assertion not acceptance—"the human will's resistance to tyranny and the human mind's masterful and insistent engagement with forms and deformations"—marked the birth, the rebirth, and the birthright of the Harlem Renaissance. Likewise, in his own scholarship and that of others, we see not only a shift from an "Anglo-American space-time," to what Baker calls "a national racial expressivity," but a linking of this cultural emphasis to the larger universe of African culture.

Freed themselves, these scholars have found in others a freedom and a vitality earlier scholars all but failed to imagine. The "discovery" of the Harlem Renaissance itself mirrors this renaissance of the imagination and serves, in turn, to sustain these imaginative revisions. However, just as Baker's scholarship both nourishes and is nourished by the challenges to intellectual and political authority presently sweeping the world, there remains an inner tension, at least a question, that is not easily resolved and opens onto an understanding of the past, of the Harlem Renaissance, that has yet to be addressed.

In *Modernism and the Harlem Renaissance*, Baker employs the term "*marronage*"—"the bonding together [of fugitives from slavery] to create independent communities of their own"—so as to establish the historical and cultural contours of the Harlem Renaissance. Thus, Baker speaks of the renaissance generally and Alain Locke's *The New Negro* (1925) in particular as the representation of "a unified community of national interests set in direct opposition to the general economic, political, and theological tenets of a racist land."[25] This "inner-objective" ("the founding of a nation of Afro-Americans on the basis of Race") rests upon the bed-rock of "self-in-*marronage*"—"the always already AFRICAN SELF that has its being in community and cultural/racial/tribal interiority."[26] Not only does Baker ground the Harlem Renaissance culturally and racially but in so doing he controls or stabilizes the "deconstructionist activities" of his trickster figures. As a consequence, ambiguity is understood to have purpose, disorder is not without order, and performance springs from conviction. For others, however, for James Clifford and for George Hutchinson, for example, this "always already AFRICAN SELF" is no less problematic than other efforts to authenticate identity and to authenticate the ethnic and cultural boundaries of the Harlem Renaissance.

Although Clifford has little directly to say about the Harlem Renaissance, he traces in *The Predicament of Culture: Twentieth-Century Ethnography, Literature, and Art*, "the formation and breakup of ethnographic authority in twentieth century anthropology."[27] In so doing, he, like Baker, applauds as well as contributes to this "critique of deep-seated Western habits of mind and systems of values." For this helps Clifford to realize his primary goal, "to open space for cultural futures, for the recognition of emergence."[28] However, the predicament Clifford addresses includes not only those whose work is in question, and the work itself, but also those (like himself) who now question this work. For if, "there is no neutral standpoint in the power-laden field of discursive positionings," isn't this equally true for those who counter the "truths" others have fashioned?[29] Thus, Clifford concludes, "if authenticity is relational, there can be no essence except as a political, cultural invention, a local tactic."[30]

Clifford has no final answer for the questions he raises, but he finds in the writing of Aimé Césaire and the "creolized" culture and consciousness of Carribean peoples an analogue and a strategy to apprehend as well as represent both one's cultural identity and modernity itself—"For Césaire culture and identity are inventive and mobile. They need not take root in ancestral plots; they live by pollination, by (historical) transplanting."[31] Airborne inspiration, pollination, and not root-deep certainties nourish his being and his poetics. As a consequence, Clifford suggests that for Césaire the term "*marron*" or "*marronage*" as a noun was insufficient to fully convey his and his peoples inner being. For this reason, Césaire turns noun into verb, coining the new word "*marronner.*" In so doing, he shifts the emphasis from the historical fact of cultural displacement (context) to the creative act of cultural construction (consciousness). As a consequence, the geography of his imagination—West Africa, France, Hispanic America, Brazil, Haiti—now becomes the alembic of imagination itself.

On a more personal note, James Baldwin anticipated the concerns that inform Clifford's reading of Césaire. Many years before Césaire had written the poem "The Verb '*Marronner*'/for René Depestre, Haitian Poet," Baldwin stood riveted by Césaire's electrifying speech given at the "The Conference of Negro-African Writers and Artists" in Paris (1956):

We find ourselves today in a cultural chaos. And this is our role: to liberate the forces which, alone, can organize from this chaos a new synthesis, a synthesis which will deserve the name of culture, a synthesis which will be the reconciliation—*et dépassement*—of the old and the new. We are here to proclaim the right of our people to speak, to let our people, black people, make their entrance on the great stage of history.[32]

Baldwin was thrilled with Césaire's "water tight" case against Europe. But he was also puzzled, even "stirred in a disagreeable way." For in his opinion, "Césaire's speech left out of account one of the great effects of the colonial experience: its creation, precisely, of men like himself."[33] Thus, questions implicit in Baldwin's concern have become, as seen, others concern as we puzzle "conjectural" identities as well as languages and voices no less conjectural. At the same time, Baldwin's question also reaches backward in time to the men and women of the Harlem Renaissance and provides, along with Clifford's response, support for, as well as a critical counterpoint to, the most recent interpretation of the Harlem Renaissance, George Hutchinson's *The Harlem Renaissance in Black and White*.

In *The Harlem Renaissance in Black and White*, Hutchinson challenges all previous interpretations of the Harlem Renaissance, grounding its significance and meaning in the search for an American national identity commonly pursued and contested by white and black intellectuals in the initial decades of the twentieth century. As Hutchinson writes,

The issue of American national identity was, in any case, the dominant *problematic* structuring the literary field relevant to the Harlem Renaissance. . . . The attempt, overall, came down to an effort to expand the notion of "the people" who compose the American national community, and thus who, in a liberal democratic state, have an acknowledged, socially *legitimated* right to help set the general direction and specific policies of that community—have a moral claim, according to that community's self-understanding, upon the common conscience and the structuring of the social order.[34]

To achieve this perspective, however, to see both the concern for an American national identity and the equally compelling effort to construct a pluralistic vision of American culture, Hutchinson argues that it is first necessary to come to terms with "traditional conceptions of American modernism." For, as he writes, "the limitations and exclusions built into traditional views of modernism have much to do with the problems afflicting understandings of the institutional contexts and intellectual trajectories of the Harlem Renaissance."[35] Thus, modernism is key to a conceptual understanding of the Harlem Renaissance and key, as well, to the intellectual and institutional dynamics that mark these years—"To enter the history of American modernism by way of an interracial perspective, I believe, can offer a new vision of the period."[36]

To make his case, Hutchinson draws upon Daniel Joseph Singal's "Towards a Definition of American Modernism" to help distinguish European "high" modernism and American "lost generation" modernism from the thought and work of those who, for the most part, remained on American shores. In particular, Hutchinson claims that "the drifting apart of social and personal spheres typical of high modernism is not typical of New Negro writing; nor is it typical of the writing of the socialists, cultural nationalists, and regional realists who responded to their work and with whom they affiliated."[37] On this basis, Hutchinson critiques Baker as well as Huggins (indeed, all interpretations) that employed "high" modernism in one way or another as if it was a relevant concern:

Indeed, it is still the case that discussions of modernism and the Harlem Renaissance often pit black writers against white writers like Eliot, Pound, and Stein, who inhabited a very different space (literally!) in the modernist landscape, while ignoring or giving little careful attention to the forms of uncanonical, "native" (white) modernism with which the African American renaissance was intimately related.[38]

Thus, Hutchinson opens the way to see the Harlem Renaissance in a new perspective, a perspective that importantly challenges his readers to realize the commonalities that sustain cultural diversity as well as the diversity needed to strengthen what a people have in common.[39]

The challenge "to appreciate a once-acknowledged but long-forgotten and repressed kinship," however, is not the only challenge the renaissance or Hutchinson's argument presents. For the sense of consciousness, even self-consciousness, addressed by both Clifford and Baldwin is no less the legacy of the Harlem Renaissance. As seen, Hutchinson argued that for present-day Americans, white and black, to realize their shared identity, it was first necessary, "to reconceive what 'American modernism' is, and also to begin thinking of American literature less as a tradition (or set of separate traditions) following noble lines of descent than as the continually reforming product of historical fields of action, power, and experience."[40] It is my argument, however, that American modernism was not only (was more than) an imaginative field that evolved from and upon which competing notions of a national American cultural identity were fought. For woven into the very texture of American modernism was both a search for and a questioning of all forms of collective identity.

At issue was the question of identity, often conceptualized as the personality, of the individual. For in the very search for a meaningful structure or a set of relationships for personality to develop there existed a simultaneous questioning of the very grounds that one imagined how personality might be achieved. In other words, American modernism is marked by an inner tension that structured as well as complicated this critical discourse. Hutchinson is right. American modernism is not best defined as "the drifting apart of social and personal spheres." No one argued, for example, as did T. S. Eliot, for an extinction of personality.[41] In contrast to Eliot, Van Wyck Brooks argued that "the essence of art, religion, literature—the essence of personality itself—since the beginning of things" had to be engaged if one was to think seriously about society and social reform.[42] And Alain Locke declared that

So for generations in the mind of America, the Negro has been more of a formula than a human being. . . . The thinking Negro even has been induced to share this same general attitude . . . to see himself in the distorted perspective of a social problem. His shadow, so to speak has been more real to him than his personality.[43]

However, if a concern for personality was central to the general idea of a cultural renaissance, the link between personal and social spheres was problematic at best.

To help suggest this tension between the individual and forms of collective identity, it is important to briefly address three key intellectual concerns that Hutchinson claims link the Harlem Renaissance and American modernism—cultural pluralism, Boasian anthropology, and philosophical pragmatism.[44]

Cultural Pluralism. In "William James and Twentieth Century Ethnic Thought," Larry C. Miller explores the degree to which James's pluralistic philosophy might have influenced the emphasis on cultural pluralism and ethnic diversity articulated by Horace Kallen, Robert Park, and W.E.B. Du Bois. Although James's ideas were, as Miller claims, "relevant" to their work, the primary thrust of his own thinking was to link pluralism with individualism and voluntarism.[45] In a somewhat similar vein, John J. Mc Dermott argues in "The Promethean Self and Community in the Philosophy of William James," that James has much to teach us about a "doctrine of community" so long as we understand that the individual and the community (society in general) are for James in an interdependent yet problematic relationship. If the self is a social construct so too is society an individual construct. As Mc Dermott quotes James, "Individuality is founded in feeling; and the recesses of feeling, the darker, blinder strata of character, are the only places in the world in which we catch real fact in the making, and directly perceive how events happen, and how work is actually done."[46] The language is that of James, but the emphasis is not too different from that of Alain Locke in "The Problem of Classification in Theory of Value," Locke's dissertation written at Harvard, and the intellectual groundwork for his critical writings in the 1920s. Finally, John P. Diggins argues in *The Promise of Pragmatism: Modernism and the Crisis of Knowledge and Authority* that James's commitment to "self-sovereignty" not only distinguished his intellectual thought but provoked John Dewey, as well as Charles H. Cooley and George H. Mead, to formulate alternative social philosophies.[47]

Boasian Anthropology. Franz Boas, whose concepts, Hutchinson claims, "became bedrock assumptions among 'New Negro' authors of virtually every persuasion," was no less challenged to locate the individual within the understanding of culture he did so much to pioneer. Thus, in "The Aims of Anthropological Research," Boas wrote, "The problems of the relation of the individual to his culture, to the society in which he lives have received too little attention. The standardized anthropological data that inform us of customary behavior, give no clue to the reaction of the individual to his culture, nor to an understanding of his influence upon it."[48] Four years later, Boas argued that although "it seems most desirable and worthwhile to understand each culture as a whole and to define its character," he doubted that "it is possible to give a picture of the culture which is at the same time a picture of a personality."[49] In addition to the methodological problem posed by Boas, his students also struggled to find their own personal voice as that voice was shaped, in part, by their theoretical concerns. As Richard Handler has argued, "In my work on the literary endeavors of Boasian anthropologists, I have examined a similar tension [the tension between the quest for self-expression and the desire to recover a viable tradition] in the development of a cultural theory that could accommodate both cultural holism and human individuality."[50]

Philosophical Pragmatism. In addressing "the central role of aesthetic experience in the achievement of new forms of solidarity and understanding," Hutchinson singled out Van Wyck Brooks and the impact his influential work, *America's Coming of Age*, had on Locke, his classmate at Harvard.[51] As Hutchinson concludes, "Brooks and his cohorts at *The Seven Arts* provided a cluster of terms that helped shape the discourse not only of the 'Little Renaissance' but of the New Negro movement."[52] At the same time, Hutchinson argues that "Locke's incorporation of *The Seven Arts* critics' ideas foreshadowed the development of related positions by younger authors such as Langston Hughes and Jean Toomer."[53] The impact of these terms, however, had a double edge. As Casey Nelson Blake argues in *Beloved Community*, Brooks, along with Randolph Bourne, came to realize that "if culture was immediately equated with community life . . . it would have little to contribute to personalities engaged in reshaping their world" precisely because community itself threatened to obliterate the independence of mind they sought to achieve.[54] As a consequence, it was necessary for "intellectuals [to exploit] the tensions between the two, honing their ideas into a critical discourse of social transformation."[55] Blake goes on to argue that this tension between personality and community was central to the thinking of all the "Young Americans," though it was most fully recognized by Lewis Mumford that "it was precisely that tension that held the greatest promise for a genuine Beloved Community."[56]

Perhaps this emphasis on personality, the place and fulfillment of the individual in tension with the search for a sustaining organic culture, especially marks American modernism. If so it is partly a question of degree. As Charles Taylor argues in *Sources of the Self: The Making of the Modern Identity*, "expressive individuation [is] one of the cornerstones of modern culture."[57] Taylor traces this "inward turning," this retrieval of "experience or interiority," back to European thought in the late eighteenth century.[58] In this context, the intellectual influence of the German philosopher Johann Gottfried Herder deserves special attention.[59] However, tracing lines of influence, a problematic quest at best, is not my particular concern. It is more suggestive to note that in Herder's effort to conceptualize the one and the many one can see the same tensions surface that surface in the Harlem Renaissance. In our own more recent time, one can see this ongoing tension in the thought of those (Kwame Anthony Appiah and Hazel Carby, for example) who are concerned with the creative act of cultural construction.

In "Identity, Authenticity, Survival: Multicultural Societies and Social Reproduction," Appiah asks "What is the relationship between this collective language and the individualist thrust of the modern notion of the self?" His answer is that identity is dialogical, something negotiated, a process both reflective and self-reflective. Thus, he argues, "Too much multi-cultural talk presupposes concepts of collective identity that are remarkably unsubtle in their understandings of the process by which identities, both individual and collective, develop.[60] When he turns his attention to Africa and African writers, Appiah notes a similar tension. Writing of Wole Soyinka, Appiah argues, "This struggle [that of the authorial 'I' with that of the 'we' of oral narration] is as central to Soyinka's situation as it is to that of African writers generally. . . . Once again the 'I' seeks to escape the persistent and engulfing 'we.' "[61]

No less concerned with the boundaries of cultural construction and individual consciousness, Hazel Carby is interested in "The Politics of Fiction, Anthropology and the Folk: Zora Neale Hurston" in Hurston's existential relationship as an intellectual to the various narrative voices she employed to fashion her fine work *Their Eyes Were Watching God*:

Hurston . . . was concerned with the relationships among the lives and cultures that she reconstructed and her own search for a construction of the self. She lived the contradictions of the various constructions of her social identity and rewrote them in *Their Eyes Were Watching God*. Her anthropological "spyglass" which she trained on the society that produced her, allowed her to return to that society in the guise of being a listener and a reporter. In her fictional return, Hurston represents the tensions inherent in her position as an intellectual—in particular as a writer—in antagonistic relation to her construction of the folk community. It is in this sense that I think Hurston is as concerned with the production of a sense of self as she is with the representation of a folk consciousness through its cultural forms.[62]

When Carby turns her attention more generally to the Harlem Renaissance, she argues in "Quicksands of Representation: Rethinking Black Cultural Politics" that what we presently would like to believe about the past doesn't hold up under close inspection: "Indeed, the Harlem renaissance is frequently conceived as a unique, intellectually cohesive and homogeneous historical moment, a mythology which has disguised the contradictory impulses of the Harlem intellectuals."[63] For both Carby and Appiah, the "production of a sense of self" is inherently problematic, a challenge rooted in the past yet no less compelling for those who live in the present.

This study is focused on five important individuals of the Harlem Renaissance who struggled to come to terms with the tension between the one and the many—W.E.B. Du Bois, Alain Locke, Claude McKay, Jean Toomer, and Zora Neale Hurston. For Du Bois and Locke, the imaginative construction of a cultural identity was simultaneously an act of self-reflection. For Du Bois this took the form in *The Souls of Black Folk* of a self-conscious narration historically as well as personally grounded, whereas Locke explored in various writings and *The New Negro* the complex sense of culture as both an objective construct and a subjective experience. As for McKay, Toomer, and Hurston, all three struggled with what Hazel Carby has called "the production of a sense of self." Although this meant very different things to each of these writers, all sought to establish the self that challenged the claims others sought to impose.

NOTES

1. Harold Cruse, *The Crisis of the Negro Intellectual* (New York: William Morris and Co., 1967), 21–22.

2. Ibid., 63.

3. Nathan Huggins, *Harlem Renaissance* (New York: Oxford University Press, 1971), 306–7.

4. Ibid., 308.

5. Cruse, *Crisis*, 7.

6. Huggins, *Harlem Renaissance*, 241.

7. Robert Bone, *Down Home* (New York: G. P. Putnam's Sons, 1975), xix

8. Ibid., 125.

9. David Levering Lewis, "The New Negro, 1920–1935," *Prospects* 3 (1997): 251.

10. Ibid., 120–21.

11. See Steven Watson, *The Harlem Renaissance: Hub of African-American Culture, 1920–1930* (New York: Pantheon Books, 1995).

12. David Levering Lewis, *When Harlem Was in Vogue* (New York: Vintage Books, 1982), 257.

13. Alain Locke, "Harlem: Dark Weather-Vane," *Survey Graphic* 25 (August 1936): 457. George Hutchinson makes the following important point—"Contrary to popular belief, publishers did not suddenly lose interest in black authors with the onset of the Depression. None of the publishers that survived stopped publishing the New Negro writers they had picked up in the 1920s. Indeed, one of the strangest charges against the Harlem Renaissance is that, having been buoyed by white fascination for the primitive, it crashed with the stock market in 1929. Simply consulting the standard bibliographies disproves this notion." However, as Hutchinson goes on to argue, there was a distinct shift in intellectual and social focus, a shift that even ridiculed "the Harlem Renaissance interest in recuperating African cultural traditions as well as what came to be regarded as the outmoded racialism of the New Negro intellectual leaders." Hutchinson, *The Harlem Renaissance in Black and White* (Cambridge: Harvard University Press, 1995), 384, 435.

14. Locke, "Harlem," 457.

15. Ibid., 457.

16. Houston A. Baker, Jr., *Modernism and the Harlem Renaissance* (Chicago: University of Chicago Press, 1987), 10.

17. Ibid., xvi.

18. Ibid.

19. Ibid., 17. Thus, Baker grounds "renaissancism in Afro-American culture as a whole" in Washington's famous address and not in the more conventional modernist time line (c. December, 1910) suggested by Virginia Woolf.

20. Ibid., xiv–xv.

21. In his earlier work, *Blues, Ideology and Afro-American Literature*, Baker singled out for special praise the readings of Frederick Jameson, Hayden White, and Marshall Sahlins and linked their critical importance for him with that of Hegel's "Phenomenology of the Spirit." Houston A. Baker, Jr., *Blues, Ideology and Afro-American Literature* (Chicago: The

University of Chicago Press, 1984). These names, together with those of the French structuralists and deconstructionists who appeared in *Modernism and the Harlem Renais-sance*, reflect that this rethinking of the past is, itself, part of a widespread reconceptualization of intellectual activity that has profoundly altered scholarship in the humanities and the social sciences in the last few decades. The following titles, by name alone, suggest the widespread attention now given to the problematics of intellectual discourse and analysis: *The Invention of Primitive Society: Transformations of an Illusion* (1988), *The Invention of Tradition; The Invention of Culture; The Invention of Africa: Gnosis, Philosophy and the Order of Knowledge* (1990), *The Invention of Ethnicity* (1989).

Invention suggests discovery as well as fabrication, and the most significant discovery is the fact or act of fabrication itself. As Adam Kuper writes in *The Invention of Primitive Society* (London: Routledge, 1988), "The anthropologists took . . . primitive society as their special subject, but in practice primitive society proved to be their own society (as they understood it) seen in a distorting mirror." And, as Marianna Torgovnick writes in *Gone Primitive: Savage Intellects, Modern Lives* (Chicago: University of Chicago Press, 1990), "The real secret of the primitive in this century has often been the same secret as always: the primitive can be—has been, will be (?)—whatever Euro-Americans want it to be." As these comments suggest, power no less than "problematics" is at issue, for the authority to write about others reflects not only the power of those in authority but serves itself to subordinate those written about to the terms and terminology one employs.

22. Baker, *Blues*, 10.

23. Baker, *Modernism*, 10.

24. One only needs to compare Stanley Elkins, *Slavery—A Problem in American Institutional and Intellectual Life* (1959) with Blassingame's, *The Slave Community—Plantation Life in the Antebellum South* (1972) or Sterling Stuckey's, *Slave Culture* (1986) to see this shift in emphasis, a people once presented as objects or victims now seen as actors affirming their humanity within the constraints that existed.

25. Baker, *Modernism*, 77.

26. Ibid., 114.

27. As Clifford writes, "The development of ethnographic science cannot ultimately be understood in isolation from more general political-epistemological debates about writing and the representation of otherness." Clifford, *The Predicament of Culture: Twentieth-Century Ethnography, Literature, and Art* (Cambridge: Harvard University Press, 1988), 24.

28. Ibid., 15–16.

29. Here Clifford is paraphrasing Jeanne Favret-Saada's argument in *Les mots, la mort, les sorts* (1977), 42. Thus, Clifford asks of Edward Said's *Orientalism*, "if criticism must struggle against the procedures of representation itself, how is it to begin? How, for example, is an oppositional critique of Orientalism to avoid falling into 'Occidentalism'?" Clifford, *Predicament of Culture*, 259.

30. Ibid., 12.

31. Ibid., 15.

32. James Baldwin, "Princes and Powers," in *Nobody Knows My Name* (New York: Dell, 1961), 40.

33. Ibid., 41.

34. Hutchinson, *The Harlem Renaissance*, 13.

35. Ibid., 14.

36. Ibid., 31.

37. Ibid., 119. To support this distinction—"the division between social and personal spheres in 'high' modernism"—Hutchinson calls attention to J. P. Stern's, "The Theme of Consciousness: Thomas Mann," in *Modernism, 1890–1930*, ed. Malcolm Bradbury and James McFarlane (Harmondsworth: Penguin, 1976).

38. Hutchinson, *The Harlem Renaissance*, 14.

39. "The literary renaissance was in part an attempt to augment the value of black culture within the national cultural field . . . it remains a primary concern among all parties to the debate over multiculturalism in the United States today." Ibid., 12–13.

40. Ibid., 447.

41. As Eliot writes, "The progress of an artist is a continual self-sacrifice, a continual extinction of personality." "Tradition and the Individual Talent," in *The Sacred Wood* (London: The Thanet Press, 1928), 53.

42. Van Wyck Brooks, "Highbrow and Lowbrow," in *America's Coming of Age* (New York: Doubleday, 1958), 18.

43. Alain Locke, *The New Negro* (New York: Atheneum, 1968), 3–4.

44. Hutchinson writes, "The Harlem Renaissance was in fact a striking experiment in cultural pluralism, with pervasive connections to philosophical pragmatism and Boasian anthroplogy." Hutchinson, *The Harlem Renaissance*, 90.

45. "For James, individualism, voluntarism, and pluralism were inseparable principles. He believed that each person through an exertion of will added something to the world not knowable before hand to any external or superhuman consciousness and not predictable from the properties of atoms. However small this addition, it sufficed to maintain the dignity of human effort. James also held that when more or less unpredictable individuals accidentally formed stable groups, the average behavior of all members of the group was predictable even though the behavior of each member was not. In arguing for individual freedom, he thus stressed groups to account for scientific laws that were neither implicit in atoms nor in some kind of superhuman consciousness."

Larry C. Miller, "William James and Twentieth Century Ethnic Thought," *American Quarterly* 31, no. 4 (Fall, 1979): 536–37.

46. John J. Mc Dermott, "The Promethean Self and Community in the Philosophy of William James," in *Streams of Experience: Reflections on the History and Philosophy of American Culture* (Amherst: University of Massachusetts Press, 1986), 58.

47. Diggins, for example, writes, "To Dewey James's position seemed to rely on an emotional inwardness that had little reference to either public awareness or the uses of cool, reflective intelligence. . . . What troubled Dewey was James's subjective individualism, which seemed almost oblivious to any social context." *The Promise of Pragmatism: Modernism and the Crisis of Knowledge and Authority* (Chicago: University of Chicago Press, 1994), 140.

48. Franz Boas, "The Aims of Anthropological Research," in *Race, Language, and Culture* (New York: The Free Press, 1966), 260.

49. Franz Boas, ed. *General Anthropology* (Boston: D. C. Heath, 1938), 680–81.

50. Richard Handler, "Ruth Benedict and the Modernist Sensibility," in *Modernist Anthropology: From Field Work to Text,* ed. Marc Manganaro (Princeton: Princeton University Press, 1990), 163.

51. Hutchinson notes that "Locke would later speak of the Negro's coming of age." He also notes that S. P. Fullinwider referred to Locke as "the Van Wyck Brooks of the black Americans," "and briefly compared the Harlem Renaissance with the 'Little Renaissance'

of New York in which Brooks figured so prominently." Hutchinson, *The Harlem Renaissance,* 99.

52. Ibid., 100. In his important book, Hutchinson gives attention to John Dewey, Josiah Royce, and William James; Franz Boas; Randolph Bourne, Van Wyck Brooks, Waldo Frank, and Lewis Mumford. A second or middle section gives extended attention to the politics of the many new journals and publishing houses that flourished in these years—*The New Republic, The Liberator, The Seven Arts, American Mercury, Modern Quarterly, The Crisis, Opportunity,* to name but a few. A third and final section gives an interpretive reading as well as detailed genesis of *The New Negro,* that unprecedented anthology of readings put together by Alain Locke, which appeared in 1925.

53. Ibid., 99.

54. As Blake writes of Randolph Bourne, "The collapse of competitive individualism in an age of large-scale bureaucracies and corporations had led Bourne to develop his own theory of a personality that gained independence and self-knowledge in exchanges with friends. Yet Bourne also seemed to suggest that the independence necessary to the life of irony was finally impossible because there existed no irreducible core of personality free of the pressures of group life." Casey Nelson Blake, *Beloved Community: The Cultural Criticism of Randolph Bourne, Van Wyck Brooks, Waldo Frank, and Lewis Mumford* (Chapel Hill: University of North Carolina Press, 1990), 71.

55. Ibid., 118.

56. Ibid., 264–65.

57. Charles Taylor, *Sources of the Self: The Making of the Modern Identity* (Cambridge: Harvard University Press, 1989), 376.

58. "What we can describe as a new moral culture radiates outward and downward from the upper middle classes of England, America, and (for some facets) France. In making the transition to new societies and strata, it is frequently transformed; so that what we end up with is a family of resembling moral cultures, or certain civilization-wide traits with important variations among nations and social classes. . . . But through all the variations, some common themes are visible. It is a culture that is individualist in the three senses I invoked earlier: it prizes autonomy; it gives an important place to self-exploration, in particular of feeling; and its visions of the good life generally involve personal commitment." Ibid., 305

59. As Taylor writes in "The Politics of Recognition, "This [the principle of originality] is the background understanding to the modern ideal of authenticity, and to the goals of self-fulfillment and self-realization in which the ideal is usually couched. I should note here that Herder applied his conception of originality at two levels, not only to the individual person among other persons, but also to the culture bearing people among other peoples. Just like individuals, a *Volk* should be true to itself, that is, its own culture." Taylor, *Multiculturalism,* ed. Amy Gutman (Princeton, NJ: Princeton University Press, 1994), 31. Also see Ingeborg Solbrig, "Herder and the 'Harlem Renaissance' of Black Culture in America: The Case of the '*Neger-Idyllen,*' " in *Herder Today,* ed. Kurt Mueller-Vollmer (Berlin-New York: Walter de Gruyter, 1990), 402–14. Also, Paul Gilroy, *The Black Atlantic: Modernity and Double Consciousness* (Cambridge: Harvard University Press, 1993).

60. Kwame Anthony Appiah, *Multiculturalism,* ed. Amy Gutman (Princeton, NJ: Princeton University Press, 1994), 149–50.

61. Kwame Anthony Appiah, *In My Father's House: Africa in the Philosophy of Culture* (New York: Oxford University Press, 1992), 83.

62. Hazel Carby, "The Politics of Fiction, Anthropology and the Folk: Zora Neale Hurston," in *New Essays On Their Eyes Were Watching God*, ed. Michael Awkward (New York: Cambridge University Press, 1990), 80–81.

63. Hazel Carby, "Quicksands of Representation: Rethinking Black Cultural Politics," in *Reconstructing Womanhood: The Emergence of the Afro-American Novelist* (New York: Oxford University Press, 1987), 163.

Chapter 2

"One Ever Feels His Two-Ness": W.E.B. Du Bois, Johann Gottfried von Herder, and Franz Boas

In February 1887 Franz Boas left Germany and soon after settled in New York City, eager to begin a new life free of the limited opportunities and anti-Semitism he had faced in the land of his birth. Seven years later, after two stimulating years of graduate study at the University of Berlin, W.E.B. Du Bois "dropped back into 'nigger-hating' America."[1] Soon, each man—brilliant, demanding, even imperious—would emerge as the preeminent voice in his field, commanding national, even international attention, and shaping opinion far into the twentieth century. Field, however, is perhaps stating their importance too narrowly. For both men presented a way of seeing the world that challenged some of the deepest convictions (and prejudices) of their contemporaries. Not only did they share many of the same concerns, but they would learn to know, to respect, and even to depend upon one another. If not exactly soul-brothers, they at least shared in the words of the German social philosopher Johann Gottfried von Herder a concern for "the cognitive governing power of the soul."[2]

Questions of race, racial identity, and racial prejudice were the core concerns that linked Du Bois and Boas. Each man had personally experienced prejudice. Each grew to understand that the prejudices he confronted were deeply rooted in the social and intellectual soil of Western culture. At the same time, in an effort to combat these prejudices, each drew upon and shared the intellectual legacy of Herder. For just as Herder thought the cultural anthropologist to be the ideal philosopher so, in turn, did he himself become philosophical grounding for subsequent thinking about culture. As George Stocking remarks, the anthropological tradition established by Boas had its deepest roots in the German romantic tradition voiced by Herder.[3]

Herder's philosophical and social theories were importantly related to notions of group life as organic wholes.[4] Central to this emphasis was the privileging of *das Volk* (the folk) as the spiritual focus and strength of a people's collective experience. As Thomas de Zengotita has written,

In *Folk Songs* (1778) Herder did for Germans and Celts and Slavs what he did for Judeo-Christians—and he did it also for Incas and Iroquois and Hottentots. He raised the voice of the unlettered to be heard—and the living Word was revealed again. Called the "Silver Book" when begun as a scrap-collecting hobby for family and friends, *Folk Songs* eventually inspired Bopp, the Brothers Grimm, and the whole folkloric tradition in the nineteenth century. Long before anthropologists went to the field to invalidate an image of humanity's origins, and long before later anthropologists cast all images into doubt, this Romantic Speaker conceived the anthropological tradition as translation. As Wordsworth turned to the rustic "speech of men" so Herder turned to folk songs for what all poetic language provided: being—articulated, known.[5]

At the same time, as Isaiah Berlin argues, there is in Herder's thought a central and unresolved tension of the "one and the many."[6] This tension, as Michael Morton suggests, results from "the apparent antimony between the ideas of cultural and individual autonomy on the one hand and development toward the realization of universal humanity on the other."[7] Within this dialectic, as a consequence, the role of the individual was crucial yet problematic. As mediator and as catalyst of the particular and the general, the individual constrained as well as embodied the tension of these opposites. Both as object (one situated in the context of others) and subject (one who sought to bring others and, in so doing, one's self into being) the individual, as a consequence, was "at once identical with his *Volk* and distinct from it." No less problematic was the world one sought to fashion—"how is one to reconcile both for oneself and for one's *Volk,* the competing demands of nationality and *Weltburgertum?*"[8]

In the year Du Bois returned to America, Boas initiated a probing critique of the racial science of his illustrious peers together with various considerations of the social and historical identity of black Americans. In "Human Faculty as Determined by Race" (1894), Boas's address to the American Association for the Advancement of Science, Boas raised serious doubts that "human faculty" was determined by race. Presumptions of racial superiority, he claimed, rested upon two fundamental yet erroneous assumptions: (1) "achievement and the aptitude for an achievement have been confounded." (2) "every deviation from the white type is considered a characteristic feature of a lower type."[9] In breaking with the logic of his contemporaries, Boas used historical comparisons and statistical evidence, (both psychological and physical) to suggest that achievements, as well as the lack of achievements, were the result more of historical and social conditions than mental ability. Thus, in discussing "the inferior position held by the negro race of the United States" Boas emphasized that "the old race-feeling of the inferiority of the colored race is as potent as ever and is a formidable obstacle to its advance and progress"[10] At this point in his thinking, Boas did think there were anatomical differences that might be of some consequence. But, he was cautious about making generalizations, for it was clear that among the various peoples of the world there was a great overlap in abilities.[11] Seven years later, however, Boas approached the question of race from a somewhat different perspective.

In "The Mind of Primitive Man" (1901), Boas again addressed the significance of race and the significance it played in social and intellectual development—"One of the chief aims of anthropology is the study of the mind of man under varying conditions of 'race' and 'environment.' "[12] Only now "race" and "environment" were somewhat subordinate concerns. Boas's immediate goal was to address the inner dynamics of human consciousness itself. What was unique to human beings, Boas argued, was the capacity to form abstract ideas and to experience the world through the forms and meanings of the abstractions created. Although the architecture of these forms (language, number, art, and ethics) varied considerably, the construction of a world of meaning was "common to the whole of humanity." In this way, Boas distinguished between "the organization of the mind" and the "achievements of the mind." These achievements, while the stuff with which the mind was filled, were the fabric of meaning that constituted a people's collective past and present.

Again Boas distinguished between faculty and race. Only now, race was more than a foil to critique arguments emphasizing the inherent biological differences that distinguished peoples. In "Human Faculty as Determined by Race," Boas had made the important point that all peoples had contributed to the development of civilization: "We must bow to the genius of all, whatever race they may represent: Hamitic, Semitic, Aryan, or Mongol."[13] Now, however, genius suggested not only contribution but integration, "the expression of [the] mental activity of a community."[14] Although Boas had not completely disassociated race and the idea that civilization was a series of stages through which all peoples must advance, race had now begun to merge with the alternative understanding that cultures (the "genius of a people") were diverse, independent, and had an internal integrity of their own.

Three years later, Boas drew upon these various theoretical considerations to provide a perspective on the racial situation in America. In an article titled, "What the Negro Has Done in Africa" (1904), Boas argued that because of the oppressive nature of American slavery it was impossible to know the true capabilities of American blacks. When viewed, however, in the larger context of their African past—in particular, the medieval kingdoms of Ghana and Songhai—it was clear that black Americans (peoples of African descent) were no less capable than others in creating complex social and cultural worlds.[15] Not only had Boas challenged Hegel's insidious notion that Africa was a continent without history, but equally important he had challenged the context in which comparative judgments were to be made.[16] Instead of the emphasis on evolutionary "stages of growth"—the bedrock assumption that supported the thoughts of scientists, philosophers, theologians, and politicians—Boas argued that culture(s) must be understood historically and individually.

Alerted to the presence of a powerful ally, Du Bois wrote to Boas asking for information on the "best and latest works bearing on the anthropology of the Negro—particularly his physical measurements, health, etc."[17] In an effort to entice Boas to address a forthcoming conference ("African Physique") to be held at Atlanta University, Du Bois added that "We have in Atlanta over 2000 Negro pupils and students who could be carefully measured."[18] Not only did Boas address the conference, but two days later he gave the commencement address "The Outlook for the American Negro" to the class of 1906.

Speaking "from the standpoint of the anthropologist," the outlook Boas offered was one of freedom and hope. The freedom he offered, most importantly, was freedom from the crippling weight of ignorance and prejudice that had long passed as truth. Drawing upon his earlier writings, Boas attacked the notion that the potential of human beings was determined by race.[19] To support this assertion, Boas offered not only a panoramic view of Africa as a land and a people with a history, but a history steeped in accomplishments that Europeans at a comparable period in time had yet to achieve—achievements in metallurgy, agriculture, and the domestication of animals, political and military organizations, market systems, and "the artistic industry of native Africa."[20] Since history and anthropology did not support charges of racial inferiority, it was clear that the problems black Americans confronted resulted from social conditions rooted in America's own peculiar racial past—conditions that, with courage and perseverance, could be changed.[21]

From the day of their first exchange of letters, until Boas's death in 1942, Du Bois would seek his advice and that of his student Melville Herskovits. Their correspondence ranged over questions dealing with I.Q. tests and intelligence; genetics; intermarriage between blacks and whites; international and national conferences on race; and various projects regarding the history and achievements of black Americans. Related to these questions were confidential exchanges concerning the locating and training of capable black men and women to help research the measuring of blacks as well as the collecting and study of urban and Southern black folklore.[22] Throughout the 1920s and 1930s other prominent black intellectuals as well—Walter White, Carter G. Woodson, Alain Locke, Charles S. Johnson, Arthur Schomburg, and Zora Neale Hurston—would also seek Boas's counsel.[23] For nearly four decades there would be a line of communication from Morningside Heights to Harlem, Atlanta, Washington, DC (Howard University), and Nashville (Fisk University). Depending upon Hurston's inspiration, her financial situation, and the advice of Boas and/or Herskovits, correspondence also made its way to New Orleans; Eatonville, Florida; and Port Au Prince, Haiti.

For Du Bois, Boas's commencement address was electrifying. Years later he recalled the importance of what he heard: "Franz Boas came to Atlanta University where I was teaching history in 1906 and said to a graduating class: You need not be ashamed of your African past; and then he recounted the history of black kingdoms of the Sahara for a thousand years. I was too astonished to speak. All of this I had never heard and I came then and afterwards to realize how the silence and neglect of science can let truth utterly disappear or even be unconsciously distorted."[24] Here, finally, was proof that science had more to offer than the continual drumbeat that peoples of Africa and African descent were racially inferior to others. Boas also represented for Du Bois affirmation of the intellectual direction his own life had taken.

At Harvard, after initial thoughts of pursuing philosophy with William James, Du Bois studied history under the guidance of Albert Bushnell Hart. Partly because of Hart's influence, Du Bois vowed in his third year to "study the Negro scientifically . . . and to find the truth beneath the black experience." It was in Germany, however, that "[Du Bois] began to grasp the idea of a world of human beings whose actions, like those of the physical world, were subject to law."[25] As Francis Broderick suggests, Du Bois's two years in Germany marked an important intellectual turning point. Under the influence of Adolph Wagner and most importantly Gustav von Schmoller, "Du Bois went to Europe an historian (1892) and returned two years later a sociologist"[26] About his own landmark study, *The Philadelphia Negro* (1899), Du Bois would echo Schmoller's classroom teaching, "We simply collect the facts; others may use them as they will."[27] Once a disciple of Herbert Spencer, Du Bois now saw the likes of his hero as "metaphysical lay figures" whose theories "bore little relation to observable fact." Franz Boas, however, was not a metaphysician but a figure who stood on solid ground. "There are two kinds of people," Boas wrote, "those who have to have general conceptions into which to fit the facts; those who find the facts sufficient. I belong to the latter category."[28] Du Bois had found his man.

As Du Bois's response to Boas's graduation address suggests, Boas offered more than the importance of science and the self sufficiency of factual evidence. Other forms of identification, the identification of other forms of meaning, were equally significant. Not only did Africa have new meaning, but black Americans were encouraged to see themselves in the larger contours of their African past. Within their more immediate national experience, as well, Boas suggested that there were traditions and forms of expression unique to black Americans.[29] Central to Boas's encouragement to the students to see themselves both historically and culturally was the notion of race. Only now, race served to suggest boundaries of affection, common understanding, and moral purpose. To understand the importance of this emphasis, and its importance for both Du Bois and Boas, it is necessary to see both of these men in a wider tradition of thought than either the empirical scholarship of Gustav von Schmoller or Boas's early training as a physicist and geographer. After all, by the time Boas had appeared on the commencement stage at Atlanta University, he had already puzzled the truths of subjective understanding. Du Bois, in turn, had already written *The Souls of Black Folk*.

Once back in America and at work on *The Philadelphia Negro*, Du Bois began to have doubts that social science would, in and of itself, be sufficient to change public and political opinion. Equally important, he was now convinced that something more was needed than a dispassionate documentation of the social life of black Americans, something that spoke directly to African Americans themselves. Two important statements Du Bois made in 1897, "The Conservation of Races," and "Strivings of the Negro People" reflect this conviction and his effort to provide this inspiration.

To the American Negro Academy, Du Bois matter-of-factly declared in "The Conservation of Races" that science and history show that "the history of the world is the history not of individuals, but of groups, not of nations but of races."[30] Although the physical differences that distinguished peoples were essentially unimportant, there were spiritual or psychical differences that, while they might "transcend scientific definition," were clearly visible to the historian and the sociologist. What bound peoples together, in fact what distinguished them as a people, was an inner spiritual cohesion, a genius, that would ultimately manifest itself through various forms of collective expression. By birth, citizenship, language, and religion, American blacks were American. On a deeper level, however, they were a people, potentially a "mighty nation," united by ties of experience and consciousness that cut across the grid of traditions and values rooted in America's Anglo-Saxon past. At the same time, as the vanguard of a dispersed people, a "vast historic race" whose roots traced back to the "African fatherland," American blacks stood poised to "take their just place in the 'van of Pan-Negroism.' " To do this, however, it was first necessary for blacks to conserve their special identity in white America.[31]

Although "the Negro race" had yet to contribute "a full clear spiritual message" to the world, it was clear, Du Bois argued, that blacks would discover within themselves their moral strength as a people: "For the development of Negro genius, of Negro literature and art, of Negro spirit, only Negroes bound and welded together, Negroes inspired by one vast ideal, can work out in its fullness the great message we have for humanity."[32] Not only did blacks have something to contribute to "civilization and humanity" but as a culture, a people, they had a "contribution to make which no other race [could] make."

In making his argument, Du Bois drew upon the names of Charles Darwin and Thomas Huxley to speak for "the whole scientific doctrine of Human Brotherhood." Du Bois, however, hardly speaks as the careful scientist, as one who trembles that "some personal bias, some moral conviction might distort his understanding." His tone, at times measured and cautious, is also morally and emotionally charged. Visions of glory and prophecies of greatness alternate with warnings of moral and intellectual corruption. In the "Strivings of the Negro People," Du Bois addressed the reader in even more personal, more private terms. His own childhood served to reveal as well as represent a defining existential moment: "How does it feel to be a problem?" This revelation, so unexpected yet so devastating, opens onto Du Bois's most famous generalization regarding the moral psychology and social consciousness of black Americans:

It is a peculiar sensation, this double consciousness, this sense of always looking at one's self through the eyes of others, of measuring one's soul by the tape of a world that looks on in amused contempt and pity. One ever feels his two-ness, two thoughts, two unreconciled strivings; two warring ideals in one dark body, whose dogged strength alone keeps it from being torn asunder. The history of the American Negro is the history of this strife—this longing to attain self-conscious manhood, to merge his double self into a better and truer self.[33]

Du Bois's remarks, eloquent as well as elegant, capture the ambivalence, the tension, the irony and the pride of being "both a Negro and an American." At the same time, Du Bois also makes clear that consciousness itself, the inner landscape of one's moral and emotional being, is of central importance.

No doubt Professor Schmoller would have been sympathetic when Du Bois wrote that *The Philadelphia Negro* was written with the understanding that "convictions on all great matters of human interest . . . will enter to some extent into the most cold-blooded scientific research."[34] But what would Schmoller have thought of "The Conservation of Races"? The "Strivings of the Negro People"? And what would he have thought of *The Souls of Black Folk* written, Du Bois claims, in "tears of blood"? Clearly, Germany had stimulated more in Du Bois than a passion for pure science.

In his contribution to *The New Negro* (1925), "The Negro in American Literature," William Stanley Braithwaite saluted *The Souls of Black Folk* as the book that had "more profoundly influenced the spiritual temper of the race than any other written in its generation."[35] Of Du Bois himself, Braithwaite sensed "that I am witnessing the birth of a poet, phoenix-like, out of a scholar." Braithwaite's general observations continue to intrigue critical opinion. However, whereas Braithwaite sees a general evolution (even conflation) of scholar and poet, more recent critics sense a tension, even conflict, that needs explanation. As Wilson J. Moses asks, "can Du Bois the social scientist be reconciled with Du Bois the poet and prophet of race?"[36] Bernard Bell posed the question in somewhat different terms: "Could Du Bois, the controversial social scientist, political leader, and man of letters . . . appreciate black folk art? Could he draw on both cultural traditions [elite and folk] for creative inspiration and expression?"[37] Houston Baker, turning Bell's question somewhat around, suggests that because Du Bois "was able to survey the black American experience through the lenses of sociology, philosophy, history and creative literature" he was able "to grasp the essential character of the black American folk experience."[38] Although each critic resolved the question he posed somewhat differently, the answer in each case was to be found somewhere in Du Bois's response to German scholarship and culture—for Moses, the Ethiopian tradition rooted in nineteenth-century *Volksgeist* mythologies; for Bell, the ideas of the philosopher and folklorist Johann Gottfried von Herder; and for Baker, the "critical objectivity" learned in the class room of Gustav Schmoller.[39]

Each of these several considerations is valuable, for collectively they relate elements of Du Bois's complex vision to the larger dilemma of cultural identity he first voiced in "Strivings of the Negro People" (1897). At the same time, each critic provides valuable insight into Du Bois's effort to construct a sense of group or collective identity—the souls of black folk— so that black Americans might see themselves through their own eyes and not the contemptuous or hostile eyes of others. However, what is missing in these several interpretations is the tension implicit in the very role Du Bois sought to play as the intellectual Bismarck of his people.[40] Du Bois's vow, made while a student in Berlin—"these are my plans: to make a name in science, to make a name in art and thus raise my race"—both frames his ambitions and the terms in which these ambitions are to be realized.[41] However, the elements of this vision—art and science—themselves embedded in the intellectual tradition that nurtured Franz Boas, embraced contradictions that Boas addressed but failed to resolve. Ultimately, his students—Edward Sapir, Alexander Goldenweiser, Alfred Kroeber, Clark Wissler, Ruth Benedict, Margaret Mead, and Melville Herskovits—had to confront the tensions implicit in his teachings. Their personal efforts to come to terms with their intellectual inheritance mirror the challenge that Du Bois would confront as "poet and scholar."

After spending the year (1883–84) in the frozen arctic of Baffinland (Canada) and a subsequent summer in Hudson Bay, Boas reflected upon the nature and study of geography. His deeper interest, however, given the somewhat anomalous identity geography had as both an empirical and descriptive science, had to do with different ways of knowing, different ways of apprehending the world. Although Boas's observations were, as he noted, part of an "old controversy between historical and physical methods" he was, nevertheless, exploring concerns in "The Study of Geography" (1887) that mark an important stage in his own intellectual transition from a student of physics and geography to one of ethnology.[42] Between the historian (or cosmographer) and the physicist Boas saw a profound difference in orientation and understanding—the one subjective and holistic, the other objective and universal.[43] Although both were sciences in that they began with "facts," cosmography was more closely related to the arts, "as the way in which the mind is affected by phenomena forms an important branch of the study."[44] Thus, whereas the physicist sought to provide "an objective connection" between the phenomena of the world, the historian or cosmographer provided connections that seemed to originate only "in the mind of the observer." As to which approach was best, Boas argued that each was equally valuable. For the one (what he called the "aesthetic" impulse), led to "laws, systems, and hypotheses" while the other (what he called the "affective" impulse), served to gratify as well as express the need for a sense of place.

Boas's effort to distinguish as well as legitimize two modes of knowing initiated what would prove to be essential elements (both epistemological and methodological) in his own anthropological vision. However, although Boas calls attention to the subjectivity of the observer, and those who are observed, he doesn't fully address his own subjectivity. He writes as if from some neutral space, his point of view ostensibly the measured reflections of an open mind. He is content, simply, to suggest that both approaches are equally valuable. Two years later, however, Boas directly addressed the tensions implicit in these two approaches when he turned his attention to the subjective connections that "seemed to . . . originate in the mind of the observer."

In the summer of 1888, Boas made his second field trip to British Columbia (Vancouver Island). Puzzled by errors he had made in recording the sounds he had heard, he began to consider the phenomena of sound itself and the manner in which one hears or mishears. In so doing, he came to realize that what one heard had a lot to do with how one heard. The act of hearing was deeply conditioned by one's own linguistic and cultural traditions. As a consequence, not only was his own role as an observer understood to be somewhat problematic but so too was his effort to give meaning to what he heard. Ironically, it seemed, conscious awareness was conditioned by conventions and assumptions below the threshold of conscious understanding. As George Stocking asserts, it is impossible to exaggerate the significance of Boas's article. Not only did it mark a turning point in his intellectual life, but it helped to establish the modern meaning and understanding of culture:

by implication it sees cultural phenomena in terms of the imposition of conventional meaning on the flux of experience. It sees them as historically conditioned and transmitted by the learning process. It sees them as determinants of our very perceptions of the external world. And it sees them in relative rather than in absolute terms. Much of Boas's later work, and that of his students after him, can be viewed simply as the working out of implications present in this article.[45]

One sees in these two articles, "The Study of Geography" (1887) and "On Alternating Sounds" (1888), the seeds of Boas's break with the evolutionary and racial assumptions of the nineteenth century as well as the genesis of key ideas that would soon attract the attention of Du Bois. However, whether culture and the study of culture was a science or an art, something constructed analytically or apprehended subjectively, remained an unresolved challenge.[46] In looking back to her graduate days, Margaret Mead writes "we lived, in a sense, lives in which the arts and the sciences fought uneven battles for pre-eminence."[47] At the same time, no matter how defined, the sense of culture as an integrated whole (an organizing spirit or genius) was somehow to be balanced with the understanding that the individual continued to have a certain moral and intellectual autonomy. As Melville Herskovits recorded in his notes, taken while studying with Boas, "One of the driving forces in cultural change must be looked for in the interrelations of individuals, which means the tribe must not be considered as a unit, but as a complex of inter-acting individuals. It is the lack of recognition of this that makes so many generally stated sociological propositions barren of result."[48] As a consequence, not only was the relationship of the individual to the whole somewhat problematic but so too was that of the whole to the individual. This ambiguity was as true for the observer as it was for those observed. Not only did the observer have to account for the consciousness of others but, in so doing, had to allow for his or her own point of view. Consciousness and self-consciousness were inextricably linked, contained and constrained within the concept of culture.

Although these various considerations were of immediate concern to those who studied with Boas, they were also issues broadly resonant in the larger culture.[49]

More than resonance, however, is involved. As F. H. Matthews notes, "The anthropologists spoke with a new relevance just because they offered answers to the questions asked by so many intellectuals in the twenties and after."[50] The anthropologists Matthews has in mind were those who studied "under the direction of the emigré scholar Franz Boas." Not only did Boas and his students provide a new vocabulary, at least a new authority, with which to critically view one's own society, they also offered ethnographic accounts of peoples who seemed to "belong to a living organic believing community."[51] Matthews's argument, however, is primarily focused on the "message" that Boas and his students provided. As a consequence, given the terms in which he sees this message (the tension between holistic and atomistic or individualistic theories of human behavior), he takes little note of the tension embedded within Boasian discourse itself.[52] However, two prominent students of Boas, Edward Sapir and Ruth Benedict, struggled to reconcile their intellectual training with deeply felt aspects of their individual lives. In so doing, they reveal tensions that others too would confront as they sought to reconcile holistic visions of cultural identity with the individual complexities of their imaginative and subjective lives.

In a celebrated article that initially appeared in *The Dial* (1919) and *The Dalhousie Review* (1924), Sapir argued in "Culture, Genuine and Spurious" that a genuine culture was not simply the "sum of abstractly desirable ends," a patchwork of separate elements, but "must be looked upon as a sturdy plant growth, each remotest leaf and twig of which is organically fed by the sap at the core."[53] To be genuine, to not be what Sapir called "external," a living, vital culture must embrace "those general attitudes, views of life, and specific manifestations of civilization that give a particular people its distinctive place in the world."[54] Sapir took pains to emphasize, however, that this integration was not to be achieved at the expense of diversity and the integrity of the individual—"a genuine culture refuses to consider the individual as a mere cog, as an entity whose sole *raison d'être* lies in his subservience to a collective purpose that he is not conscious of or that has only a remote relevancy to his interests and strivings."[55] Rather than the individual merely fitting into the formal needs of society what was important was to have these needs be an extension of "the central interests and desires" of the individual.

This ideal, the realization that the relationship of the individual to the group must be based on the understanding of the "spiritual primacy of the individual soul," was the challenge that confronted Americans. How to come to this understanding, how to achieve "a richly varied and yet somehow unified and consistent attitude toward life," was not entirely clear. Perhaps through art, "the form of consciousness in which the impress of the self is most direct, least hampered by outward necessity," might be provided the forms of expression to relate the deepest levels of the self to "others and make us live again in these others." However this integration might be achieved, it was Sapir's contention that the "development of culture" took place in "comparatively small, autonomous groups." For this reason, he looked forward to a series of "linked autonomous cultures" to take root in such urban centers as New York, Chicago, and San Francisco.

Sapir's critical vision importantly drew upon Boas's definition of culture as the "genius" or "spirit" of a people. However, whereas "genius" had a collective meaning, it also had an individual meaning. Sapir embraced both, seeking to integrate as well as distinguish the two. The resulting tension served to frame social and historical experience as well as to evaluate that experience. It also served as imaginative ground for Sapir's ethnographic and literary or aesthetic concerns.[56]

In his review of *American Indian Life*, for example, Sapir writes, "It [American Indian life] poses an interesting question. To what extent can we penetrate into the vitals of primitive life and fashion for ourselves satisfying pictures on its own level of reality?" Can the conscious knowledge of the ethnologist be fused with the intuitions of the artist? However, few artists, he argued, "possess[ed] so impassioned an indifference to the external forms of conduct as to absorb an exotic milieu only to dim its high visibility and to make room for those tracks of the individual consciousness which are the only true concern of literary art."[57] At the same time, intellectual constructs could be no less inhibiting than the "dry rot of social [and artistic] habit." Thus, in his criticism of Alfred Kroeber's "The Superorganic," Sapir objected that Kroeber had so reified culture as a total system that he had negated "the peculiar influence [and presence] of individuals." In contrast, what Sapir called "experiential irresolvability" not only allowed for the individual's self consciousness but, pointedly, that of Kroeber's as well. Thus, in his effort to construct a unified social order in "conformity with the essential nature of one's own personality," Sapir reflects his own personal struggle to achieve and sustain an individual consciousness integrated with but not subordinate to the forms employed to express that awareness.

In June 1922 Sapir wrote to Ruth Benedict, warmly praising her dissertation ("The Concept of the Guardian Spirit in North America") recently completed under the direction of their common mentor Franz Boas. In the same letter he encouraged her to seriously consider (to further consider) the concerns he had already addressed in his poetry, literary criticism, and his critique of Kroeber—"I should like to see the problem of individual and group psychology boldly handled, not ignored, by someone who fully understands culture as an historical entity."[58] Thus began a friendship, both personal and intellectual, that was to lead to their prominence as major figures in the "Culture and Personality" movement soon to distinguish American anthropology.[59]

Benedict's efforts to come to terms with the individual's relationship to culture and the analytical means to present this relationship were, as were Sapir's, rooted in and were a reaction to the intellectual legacy of Boas. At the same time, Benedict was also responding to, and importantly contributing to, the more general discourse of cultural criticism that marks these years. F. H. Matthews, for example, sees Benedict as a major exponent of cultural pluralism and her work a plea for a more tolerant social order.[60] Clifford Geertz, in turn, characterizes Benedict's work as a strategy to portray "the alien as the familiar" so as to see our own selves (our own world) critically and not worshipfully or complacently.[61] Both Matthews and Geertz, however, paid little attention to deep feelings of personal alienation that also motivated Benedict in her efforts to come to terms with her "fragmented neurotic civilization" as well as her chosen profession.

Margaret Caffrey's title for her study of Benedict, *Ruth Benedict: Stranger in This Land*, perfectly captures the emotional and moral isolation that Benedict experienced in her adult life. In this light, one notes that Benedict's *tour de force*, *Patterns of Culture*, has a very personal dimension that frames as well as is framed by the content of the argument. Benedict begins, for example, by noting that "The life history of the individual is first and foremost an accommodation to the patterns and standards traditionally handed down in his community."[62] This generalization, however, serves throughout her discussion of the Zuni, the Kwakiutl, and the Dobu to illuminate, not subordinate, the full humanity of the individual. As a consequence, the reader is asked to be doubly reflective—to realize "a greatly increased tolerance toward their divergencies" and, in so doing, to "train ourselves to pass judgment upon the dominant traits of our own civilization."[63] This appeal is especially marked in Benedict's discussion of homosexuality:

When the homosexual response is regarded as a perversion, however, the invert is immediately exposed to all the conflicts to which aberrants are always exposed. His guilt, his sense of inadequacy, his failures, are consequences of the disrepute which social tradition visits upon him, and few people can achieve a satisfactory life unsupported by the standards of society. . . . The weakness of these aberrants is in great measure illusory. It springs, not from the fact that they are lacking in necessary vigor, but that they are individuals whose native responses are not reaffirmed by society. They are, as Sapir phrases it, "alienated from an impossible world."[64]

Whether presenting others as a mirror to better see one's self or critically evaluating this double perspective, Benedict drew upon her deepest emotional and intellectual resources so as to allow for the individual she knew herself to be.

Early in his career, Sapir reviewed in *Modern Philology* (1907) Herder's "Treatise on the Origin of Language," written in 1770. Just as this treatise was a seminal point in Herder's intellectual development so too was Sapir's review an important stage in his own critical thinking. Benedict's debt to Herder is less clear, although Matthews and others locate in Herder the "organicist theory of cultural uniqueness," which she later "reproduced" in *Patterns of Culture*.[65] For both Sapir and Benedict, however, Boas's teachings were the immediate filter through which they encountered Herder's commanding ideas. However, as Isaiah Berlin suggests, beyond any specific influence Herder's intellectual legacy underpins the thinking of all those who locate the "genius of a people" in national and/or ethnic forms, especially those who privilege folk expressions to be the vital nucleus of a people's cultural identity: "All regionalists, all defenders of the local against the universal, all champions of deeply rooted forms of life . . . owe something, whether they know it or not, to the doctrines which Herder . . . introduced into European thought."[66] At the same time, however, Herder was no less a champion of the fullest, most far-ranging intellectual thought and this commitment was premised on his deep faith in freedom and the free flow of the human imagination.[67] Thus, just as Herder championed that all peoples manifested (at least potentially) an intrinsic and unique integrity, so too did he equally encourage the fullest integrity of the individual. Ideally, the one was a grounding for the other.[68] But tradition could be stultifying, and one had to allow for the contingent and the arbitrary. In addition, as Berlin makes clear, Herder's vision of community and his envisioning of community were grounded in deep personal and intellectual tensions, tensions that Sapir, Benedict, and Du Bois also experienced in their efforts to construct imaginative visions of "collective individuality."[69]

In the "Forethought" to *The Souls of Black Folk*, Du Bois boldly maps the range and importance of his great work: "the problem of the Twentieth Century is the problem of the color line," a line that extends to the "relation[s] of the darker to the lighter races . . . in Asia and Africa, in America and the islands of the sea."[70] Within this geography, however, lies buried Du Bois's true subject, the psychological landscape he calls "the strange meaning of being black."[71] This landscape is strange because one soon learns that he is a stranger in the land of his birth as well as a stranger even to himself—"one ever feels his two-ness, an American, a Negro, two souls, two thoughts, two unreconciled strivings; two warring ideals in one dark body." At the same time, the "meaning of being black" is strange to whites, foreign to their understanding though configured in great part by their very ignorance and indifference. Thus, Du Bois's strategy is to take his reader into veiled territory so as to "view faintly its deeper recesses—the meaning of its religion, the passion of its human sorrow, and the struggle of its greater souls." In so doing, however, Du Bois also initiates his own effort to discover these "deeper recesses." Equally important, this act of discovering others is simultaneously a discovery of self. Although Du Bois assures us that he is "bone of the bone and flesh of the flesh of them that live within the Veil," this identification barely suggests the complex turns of his own inward journey.

History frames as well as sustains the narrative of *The Souls of Black Folk*. In lifting the veil that separates black and white, Du Bois provides a historical setting, figures of historical importance, and his own personal history in Tennessee and Georgia to carry the narrative to the penultimate chapter, "The Sorrow Songs." Not only are we provided with a perspective that links past and present but a perspective that mirrors and is a mirror for the historical experience of other peoples. We learn to see, for example, that "Sambo's history" has also been that of "John and Hans, of Jacques and Pat," that "the efficiency or temper of the mass of black laborers" is little different from that of "all ground-down peasantries."[72] At the same time, Du Bois draws upon cultural phenomena whose origins, though outside the immediate contours of the American experience, link with and become an integral part of that experience. Thus, in discussing the importance of the Negro church we see its roots in, retention of, and transformation from African forms of spiritual worship. Likewise, European forms and values infuse the narrative, especially as they resonate in Du Bois's own imagination, and provide a critical as well as liberating perspective. Not only does a cotton field call to mind "the ancient and the modern

Quest of the Golden Fleece" but a Negro folk song echoes feelings toward life and death to be found in German folk songs. Through comparison, diffusion, and/or transformation Du Bois links the experience of African Americans to an historical framework that transcends the immediate boundaries of the nation itself. In so doing, he broadens as well as particularizes their experience while challenging "the arrogance of peoples irreverent toward Time and ignorant of the deeds of men."[73]

But most important, Du Bois's focus is on the experience of African Americans within the historical contours of America itself. The "Negro" might be a "sort of seventh son" cursed and spit upon by his "fellow" Americans, but he was not cursed by God and his race was not a curse. The limits and abuses that blacks experienced were the very fabric of the American experience itself. Slavery was a system that exploited as well as shaped, a system in which legally, politically, and economically North and South were "co-partners in guilt." It was also a system recently converted to new forms of power, though built on the past foundations of exploitation and prejudice. If, as Du Bois tells us, Georgia was "historic ground . . . the centre of the Negro problem—the centre of . . . America's dark heritage from slavery and the slave trade," Georgia was also common ground, one whose circumference was the nation itself.

Important as it was to historicize "America's dark [as well as white] heritage," to objectify the "Negro problem," Du Bois suggests the limits of historical generalization. In "Of the Sons of Master and Man" he writes, "outside of written history and outside of printed law, there has been going on for a generation as deep a storm and stress of human souls, as intense a ferment of feeling, as intricate a writhing of spirit, as ever a people experienced."[74] While, in "Of the Quest of the Golden Fleece," he warns us that "we often forget that each unit in the mass is a throbbing human soul."[75] Although Du Bois, here, calls attention to "written history" and "printed law" his deeper point is that black Americans were not simply objects of history itself, not simply victims of a dehumanizing system.[76] Most important, they were conscious beings, a people whose inner thoughts and spiritual resources constituted a shared moral and emotional landscape. In a word, these were people with a culture. Individually and collectively they were a folk. It was Du Bois's challenge to reveal this inner world of meaning, all but invisible to whites and not always fully visible to blacks, and to link this meaning with the expressive and symbolic forms that sustained these black folk.[77] Close up (the Burkes, the Dowells, Josie); from a distance (Du Bois's "grandfather's grandmother" . . . [who] often crooned a heathen melody to the child between her knees"); and anonymously (chapters framed with "weird old songs in which the soul of the black slave spoke to men") we see a people vulnerable in their "half-awakened common consciousness" and resourceful in their "common joy and grief."

Although the distinction between peasant and folk (between object and subject) importantly serves to distinguish Du Bois's point of view, it is a distinction that has been a source of controversy. Arnold Rampersad, for example, flatly asserts that "beyond his deep admiration for the religious songs, Du Bois was no champion of folk expression."[78] While Bernard Bell argues that Du Bois "transformed folk materials into formal art" and in so doing importantly contributed to the "struggle to reconcile his [and his peoples] double-consciousness as a black American."[79] Both Rampersad and Bell trace Du Bois's thinking to that of Herder, though clearly drawing significantly different conclusions. In neither argument, however, is the tension manifest in Herder's self-conscious consciousness, in consciousness itself, related to Du Bois's formulations of a collective black identity.

Prior to going South, prior to "leaving . . . the world of the white man," Du Bois recalls that in childhood he felt a deep identification with those who lived within the Veil—"Ever since I was a child these [Sorrow] songs have stirred me strangely. They came out of the South unknown to me, one by one, and yet at once I knew them as of me and of mine."[80] These remarks, which both culminate and retrospectively initiate *Souls*, serve to validate as well as unify the experience that unfolds. At the same time, Du Bois's own unfolding experience is telescoped within the unfolding historical experience of his people. Thus, he sees in the immediate aftermath of the Civil War a similar childhood awakening: "it changed the child of Emancipation to the youth with dawning self-consciousness, self-realization, self-respect."[81] Identification, however, also served to stimulate self-awareness, an awareness of self that no less than other concerns was object and subject of *The Souls of Black Folk*.

Whether addressing blacks as "peasants," as a "folk," or inscribing a folk identity with and within elite forms and meaning, Du Bois calls attention to his own interpretive presence. At times he points to differences in experience due to his New England birth—his quiet and subdued Sabbaths, for example, little prepared him for the "pythian madness" of a Southern Negro revival. At other times, he thinks more generally of the interpretive frames of the social scientist, positioning himself somewhere outside the veils of misapprehension presently shrouding sociological "understanding."[82] This distancing, however, contrasts with other moments wherein Du Bois questions "truths" he once shared with others but now must abandon. Throughout his journey Du Bois not only guides us into unfamiliar territory but consciously calls attention to the role he plays.[83] These moments of self reflection serve to personalize what Du Bois more generally called the "contradiction of double aims" that the "would-be black savant" experienced no less than other black Americans. However, in calling attention to himself Du Bois was not simply addressing the constraints that he and others commonly experienced. Reflection was also assertion. The "dim feeling" that Du Bois saw emerging in his people's consciousness—"that, to attain his place in the world, he must be himself, and not another"—was doubly his own. The self in one's self, that "higher individualism" together with "the sovereign human soul that seeks to know itself and the world about it," were central to Du Bois's message and his search. Although Booker T. Washington might not understand "a lone black boy poring over a French Grammar amid the weeds and dirt of a neglected home," might not understand Du Bois himself, Frederick Douglass and Alexander Crummell certainly would. For each of these men represented, as few others, that "transfigured spark of identity which we call Myself." It was this "myself," the integrity of Du Bois's own spark of identity, which not only identified with but identified those "of me and mine."

In the concluding paragraph of *The Souls of Black Folk*, Du Bois reflects on the songs of his father as he sits listening to "fresh young voices welling up . . . from the caverns of brick and mortar below—swelling with song, instinct with life, tremulous treble and darkening bass." Their words—"Let us cheer the weary traveler"—fuse with his own traveler's role as he "girds himself, and sets his face toward the Morning, and goes his way." In *Modernism and the Harlem Renaissance*, Houston Baker reads this passage as signaling the "conflation of African and American selves on the ritual ground of a black southern university." This reading, "the merger of old disjunctions and the forecast of a future unity of aims," only makes sense, Baker claims, if we regard *"The Souls of Black Folk* as a profoundly southern book."[84] Looming in the background of Baker's response, preceding and prefiguring both Du Bois and Baker himself, is the figure of Shakespeare's Caliban, not simply a possessed being but a being in possession. One who knows his way and what to say.[85]

Baker, however, should not overlook Franz Boas and Boas's efforts to transcribe the language of the Eskimos, his research on "sound-blindness," and his seminal article "On Alternating Sounds." One should also not overlook Herder for whom sounds (language) were both the essence of consciousness and the means to achieve a consciousness of one's essence. As Thomas De Zengotita has noted, "Herder's 'Essay on the Origin of Language' (1769) is his Book of Genesis."[86] However, if this essay gave birth to Herder's original vision of man as a *"sensorium commune"* it also pointed to the *"coincidentia oppositorum"* as his ideal answer.

Du Bois might hear himself in the "fresh young voices" beneath his window. But it is important to note that he heard other voices as well. In the conclusion "Of the Training of Black Men," high above "the dull red hideousness of Georgia," Du Bois confidently claimed, "I sit with Shakespeare and he winces not." Soul brothers in the deepest sense, their fraternity was that of enlightened individuals. Others, too, found Shakespeare a kindred soul. In "Do We Need a Superorganic?" (1917), Edward Sapir expressed essential agreement with the distinction Alfred Kroeber made between organic heredity and social tradition. Nevertheless, Sapir insisted, "it is always the individual that really thinks and acts and dreams and revolts." Shakespeare, he dryly noted, was not simply "the cat's paw of general cultural drifts."[87] And in "Shakespear" (1772) Herder historicized as well as individualized England's dramatic genius. For each scholar, Shakespeare served significantly different purposes. However, all three saw in this "speaker of being," in themselves, and in the world they inhabited the "tensions of the One and the Many" that each in his own way sought to reconcile and to voice.[88]

Throughout *Souls*, Du Bois pauses to reflect on what he sees and the spell these experiences cast upon his imagination: "How curious a land is this,—full of untold story, of tragedy and laughter, and the rich legacy of human life, shadowed with a tragic past and big with future promise."[89] Du Bois's words proved to be both inspiration and prophecy, for, as the new century lengthened into the 1920s, into what became known as the Harlem Renaissance, story upon story began to be told. Du Bois, no less than others, championed and sought to shape this "rich legacy of human life . . . big with future promise." In 1920, writing in *Crisis*, he sharpened his earlier musings: "A renaissance of American Negro literature is due; the material about us in the strange, heart-rending race tangle is rich beyond dream and only we can tell the tale and sing the song from the heart."[90] Five years later, in "The Social Origins of American Negro Art," (1925) Du Bois encouraged as well as cautioned a balance between individual and group expression: "The art instinct is naturally and primarily individualistic . . . [but] in most cases individual impulse was combined with a certain group compulsion."[91]

By then, however, Du Bois found himself at odds with many of the very writings he so eagerly encouraged. Claude McKay's *Home to Harlem* (1928) nauseated Du Bois and "after the dirtier part of its filth [he felt] distinctly like taking a bath."[92] Hopefully, McKay would someday "rise above" all this and provide "in fiction [a] strong, well-knit as well as beautiful theme."[93] Likewise, Du Bois complained that in *The Walls of Jericho* (1928) Rudolph Fisher "has not depicted Negroes like his mother, his sisters, his wife, his real Harlem friends. He has not even depicted his own soul."[94] Ironically, the very tensions that Du Bois himself had felt and had so eloquently voiced continued to stimulate imaginative expression. Only now, self expression had taken a path he was reluctant to follow.

NOTES

1. W.E.B. Du Bois, *Crisis* 15 (1917–18), 169.

2. Robert T. Clark, *Herder: His Life nd Thought* (Berkeley: University of California Press, 1955), 308–47. Also Joe K. Fugates, *The Psychological Basis of Herder's Aesthetics* (Paris: Mouton, 1966).

3. George W. Stocking, Jr., "Franz Boas and the Culture Concept," in *Race, Culture, and Evolution: Essays in the History of Anthropology* (New York: The Free Press, 1968), 195–233. More generally, George Stocking, ed., *Volksgeist as Method and Ethic: Essays on Boasian Ethnography and the German Anthropological Tradition* (Madison: University of Wisconsin Press, 1996).

4. As Isaiah Berlin writes, "No writer has stressed more vividly the damage done to human beings by being torn from the only conditions in which their history has made it possible for them to live full lives. He insists over and over again that no one milieu is necessarily superior to any other. He assumes only that to be fully human, that is, fully creative, one must belong somewhere, to some group or some historical stream which cannot be defined save in the generic terms of tradition and milieu and culture." Isaiah Berlin, "J. G. Herder (II)," *Encounter* 25 (July, 1965): 43.

5. Thomas de Zengotita, "Speakers of Being: Romantic Refusion and Cultural Anthropology," in *Romantic Motives: Essays on Anthropological Sensibility,* ed. George W. Stocking (Madison: University of Wisconsin Press, 1989), 88–89.

6. "Indeed the notion of unity in difference, still more that of differences in unity, the tension of the One and the Many, is his obsessive idée maitresse." Berlin, "J. G. Herder," 33.

7. Michael Morton, *Herder and the Poetics of Thought* (University Park: Pennsylvania State University Press, 1989), 12.

8. Ibid., 18.

9. Franz Boas, "Human Faculty as Determined by Race," in *The Shaping of American Anthropology—1883–1911*, ed. George Stocking (New York: Basic Books, Inc., 1974), 223.

10. Ibid., 226.

11. "The variations, however, are such that we may expect many individuals of all races to be equally gifted, while the number of men and women of higher ability will differ." Ibid., 242.

12. Franz Boas, "The Mind of Primitive Man," *The Journal of American Folklore* (January–March, 1901): 14.

13. Stocking, *The Shaping of American Anthropology*, 223.

14. Boas, "The Mind of Primitive Man," 11.

15. See Marshall Hyatt, "The Struggle for Racial Equality," in *Franz Boas Social Activist: The Dynamics of Ethnicity* (Westport, CT: Greenwood Press, 1990), 83–102

16. In the introduction to *Die Philosophie der Geschichte*, G.W.F. Hegel writes "We now leave Africa never to mention it again. For it is not a historical continent, it shows neither change nor development, and whatever may have happened there belongs to the world of Asia and Europe." J. M. Ita, "Frobenius, Senghor and the Image of Africa," in *Modes of Thought—Essays in Thinking*, ed. Robin Horton and Ruth Finnegan (London: Faber and Faber, 1973), 306–37.

Neale Acherson comments in 1992 that "more than thirty years ago" one of his professor's at Cambridge sought to discourage his [Acherson's] idea to do a postgraduate thesis on Ugandan history: "The older one, a mighty anthropologist, said flatly that there was no such thing as African history. This was partly because there were no documents to speak of, and only a very little archaeology. But it was mostly . . . because the essence of Africa was that nothing much had ever changed there. Africa, unlike the rest of the world, was static. A continent with no change or development plainly had no history—although he could envisage young troublemakers going out to invent some." Acherson, *The New York Review of Books* 29 (June 11, 1992): 26–29.

17. W.E.B. Du Bois to Franz Boas, 11 October 1905, Moreland Research Library, Howard University.

18. Ibid.

19. In his address Boas stated: To those who stoutly maintain a material inferiority of the Negro race and who would dampen your ardor by their claims, you may confidently reply that the burden of proof rests with them, that the past history of your race does not sustain their statement, but rather gives you encouragement. The physical inferiority of the Negro race, if it exists at all, is insignificant when compared to the wide range of individual variability in each race. There is no anatomical evidence available that would sustain the view that the bulk of the Negro race could not become as useful citizens as the members of any other race. That there may be slightly different hereditary traits seems plausible, but it is entirely arbitrary to assume that those of the Negro, because perhaps slightly different, must be of an inferior type. Stocking, *The Shaping of American Anthropology—1883–1911*, 313–14.

20. Ibid.

21. More by implication than direct argument Boas placed blame on slavery and racism. But in *The Mind of Primitive Man* Boas writes, "The traits of the American Negro are adequately explained on the basis of his history and status. The tearing away from the African

soil and the consequent complete loss of the old standards of life, which were replaced by the dependency of slavery and by all it entailed, followed by a period of disorganization and by a severe economic struggle against heavy odds, are sufficient to explain the inferiority. In short, there is every reason to believe that the Negro, when given facility and opportunity, will be perfectly able to fulfill the duties of citizenship as well as his white neighbor." Boas, *The Mind of Primitive Man* (New York: Macmillan, 1916), 272–73.

22. Du Bois, for example, wrote to Herskovits,"I wonder if I could trouble you for a confidential opinion concerning a colored anthropologist. . . . I should like very much to get a line on him as a scientist and as a man." Du Bois to Melville Herskovits, 31 May 1935, W.E.B. Du Bois Papers, Special Collections and Archives, University of Massachusetts Amherst Library.

Herskovits replied, "My feeling concerning him [Louis King] is that he is an honest, conscientious thorough-going man of mediocre ability. I know he had great difficulty finally getting through his Ph. D examinations. . . . I contrast him with Dr. Mark Watkins who took his Ph.D. two or three years ago from the University of Chicago in anthropology, and who is, I believe, one of the finest young men, colored or white, in the subject." Herskovits to Du Bois, 5 June 1935, W.E.B. Du Bois Papers, Special Collections and Archives, University of Massachusetts Amherst Library.

23. The following from Walter White to Boas is typical of the requests he would receive: "In our work here at the office (NAACP), we are asked many questions, wise and foolish, and one which recurs frequently is this. If a child is born of one parent who is white and the other with a small admixture of Negro blood, is it not true that the child may be black? White to Franz Boas, 9 December 1925, Manuscript Division, Library of Congress.

Writing for Boas, Herskovits answered: "the chances of a child born to such a couple having distinctly Negroid characteristics would be almost infinitesimal. What might well occur would be that such a child would have one Negroid trait, such as, let me say, broad nostrils. But I doubt very much whether there would be a combination of Negroid traits which would mark such offsprings as a distinct Negro. As you may know, such occurrence of one Negroid trait is remarked often among Western Asiatic peoples who have a slight admixture of Negro blood, and among whom there will be seen an individual here and there who has Negroid hair, or nostrils, or lips. But the frequency of these occurrences has never, to my knowledge, been studied." Herskovits to Walter White, 13 December 1926, Manuscript Division, Library of Congress.

24. Marshall Hyatt, "Franz Boas and the Struggle for Black Equality: The Dynamics of Ethnicity," in *Perspectives in American History*, New Series, 2 (1985), 295.

25. W.E.B. Du Bois, *Dusk of Dawn: An Essay Toward an Autobiography of a Race Concept* (New York: Harcourt, Brace, 1940), 50.

26. Francis Broderick, "German Influence on the Scholarship of W.E.B. Du Bois," 19 *Phylon,* (winter 1958): 367. Upon his return to America, Du Bois recalls in *Dusk of Dawn* "I was going to study the facts, any and all facts, concerning the American Negro and his plight, and by measurement and comparison and research, work up to any valid generalization which I could." Du Bois, *Dusk of Dawn,* 51. For the most recent and most detailed discussion of Du Bois's years in Germany see David Levering Lewis, "*Lehrjahre*," in *W.E.B. Du Bois: Biography of a Race—1868–1919* (New York: Henry Holt, 1993), 117–50.

27. Broderick, *Phylon* (winter 1958): 370. As Broderick writes, "Du Bois's notes on Schmoler's seminar quote the German as saying: 'My school tries as far as possible to leave the *sollen* for a later stage and study the *geschehen* as other sciences have done.'" Ibid., 369.

Under Du Bois's direction, *The Philadelphia Negro* was soon followed by a series of pioneering monographs, at the time the most ambitious sociological studies of African American life ever written in America. "The object of these studies is primarily scientific—a careful search for truth conducted as thoroughly, broadly, and honestly as the material resources and mental equipment at command will allow." Du Bois, *Dusk of Dawn,* 64. Also see, Elliott Rudwick, "W.E.B. Du Bois as Sociologist," in *Black Sociologists: Historical and Contemporary Perspectives,* eds. James E. Blackwell and Morris Janowitz (Chicago: University of Chicago Press, 1974), 25–55.

28. Adam Kuper, "The Boasians and the Critique of Evolutionism," in *The Invention of Primitive Society: Transformations of an Illusion* (London: Routledge, 1988), 150. Margaret Mead's comments on Boas's teaching reveal the care and precision he expected of his students: On the one hand was Alexander Goldenweiser, "mercurial, excited by ideas about culture, but intolerant of the petty exactions of field work" . . . on the other hand, Elsie Clews Parsons, from whom "students learned that anthropology consisted of an enormous mass of little bits of material carefully labeled by time, place, and tribe—the fruits, arid and bitter, of long, long hours of labor and devotion" Mead, *An Anthropologist at Work: Writings of Ruth Benedict* (Boston: Houghton Mifflin, 1959), 8.

29. See William S. Willis, Jr., "Franz Boas and the Study of Black Folklore," in *The New Ethnicity: Perspectives From Ethnology,* ed. John W. Bennett (St. Paul, MN: West Publishing, 1957), 307–34.

30. W.E.B. Du Bois, "The Conservation of Races," in *The American Negro Academy: Occasional Papers,* no. 2 (Washington, DC: The Academy, 1897), 7.

31. "It is our duty to conserve our physical powers, our intellectual endowments, our spiritual ideals; as a race we must strive by race organization, by race solidarity, by race unity to the realization of that broder humanity which freely recognizes differences in men, but sternly deprecates inequaltiy in their opportunities of development." Ibid., 12.

32. Ibid., 10.

33. W.E.B. Du Bois, "Strivings of the Negro People," *Atlantic Monthly,* (August 1897): 194–95.

34. Du Bois, *Dusk of Dawn,* 59.

35. William Stanley Braithwaite, "The Negro in American Literature," in *The New Negro,* ed. Alain Locke (New York: Atheneum, 1968), 40.

36. Wilson J. Moses, "The Poetics of Ethiopianism: W.E.B. Du Bois and Literary Black Nationalism," in *Critical Essays on W.E.B. Du Bois,* ed. William Andrews (Boston: G. K. Hall, 1985), 102.

37. Bernard W. Bell, "W.E.B. Du Bois's Struggle to Reconcile Folk and High Art," in *Critical Essays on W.E.B. Du Bois,* ed. William L. Andrews (Boston: G. K. Hall, 1985), 106.

38. Houston A. Baker, Jr., "The Black Man of Culture: W.E.B. Du Bois and *The Souls of Black Folk,*" in *Critical Essays on W.E.B. Du Bois,* 136.

39. Moses, "The Poetics of Ethiopianism," 102; Bell, "W.E.B Du Bois's Struggle to Reconcile Folk and High Art," 110; Baker, "The Black Man of Culture," 136. ed. William L. Andrews (Boston: G. K. Hall, 1985).

40. "Bismarck was my hero. He had made a nation out of a mass of bickering peoples. He had dominated the whole development with his strength. . . . This foreshadowed in my mind the kind of thing that American Negroes must do, marching forth with strength and determination under trained leadership." Du Bois, *Dusk of Dawn,* 32.

41. Bell, "W.E.B. Du Bois's Struggle to Reconcile Folk and High Art," 110. Boas writes, "My reading of the writings of philosophers stimulated new lines of thought, and my previous

interests became overshadowed by a desire to understand the relation between the objective and subjective world." Boas, "Living Philosophies, II—An Anthropologist's Credo," *Nation* 147 (8/27/1938), 201–4.

42. George Stocking, "From Physics to Ethnology," in *Race, Culture and Evolution: Essays in the History of Anthropology*, 133–60.

43. Franz Boas, "The Study of Geography," in *Race, Language and Culture* (New York: The Free Press, 1968), 644.

44. Ibid., 646.

45. Stocking, *Race, Culture and Evolution*, 159.

46. Michael Carrithers, "Is Anthropology Art or Science?" *Current Anthropology* 31 (June 1990): 263–82.

47. Mead, *An Anthropologist At Work*, xviii.

48. Melville Herskovits, "Anthropological Methods—Franz Boas," February 23, 1923, Melville Herskovits Papers, Northwestern University Archives.

49. See Casey Nelson Blake, *Beloved Community: The Cultural Criticism of Randolph Bourne, Van Wyck Brooks, Waldo Frank, and Lewis Mumford* (Chapel Hill: University of North Carolina Press, 1990).

50. F. H. Matthews, "The Revolt against Americanism: Cultural Pluralism and Cultural Relativism as an Ideology of Liberation," *The Canadian Review of American Studies* 1 (Spring 1970): 17.

51. Ibid., 14.

52. As George Stocking writes, "so long as anthropologists continue to be interested in broadly contrastive characterizations of otherness, subjectivity will be both the object and the instrument of their endeavor. If methodological sophistication may to some extent bring that subjectivity under control, it seems unlikely that method can ever eliminate entirely the anxiety aroused by the subjective encounter with otherness; and, as Boas's opposition implies, it may in fact be that our understanding is in some profound sense dependent on that anxiety. If this is the case, then it seems unlikely that the tension between the "organic" and the "repressive" orientations—any more than that Boas postulated between the methods of analysis and understanding—will ever disappear from anthropology." Stocking, "The Ethnographic Sensibility of the 1920s and the Dualism of the Anthropological Tradition," in *Romantic Motives: Essays on Anthropological Sensibility* (Madison: University of Wisconsin Press, 1989), 268.

53. Edward Sapir, "Culture, Genuine and Spurious," in *Selected Writings of Edward Sapir in Language, Culture and Personality*, ed. David G. Mandelbaum (Berkeley: University of California Press, 1949), 316.

54. Ibid., 311.

55. Ibid., 315.

56. Handler, "The Dainty Man and the Hungry Man," in *Observers Observed: Essays on Ethnographic Field Work*, ed. George Stocking (Madison: University of Wisconsin Press, 1983), 208–31.

57. Edward Sapir, "A Symposium of the Exotic," *Dial* 73 (November, 1922): 570.

58. Margaret M. Caffrey, *Ruth Benedict: Stranger in This Land* (Austin: University of Texas Press, 1989), 127.

59. Benedict's "Psychological Types in the Cultures of the Southwest" (1928) and "Configurations of Culture in North America" (1932) were important early writings that preceded her enormously popular and provocative *Patterns of Culture* (1932). In 1931 Sapir offered a seminar at Yale on culture and personality. Soon after, under Sapir's direction, the

Social Science Research Council and the National Research Council funded research on culture and personality. Caffrey, *Ruth Benedict: Stranger in This Land,* 214.

60. "Within one's own culture, the study of other patterns might be a guide to personal action, might, by showing the range along the arc of possibility, encourage planning for a broader, more tolerant society in the future, one which would waste as few kinds of personality as possible." Matthews, "The Revolt against Americanism," 22.

Throughout the 1920s Benedict also wrote, as did Boas, for a popular audience. As Margaret Caffrey writes, "By that spring (1923) Benedict had already become engaged in the project of making American culture-conscious by writing popular articles for placement in various magazines like *Nation, New Republic, American Mercury, Scribner's, Harper's,* and *Century* in order to make anthropological ideas an important factor in American life." Caffrey, *Ruth Benedict: Stranger in This Land,* 122.

61. To account for Benedict's deconstructionist strategy, Geertz situates her, though somewhat insecurely, in the prevailing intellectual milieu: "That someone so intent to disturb should so represent herself as engaged in constructing a table raisonnée of human possibilities is mainly to be accounted for by the intellectual environment in which she worked, but to which, coming late and with a metaphorical turn of mind, she never quite properly belonged." Clifford Geertz, *Works and Lives: The Anthropologist as Author* (Stanford: Stanford University Press, 1988), 115.

62. Ruth Benedict, *Patterns of Culture* (Boston: Houghton Mifflin, 1989), 2–3.

63. Ibid., 37, 249.

64. Ibid., 262, 270.

65. Matthews, "Cultural Pluralism and Cultural Relativism," 29.

66. Isaiah Berlin, *Vico and Herder—Two Studies in the History of Ideas* (New York: The Viking Press, 1976), 176.

67. As Berlin writes, "He repeats throughout the *Ideen* that originality, freedom of choice and creation, is the divine element in man. . . . Herder, in opposition to the primitivists, welcomed invention—the arts and sciences are fruits of the creative powers of man, and through them he rises to the full height of his purposive nature." Ibid., 178.

68. "True *Fortgang* (advance) is the development of human beings as integrated wholes and, more particularly, their development as groups—tribes, cultures, and communities determined by language and custom, creating out of the "totality of their collective experience." Ibid., 191.

69. "The vision of the unity of the human personality and its integration into the social organism by 'natural' means was the polar opposite of Herder's own character and conduct. . . . His ideas seem, at times, a mirror image of his own frustrations." Ibid., 205. Also, Gordon Craig, "Herder: The Legacy," in *Herder Today* (Berlin: Walter de Gruyter, 1990), 17–30.

70. W.E.B. Du Bois, "Of the Dawn of Freedom" and "Forethought," in *The Souls of Black Folk* (New York: Penguin Books, 1989), 13, 1.

71. Du Bois, "Forethought," in *Souls,* 1.

72. Du Bois, "Of the Quest of the Golden Fleece," in *Souls,* 123.

73. Du Bois, "The Sorrow Songs," in *Souls,* 214.

74. Du Bois, "Of the Sons of Masters and Man," in *Souls,* 147.

75. Du Bois,"Of the Quest of the Golden Fleece," in *Souls,* 118.

76. As Houston Baker has written, "Du Bois's title [*The Souls of Black Folk*] suggests spirit and duration rather than a historically and materially grounded slavery." Baker, *Modernism and the Harlem Renaissance* (Chicago: University of Chicago Press, 1987), 63.

77. "We must remember that living as the blacks do in close contact with a great modern nation, and sharing, although imperfectly, the soul-life of that nation, they must necessarily be affected more or less directly by all the religious and ethical forces that are to-day moving the United States. These questions and movements are, however, overshadowed and dwarfed by the (to them) all-important question of their civil, political, and economic status. They must perpetually discuss the 'Negro problem,'—must live, move, and have their being in it, and interpret all else in its light or darkness." Du Bois, "Of the Faith of the Fathers,"in *Souls*, 164.

78. Arnold Rampersad, *The Art and Imagination of W.E.B. Du Bois* (Cambridge: Harvard University Press, 1976), 74.

79. Bell, "W.E.B. Du Bois's Struggle to Reconcile Folk and High Art," in *Critical Essays*, 106.

80. Du Bois, "The Sorrow Songs," in *Souls*, 204.

81. Du Bois, "Of Our Spiritual Strivings" in *Souls*, 9.

82. In "Of Our Spiritual Strivings" Du Bois laments the sociologists who "gleefully count" bastards and prostitutes while ignoring the "very soul of the toiling, sweating black man" and the despair experienced. But in "The Sorrow Songs" he addresses more generally the inchoate state of sociological understanding—"So woefully unorganized is sociological knowledge that the meaning of progress, the meaning of 'swift' and 'slow' in human doing, and the limits of human perfectability, are veiled, unanswered sphinxes on the shores of science." Du Bois, *Souls*, 214.

83. As he writes, "But we must hasten on our journey. This that we pass as we leave Atlanta is the ancient land of the Cherokees,—that brave Indian nation which strove so long for its fatherland, until Fate and the United States Government drove them beyond the Mississippi. If you wish to ride with me you must come into the 'Jim Crow Car.' " Du Bois, "Of the Black Belt," in *Souls*, 93.

84. Baker, *Modernism and the Harlem Renaissance*, 58.

85. Ibid., 53–69.

86. De Zengotita, "Speakers of Being," in *Romantic Motives*, 89.

87. Edward Sapir, "Do We Need a Superorganic?," *American Anthropologist* 19 (1917): 443.

88. Berlin, *Vico and Herder*, 154. Thomas De Zengotita defines Romanticism as "the effort of the alienated modern mind to refuse itself, as alienated, and so re-fuse itself, as embodied in the world." And he goes on to say, "the Speaker both expresses and creates being: he does not, like the Stewart, govern a world of objects and instruments from a position of abstraction; he participates through utterance." Zengotita, "Speakers of Being, in *Romantic Motives*, 75–76. With this definition in mind, he considers Johann von Herder and Edward Sapir, among four representative thinkers, as "speakers of being." Might we not, with some care, think of Du Bois in these terms, one who spoke to the alienation of himself and others while simultaneously asserting the integrity of their and his own identity?

89. Du Bois, "Of the Black Belt," in *Souls*, 100.

90. Du Bois, "Negro Writers," *Crisis* 19 (April 1920): 299.

91. Du Bois, "The Social Origins of American Negro Art," *Modern Quarterly* 3 (autumn 1925): 53.

92. Du Bois, *Crisis* 35 (June 1928): 202.

93. Ibid.

94. Du Bois, *Crisis* 35 (November 1928): 374.

Chapter 3

"Feeling Universality and Thinking Particularistically": Alain Locke, Franz Boas, and Melville Herskovits

I n 1925 in *The New Negro*, Alain Locke announced to the world that something new, "something beyond the watch and guard of statistics," had taken place in the racial alembic of twentieth-century America. Although the "Sociologist," the "Philanthropist," and the "Race-leader" were not unaware of this "changeling," this New Negro, they were unable to account for what they saw. A new awareness was needed, for these authorities were unable to see beyond the limits and assumptions of their professional interests. For this reason, it was Locke's intent, as a professor of philosophy at Howard University, to announce, to identify, and to help bring to life this renaissance of the spirit. Not unlike Du Bois in *The Souls of Black Folk*, Locke challenged his generation to see the world with fresh eyes. But, whereas Du Bois took his reader to the South, to "historic ground," Locke looked over the terrain of a "younger generation . . . vibrant with a new psychology." Harlem, not Georgia, was the center of his attention. Unlike Du Bois, Locke did not seek to reveal "the strange experience" of being a "problem" but celebrated the pride of being black in America.[1]

Locke's introductory essay, "The New Negro," is itself charged with all the energy and optimism that he argues to be the new consciousness of this postwar generation. His emphasis is on change, innovation, a boldness of imagination, and a willingness to confront limitations both imposed and self-imposed. And just as the forms and formal arrangements of the past are dismissed as irrelevant, so does the very form of *The New Negro* announce "a new figure on the national canvass and a new force in the foreground of affairs." Poetry, short story, and drama; the art of Aaron Douglas, Winold Reiss, and Miguel Covarrubias; and masks and statues of various African peoples constitute a richly diverse and expressive mosaic representative of the transformations that Locke sees taking place in "the inner and outer life of the Negro in America." Sustaining as well as expanding upon the cultural implications of this core of imaginative expression are a wide range of essays that explore "this deep feeling of race [which] is at present the mainspring of Negro life."

The New Negro was immediately hailed as a tour de force and has continued to serve as symbol and nucleus of the Harlem Renaissance.[2] Locke himself quickly gained national, even international prominence, his own naissance as a public figure directly linked with the renaissance he helped to nurture. In looking back upon these euphoric years, William S. Braithwaite compared Locke to Erasmus, both individuals "the propelling spirit" of a renaissance.[3] Locke's assessment of his own role, however, was considerably more modest. In the preface to his essay "Values and Imperatives," Locke was content to describe himself as "more of a philosophical mid-wife to a generation of younger Negro poets, writers, artists than a professional philosopher."[4] Subsequent scholarship has tended to side more with Locke's point of view than with Braithwaite's. "Mid-wife," however, is deceptively modest, for Locke does not simply assist another's labor.[5] His own work attempts an integrating vision, one that is itself a creative effort.

Although Locke remained intellectually active throughout his life—tirelessly promoting black writers and artists; teaching; lecturing; editing; and writing for various journals—his own involvement in the Harlem Renaissance (indeed the renaissance itself) soon all but slipped from view. In part, Locke himself had anticipated, if not contributed to, this decline in interest. In 1936, looking back on the 1920s Locke was no longer certain that "the rosy enthusiasms and hopes of 1925 were more than bright illusions or a cruelly deceptive mirage."[6] In a sense, Locke was now forced to confront an ending that history itself seemed to have fashioned. But Locke also questioned the underlying assumptions of his earlier understanding. In *The New Negro* Locke presumed that through art and literature, through cultural recognition, there would result "that revaluation of the Negro which must precede or accompany any considerable further betterment of race relationships."[7] Ten years later, however, he proposed that "there is no cure or saving magic in poetry and art, an emerging generation of talent, or international prestige and interracial recognition, for unemployment or precarious marginal employment."[8] For the next thirty years, interest in the Harlem Renaissance was at best a private concern. However, in the political and cultural ferment of the 1960s and in the deepened interest in ethnic and racial identity that marked these years both the Harlem Renaissance and Alain Locke became central to our sense of the past and our concerns for the present.

Two important studies, Harold Cruse's *The Crisis of the Negro Intellectual* (1967) and Nathan Huggins's *Harlem Renaissance* (1971), helped to initiate contemporary interest in the nineteen twenties and the recovery of a generation of black men and women only dimly remembered. Years later, in *When Harlem Was in Vogue* (1982), David Levering Lewis broadened our understanding of Locke and his role as a cultural promoter and arbiter of taste. The Harlem Renaissance and Locke's theoretical and critical interest in art and literature continued to draw attention. Most notably, so as to stimulate further study of these interests, Jeffrey Stewart provided in *The Critical Temper of Alain Locke: A Selection of His Essays on Art and Culture* (1983) a diverse selection of Locke's writings spanning the years 1923 to 1952. More recently, in *Modernism and the Harlem Renaissance* (1987), Houston A. Baker, Jr. saluted *The New Negro* as "a broadening and enlargement of the field of traditional Afro-American discursive possibilities." Baker's remarks contrast with the marginal and compromised view of the Harlem Renaissance seen by Huggins, who saw Locke as a special form of American provincialism, and Lewis, who presented Locke as a brilliant but eccentric academic "with a weakness for his male students" and a proud individual compromised by his "pleasant servitude" to the wealthy, white Mrs. Charlotte Osgood Mason. In Baker's view, *The New Negro* was a central text, "summoning concerns not of a problematical folk but rather those of a newly emergent race or nation—a national culture."[9]

In addition to this surge of scholarship, the first "Alain L. Locke Symposium," sponsored by *The Harvard Advocate,* took place at Harvard University in December, 1973. In the summer of 1978 (June 12 to August 4) participants gathered at Atlanta University for a seminar dedicated to "one of the most important black figures of the twentieth century." Both conferences were efforts to give fuller attention to the range and complexity of Locke's thought. Not only was he understood to be a neglected figure, but the attention that had been given was seen, primarily, as an effort "to use Locke as a lens through which to see black writers like Langston Hughes, Countee Cullen, Sterling Brown, [and] artists like Aaron Douglas."[10] As a consequence, Locke's interest in philosophical and anthropological issues was singled out for special attention. As Russell Linnemann stated in the introduction to the Atlanta University conference papers, later published under the title *Alain Locke: Reflections on a Modern Renaissance Man* (1982), it was the specific intent of this volume of essays to address Locke's "deep . . . involvement with anthropology in general and questions of cultural pluralism in particular."[11]

Since Linnemann's call for a "sorely needed 'renaissance' in Lockean studies," Locke has, as seen, become the focus of increased attention.[12] Johnny Washington's *Alain Locke and Philosophy: A Quest for Cultural Pluralism* (1986) is the first study to present Locke not simply as a "philosophical mid-wife," as a "lens" to see others, but as a major philosophical voice who has contributed to our theoretical understanding of cultural pluralism and its specific meaning for a democratic, ethnically diverse society. In addition to bibliographical and biographical essays that have appeared, Leonard Harris has made available in one source, *The Philosophy of Alain Locke: Harlem Renaissance and Beyond* (1989), Locke's major philosophic and social writings.[13] In addition, Harris and Ernest Mason have provided important critical essays detailing the complex patterns of Locke's philosophical ideas.[14] To a degree, then, Locke is enjoying a "renaissance" of his own. However, the central challenge posed by Linnemann and addressed, as well, at the "Alain L. Locke Symposium" remains unanswered. Nathan Huggins's concern—"we have tended to ignore the philosophical and theoretical grounds on which all of his efforts rested"—has yet to be fully explored. Locke's philosophical and anthropological concepts are still in need of clarification, and the relationship of these concepts to *The New Negro*, what Baker calls "perhaps our first national book," has not been fully addressed. Finally, as we shall see, in addition to Locke's work in value theory as a student of philosophy, this clarification must also include the intellectual presence of Franz Boas and his student Melville Herskovits.[15]

After three brilliant years as an undergraduate at Harvard (1904–7), Locke studied at Oxford University (1907–10) and then pursued a year of advanced work in philosophy at the University of Berlin (1910–11). In 1916 he returned to Harvard, receiving a Ph.D. in philosophy upon completion of his dissertation, "The Problem of Classification in Theory of Value" (1918). One is immediately struck by certain parallels in Locke's intellectual development with that of Du Bois, the first black American to have received a Ph.D. at Harvard. The differences, however, were equally great. While still thinking of studying philosophy, Du Bois offered in a paper for William James, "The Renaissance of Ethics: A Critical Comparison of Scholastic and Modern Ethics," distinctions and observations that Locke, twenty years later, would consider antithetical if not irrelevant to the notion of modernity and the challenge implicit in the term "modern ethics."[16] Their differences help to reveal not only something about the shift in intellectual focus that marks these years but differences as well in their individual intellectual sensibilities.

In his maiden effort to formulate a moral philosophy, Du Bois asserts (after first reviewing the history of scholastic ethics) that "the fundamental question of the universe, for ages past, present, and to come is Duty." However, given the split that exists between theology and science (value and fact), Du Bois argues that the only way back to ethics ("the beacon light of struggling humanity") is through science. Science lays the foundation. Science yields the facts, and "once we know the facts we can proceed to values, to ends." As Du Bois concludes, "first the What, then the Why—underneath the everlasting Ought."[17] Locke, however, radically questions what one means by science. In so doing he challenges not only the objectivity of science but the notion of objectivity itself. Not only is there no fixed point of view but there is no fixed point upon which to ground a point of view. As Locke was to write, "all philosophies, it seems to me, are in ultimate derivation philosophies of life and not of abstract, disembodied 'objective' reality: products of time, place and situation, and thus systems of timed history rather than timeless eternity."[18] The "relativity of human knowledge" that Du Bois dismissed as a barrier to truth was for Locke the nature of truth itself.

Although Locke was not concerned with the "everlasting Ought," he did address the "what" and the "why." As with Du Bois, he never lost faith that science had the potential to sort out facts and to distinguish empirical "truths" from ignorance and prejudice. Both men shared, for example, high regard for Melville Herskovits and Herskovits's carefully researched study *The American Negro* (1928): "When Melville Herskovits started anthropological measurements in Harlem, the only hope we had was that he was a pupil of Franz Boas. But he proved to be more than this. Herskovits is a real scientist. That is: a man who is more interested in arriving at truth than proving a thesis of race superiority."[19] However, Locke's praise for

Herskovits's work, as well as differences he had, were also based on his under-standing that facts did not speak for themselves. It was always somewhat problem-atic as to what, indeed, was a fact. In sum, it was not fully clear that the sequence Du Bois confidently asserted ("first the What; then the Why") was in the proper order or that it was even possible to speak in terms of an order.

The fundamental premise of Locke's philosophical concerns is that values are central to human experience, are experience itself, and that values arise from elemental states of feeling and not from some "everlasting Ought," some transcen-dent logic, or some insistent need or compelling problem. How, then, to establish a "science of values" without falsifying their inchoate and protean nature is the problem Locke addresses in his dissertation. To accomplish this, as Ernest Mason suggests, Locke's approach is both phenomenological and genetic: "Pheno-menologically, [he] attempts to explore and describe the psychological phenomena of valuational experiences; genetically, [he] traces the origin and development of these experiences in terms of the psychological processes involved. The essence of his position is that values should be classified in terms of the psychological or affective factors involved in the valuational experience."[20] Locke explores not only the subjective nature of experience but the experience of subjectivity itself. Not only does experience have meaning because one gives it meaning, but the act of meaning, deeply rooted in one's own emotional nature, is part of the experience as well. As Locke writes "the differentiated ways in which values are actually *sensed* and *felt*, though abstract and only to be traced genetically from the psychological point of view, are after all immediate and operative factors in valuation, and are, therefore, the fundamental bases for the distinctions of type among values as well as of the normative references and evaluative systematizations to which values are sub-sequently liable."[21] The certainties and boundaries Du Bois presumes to exist are no longer presumptions Locke can make. For Locke, to be modern is to understand that "values are rooted in attitudes, not in reality and pertain to ourselves, not to the world."[22] In certain respects Locke shares the emphasis of his contemporary, Ezra Pound, who argues in *"The New Age"* that to be modern is to understand that, "the artistic statement of a man is not his statement of the detached and theoretic part of himself, but of his will and of his emotions"[23] However, how to translate emotion into social and cultural forms that speak to and for black Americans distinguishes Locke's renaissance from that of Pound's *resorgimento*.

Leonard Harris and Ernest Mason both locate in Locke's philosophical thought the seeds of his social criticism and the basis upon which he provides a rationale for an alternative model of social understanding. To do so they place Locke within a specific intellectual tradition. Harris, for example, understands Locke's philo-sophical thought to be a synthesis of William James, Christian Freiherr von Ehrenfels, Alexius Meinong, Wilbur Marshall Urban, and Ralph Barton Perry. In addition to these formative inspirations, both men give special emphasis to Franz Clemens Brentano, a professor of philosophy and psychology at the University of Vienna. A quick reading of Locke's dissertation confirms the validity of their claims. In addition, so as to spell out the social implications of Locke's philosophical ideas, both of these critics more or less conflate the abstract, technical discussion of Locke's dissertation with that of its revised version "Values and Imperatives," an essay that appeared in *American Philosophy Today and Tomorrow* (1935). Finally, both Harris and Mason hear in Locke's critical voice the Gallic accent of Jacques Derrida. Harris, for example, refers to Locke's "deconstructive project," and Mason demonstrates the "deconstructive tendencies" in Locke's philosophical ideas.[24]

We should, however, take somewhat more literally Locke's admonition that "all philosophies . . . are products of time, place and situation." His graduate work at Harvard (1916–18) follows four years of teaching at Howard. The abstractions of his dissertation are not given social flesh in "Values and Imperatives" until long after his return to Howard in 1918, his friendship with Melville Herskovits, and his deep involvement with almost every individual of major importance in the Harlem Renaissance. It is a mistake, in other words, to pass too quickly from what Locke has to say in 1918 to what he concludes in 1935 without taking note of the years in between.

At the same time, suggestive as it is to view Locke through Derrida's critical concerns, isn't the "deconstructive" as well as "constructive" work of Boas and his students a more helpful context in which to understand not only Locke's philosophical and social concerns but also the links between the two? It is certainly not wrong to suggest that Locke's "code of value theory, particularly value relativism and cultural pluralism, [was] his master code of deconstruction" and that this subterranean message "served the purpose of positively evaluating features of black culture."[25] Not only does Locke link inner states of consciousness with the external world of human experience, but he seeks to formulate experience along lines of tolerance and equality—"In such a perspective, Nordicism and other rampant racialisms, might achieve historical sanity or at least prudential common-sense to halt at the natural frontiers of genuinely shared loyalties and not . . . through forced loyalties and the counter-reactions which they inevitably breed."[26] But one only needs to look to Columbia University's anthropology department in the first decades of the twentieth century, not to Paris in the 1960s, to find inspiration and perspective for his challenging words. At the same time, the tension between various schemes of classification and what Locke calls the "natural frontiers of genuinely shared loyalties" is also a tension deeply rooted in the anthropology of Boas and his students.

In 1912 Locke joined the faculty of the Teacher's College at Howard University determined to make Howard a center for the study of problems related to "race, cultural contact, and colonialism."[27] This ambition conflicted with the prevailing policy of the university that Howard would remain, as in the past, a "color-free" institution. As a result, his proposal to offer a course on race was rejected by the university's Board of Trustees. However, under the auspices of the Howard Chapter of the NAACP and the Social Science Club, Locke was able to offer "Race Contacts and Inter-Racial Relations: A Study in the Theory and Practice of Race" as an extension course. This series of lectures was grouped into five broad topics and offered in the spring of 1915 and 1916. The readings for the course ranged over history, philosophy, sociology, and anthropology. But the crucial text used to address the question of race, its scientific meaning past and present, was Franz Boas's *The Mind of Primitive Man* (1911).[28] In addition, Locke also used Boas's "The Instability of Racial Types," a paper Boas had presented at the First Universal Race Congress in London that he attended with W.E.B. Du Bois in the summer of 1911.

Locke's opening topic, "The Theoretical and Scientific Conceptions of Race," establishes the intellectual framework of the lectures to follow.[29] Most importantly, Locke addresses as well as challenges the various scientific rationales for "race" as a meaningful concept and the various uses to which "race" had been put. Not only does he argue that race is a false concept and its intellectual underpinning a "pseudo-science" but that inequalities that exist between peoples are best understood in terms of history and power (political, economic and social), not nature. Race, then, is not so much an explanatory concept as a rationalization, a way to make distinctions so as to advance the interests of some peoples and not others.

In subsequent lectures, Locke expands upon these key ideas while shifting the focus of "science" as an authoritative voice from that of biology to sociology and psychology. At the same time, in breaking the link between nature and society, Locke makes discourse itself, the categories used to frame social reality, the focus of attention. Not only does Locke suggest that the "truths" we employ are, in fact, "truths" we construct, but he uses this freedom to deconstruct the "truths" of the past that continue to claim scholarly and popular attention.[30] In effect, Locke suggests that what now needs explanation is how and why race (an *"idola theatri"*) continues to function in political and social discourse. And yet, whether an *"idola theatri"* or not, race also represents a continuing social and intellectual challenge of a more positive kind: if "race as a unit of social thought is of growing importance and necessity . . . what conception of race is to dominate in enlightened social thought and practice is the present problem."[31]

One sees here the seeds of Locke's social and cultural thinking and the future challenge of his life's work—"culture-citizenship is not acquired through assimilation merely, but in terms of a racial contribution to what becomes a just civilization."[32] One also sees in Locke's response to Boas, in Boas's *The Mind of Primitive Man* itself, methodological concerns that later inform his dissertation "The Problem of Classification in Theory of Value." Whether addressing the science of man (anthropology) or the science of values (axiology), Locke addresses not only traditional systems of classification but the problem of classification itself. In either case (method or content) Locke shifts the focus away from the presumption of a universally shared hierarchy of values to a world in which diversity, a variety of values and ways of living, is universally experienced. With this shift from the one to the many there is a shift from the certainties and constraints of objectivity to the problematics and freedom of subjectivity. We now see the world through others' eyes, and we are to understand that their vision is no less keen than our own. We are also to understand that what others see (what we ourselves see) is conditioned by "time, place and situation" and grounded as well in the quicksand of emotion and self-reflection.

Locke's dissertation, "The Problem of Classification in Theory of Value" is as abstract as the title suggests. Situated in no particular time or place, the foundation of the argument is theory and logic the architecture. However, just as Boas helped to place the outer world in meaningful perspective so too did Locke's philosophical focus help to sharpen his understanding of Boas and the world beyond the text of his dissertation. For Franz Boas, however, the concept of culture was the center piece of his thinking about human behavior and social order. Race was not to be confused with the "genius of a people." For Locke, however, how to give race the intellectual respectability that culture now had, how to make race no less the centerpiece of understanding, was the challenge he sought to meet. Locke's two important articles "The Problem of Race Classification" (1923) and "The Concept of Race as Applied to Social Culture" (1924) reflect this intellectual alchemy. They also represent a threshold in Locke's own thinking as he also began to think through George Peabody's proposal to devote an entire issue of *Survey Graphic* to Harlem as a cultural Mecca for black Americans.

The immediate stimulus for "The Problem of Race Classification" was Roland Dixon's *The Racial History of Man* (1923), in which Dixon made the familiar argument that peoples of Alpine or Nordic descent were racially superior to others. As to the specific claims of the argument, Locke spends little time, referring the reader to Boas's trenchant critique "Importance and Significance of the Human Head," which appeared in the *New York Times* (April 1, 1923). Instead, what intrigues Locke are the various and inconsistent ways Dixon uses the idea of race, at times an "abstract noun of classification" at other times meant to "represent concrete historical stocks of breeds."[33] At best, Dixon's book would serve "as a sort of reductio ad absurdum test of the purely anatomical approach to the questions of human classification."[34] But the question of classification remained and pointed to the very crux of the anthropological problem: "The problem of anthropology today is not the problem of facts but of proper criteria for the facts; the entire scientific status and future of the consideration of man's group characters rests upon a decisive demonstration of what factors are really indicative of race"[35] Dixon's book also pointed to the very crux of the problem Locke sought to resolve. If criteria for "man's group characters" were not to be found, Locke foresaw two possible choices: (1) to "throw the category of race into the discard as another of the many popular misconceptions detrimentally foisted upon science" or (2) to "divorce the idea of race in the physical sense from 'culture-group' or race with respect to ethnic traits."[36] Neither choice, however, was exactly what Locke had in mind.

The fallacy Locke saw in Dixon's "block conception of race," together with the correlation Dixon made with various "cultural capacities and attainments," pointed to the middle ground Locke sought to achieve: "the way is very open to this [Dixon's faulty reasoning] as long as one assumes that blood as mixture acts as a 'cultural leaven' and not merely as an activating agent, and that it always works from so-called 'higher' to so-called 'lower' instead of on a reciprocal basis."[37] As long as one understands, Locke argues, that "blood" acts as an "activating agent," not a "cultural leaven," and that it acts reciprocally and not hierarchically it is possible to avoid the mistakes that Dixon has made. At the same time, Locke is still intent in discovering "some criteria of true race, of finding some clue to the inter-connection between physical character, and group-behavior, psychological and cultural traits."[38] For this reason, Locke is hopeful that "history and the science of human society" can still be attained in the relatively neglected study of the "intensive anthropometric study of race hybrids," (in particular, "the inter-mixture of the Negro with Nordic stocks in America").

In effect, whether he was aware of it or not, Locke was struggling with the paradox that Boas had voiced forty years earlier. Was anthropology a science, an art, or both?[39] And were "culture areas," as Boas had written in *The Mind of Primitive Man,* a "mere convenience," or did they represent something more solid than simply one more way to configure human experience? If so, was culture (understood to be the "genius of a people") or race (understood to be an "activating agent") sufficient to anchor "man's group characters"?

For Locke, Boas would remain, until his death in 1942, an intellectual touchstone, an authority to consult and a body of ideas to help ground his own social and cultural thinking. Beginning in the 1920s, however, it was through Boas's student, Melville Herskovits, that Locke maintained most direct contact with Boas's scientific interests and the problematics of formulating some form of collective identity. And in his own right as well, Herskovits, the only student of Boas to devote his life to the study of African and African American cultures, emerged, along with Elsie Clews Parsons and Arthur Huff Fauset, as the most authoritative anthropologist in America to consult regarding questions of race and African American culture.

As Locke was completing his article, "The Problem of Race Classification," Herskovits, fresh from his studies with Boas at Columbia University, was in the process of outlining for the National Research Council plans to investigate "the problem of variability of racial crosses." His work would center on the black population of New York City and would be concentrated in Harlem. Already, he had contacted the head librarian of the 135th Street branch of the New York Public Library who had, Herskovits claimed, access to both "upper and lower economic groups."[40] Although Locke was not yet aware of Herskovits and the work he intended to pursue, they would soon meet. Locke's critique of Dixon had caught Herskovits's eye, and he mentioned to Charles S. Johnson, editor of *Opportunity* magazine, that he would like to meet its author. On January 8, 1924, Johnson informed Herskovits that Locke would soon be in New York City and that a meeting was possible.[41]

Two letters that Locke wrote to Herskovits a few months after their first meeting in January 1924 reveal the complex range of interests they personally shared and that they shared with others. In the first letter (April 14), Locke thanks Herskovits for allowing him to read his "most illuminating" paper, "The Cultural Approach to Sociology" (1923), and suggests that his own paper, "The Concept of Race as Applied to Social Culture" (1924), will show that he has "caught the distinction between the Graebnerian and the Wissler culture-area conceptions."[42] Locke goes on to encourage Herskovits to meet two students (Louis King of Howard University and Alexander Washington of West Virginia Collegiate Institute) whom Locke would like to recommend to Carter G. Woodson to help support their efforts to do anthropological work.[43] Locke concludes on a more personal note, expressing great pleasure at having run into Herskovits at the "stunning collection" of African and modern art assembled by Albert C. Barnes and housed at Barnes's private institute in Merion, Pennsylvania. Ten days later, responding to Herskovits's note that on Friday Boas would be reading a paper on race at the American Philosophical Society,[44] Locke thanks him for "the word about Boas" and promises that he will "try to connect with him in Philadelphia." At the same time, Locke notes that he had substantially revised the outline for the Harlem issue of *Survey Graphic*, and would like Herskovits to address the question "Has the Negro a Unique Social Pattern?"[45]

By this time, as correspondence began to flow between Howard University and Morningside Heights, Herskovits had become a Fellow of the National Research Council in Anthropology and was measuring the children of Public School 89 for his project "Variability under Racial Crossing with Special Reference to Negro-White Crossing."[46] Already seeking to expand his research base, however, Herskovits had inquired of Locke soon after their first meeting whether it would be possible to give "psychological tests and anthropometric measurements" at a Negro university.[47] As a result, with considerable assistance from Locke, Herskovits would spend the spring semester at Howard (1925) teaching "Introduction to Physical Anthropology" and correlating various measurements (rates of growth, head-form, skin-color, nose-form, etc.) with the psychological profiles of male students.[48]

Herskovits's paper figures importantly in Locke's "The Concept of Race as Applied to Social Culture." In addition to his particular phrasing of the argument, many of the same terms that structure Herskovits's article—trait, culture trait, trait complex, culture complex, culture-type—are also to be found in Locke's essay. At the same time, it is important to see that this further effort to define race anthropologically and culturally is very broadly grounded in the theoretical concerns of Boas, his colleagues, and his students. R. H. Lowie's *Culture and Ethnology* (1923), Alexander A. Goldenweiser's *Early Civilization* (1923), Edward Sapir's "Culture, Genuine and Spurious" (1924), and Clark Wissler's *Man and Culture* (1923) all figure prominently in Locke's argument. In addition, Herskovits's particular contribution, the distinction that Locke singled out regarding the "culture-area conceptions" of the German ethnologist F. Graebner and Clark Wissler, stems from a critique of Graebner that Boas had made in 1911.[49]

In "The Concept of Race as Applied to Social Culture," Locke immediately addresses the concepts of race and culture, the "most inevitable yet most unsatisfactory concepts involved in the broad-scale consideration of man and society."[50] In order to limit what is a very contentious and complex subject, Locke confines his thoughts to examining "their supposed relationship to one another."[51] Although he suggests that it is "too early to assume that there is no significant connection between race and culture" (too much intellectual confusion still clutters the air) Locke proceeds with his essay on the following basis: (1) although race and culture are "variables, not constants, [they] are neither organically or causally connected," and (2) that "race stands for significant social characters and culture-traits [and] represents in given historical contexts characteristic differentiations of culture-type."[52] The body of the essay that follows is an effort to clarify these distinctions, to support these various claims, and to point the way to a reorientation of understanding and a renewal of cultural discourse.

As Locke feels his way, he first plays off Lowie's "extreme cultural relativism" (wherein race has no "permanent or even uniform alignment with reference to culture-type or cultural stages") against Sapir's emphasis on "all but instinctive forms [of thought and behavior] peculiar to a people" (although Sapir too doesn't mention race). Next, Locke speaks of race and ethnic groups as equivalents and culture as variously "traits" and "types" that cohere into differing patterns having a life of their own. Locke's thoughts even carry to the point of wondering whether it might not be best "to substitute for the term race the term culture-group."[53] But, he concludes, "culture-group," is too general; it lacks that "sense of race as perhaps the most intense of the feelings of commonality."[54] As a consequence, what Locke refers to in "The Problem of Race Classification" as an "activating agent" is here defined as race consciousness, inner states of subjective awareness that take form as a core of shared values and shared notions of self and others.

Building upon the distinction Herskovits suggested regarding the cultural models of F. Graebner and Clark Wissler, though now making race itself a cultural value, Locke emphatically concludes, "Race operates as tradition, as preferred traits and values, and when these things change culturally speaking ethnic remolding is taking place. Race then, so far as the ethnologist is concerned, seems to lie in that peculiar selective preference for certain culture-traits and resistance to certain others which is characteristic of all types and level of social organization."[55] Not only does race offer a "platform of the newer science of social culture," but it also allows for an understanding of African Americans in terms of their own "intrinsic values as a vital mode of living." It is now possible, Locke argues, to initiate a discourse free of the past errors "of fact and of value." It is also now possible to understand how the sense of race "determines the stressed values which become the conscious symbols and tradition of the culture." Finally, it is now possible for Locke to turn his attention to the symbolic dimensions of racial identity.

Except for Walter Jackson's "Melville Herskovits and the Search for Afro-American Culture," little attention has been given to Locke's and Herskovits's relationship and the interplay of Boas's ideas as these ideas took shape in the form of Herskovits's own intellectual interests. In general, Jackson broadly frames their relationship in terms of Boas's dual commitment to "universalism" and "the importance of understanding each culture on its own terms."[56] Jackson's focus, however, is almost exclusively on Herskovits, and Locke gains attention to the extent that he challenges Herskovits's contribution to the Harlem issue of *Survey Graphic*.[57] Most importantly, Jackson argues that Locke's critical remarks, together with the expressive vitality and diversity of *The New Negro* itself, had an important impact in causing Herskovits to reassess his assimilationist emphasis, a shift in point of view that would eventually lead to his classic work *The Myth of the Negro Past* (1941).

As their correspondence reveals, however, the relationship of Locke and Herskovits must be seen in more complex terms than Locke's critical assessment of Herskovits's essay "The Dilemma of Social Pattern." If Locke contributed to Herskovits's rethinking of the social and cultural experience of black Americans, Herskovits also influenced Locke's own point of view. It was Herskovits's article, "The Cultural Approach to Sociology," that helped Locke to clarify distinctions he would make in "The Concept of Race as Applied to Social Culture." Ironically, it was these same distinctions that then contributed to Locke's critique of Herskovits's essay and Herskovits's rethinking his assertion that black culture and white culture "were the same pattern, only a different shade."[58] At the same time, the question of influence broadened to include the scientific interests both men shared. Locke's continuing hope for "some criteria of true race" and Herskovits's anthropometric studies in Harlem initiated prior to his first meeting Locke not only overlapped but importantly contributed to each man's conception of the cultural experience of African Americans.

Prior to his stay at Howard, Herskovits had already come to the tentative conclusion that, despite widespread racial mixing, black Americans were consolidating as a group, were producing a "homogeneous type" and not simply assimilating into the larger population.[59] Not only did his measuring at Howard help to confirm this conclusion, but after conversations with various faculty at Howard (Locke and Ernest Just in particular), Herskovits was certain that he had discovered (was "let in on") the "social factor" or mechanism that helped to explain this consolidation—that color distinctions or preferences within the black community tended to stabilize the population.[60]

For Herskovits (and for Boas) these findings were immensely suggestive and contributed to scientific studies being conducted elsewhere on various population groups as to "the extent to which variability is associated with racial purity."[61] Not only did Herskovits conclude that "the attempt to place populations in racial categories seem a waste of effort," but in thinking through the question of group identity and factors of social selection he now speculated that "there is a possibility of there being something of a differing temperamental base which has not been studied."[62] As a consequence, Herskovits increasingly turned his attention to cultural factors to help explain what science had revealed but could not fully explain. To the Board of Fellowships in the Biological Sciences of the National Research Council and to the Inter-Racial Relations Committee of the Social Science Research Council, Herskovits now mapped the research he hoped to do "in the great African collections of the major European ethnological museums" and in West Africa:

It is therefore my intention . . . to take up for study some manifestation of the culture of the West African peoples. . . . The problem of the West African wood-carving is of particular significance in the light of my particular problem, since it is in the realm of the artistic products manifested in this country particularly through the Negro spiritual that any innate connection with the African temperament might most easily be seen.[63]

However, because Herskovits's proposal to the National Research Council and the Inter-Racial Relations Committee was turned down, his search for "innate connections" began in the Dutch colony of Suriname. With financial assistance from Elsie Clews Parsons, Herskovits and his wife Frances studied the Saramaka in the summers of 1928 and 1929. Thus, what "began in 1923 with the inquiry into Negro-white crossing in the United States," led to fieldwork among the descendants of runaway slaves and an almost novelistic rendering—*Rebel Destiny* (1934)—of that elusive "temperamental base."[64] Science had helped Herskovits to find his way to art, and art now helped to enrich the science he sought to practice.

For Locke, and for Du Bois as well, the question implicit in Herskovits's work—"who and what is Negro?"—remained of continuing importance. Thus, the work Herskovits was doing, first in Harlem and subsequently at Howard, served to reinforce Du Bois's and Locke's own response to what Locke would call that "Janus-faced question,—who and what is Negro—[that] sits like a perennial sphinx at the door of every critic who considers the literature or the art of the Negro."[65] In 1927, for example, Du Bois wrote an angry letter to A.V. Kidder, the chairman of the Division of Anthropology and Psychology of the National Research Council:

It seems to me almost incredible that American universities and scientific associations presume to make scientific studies of the Negro without any preliminary attempt to ascertain what is meant by the term "Negro." Here is a persons [sic] practically white, whose great great grandfather was a Negro and he is classed with a modern banto [sic] and the resulting measurements are put down to the credit of the Negro race in America. This is, of course, balled nonsense, and nine-tenths of the so-called measurements of the Negro race in America are vitiated by facts like this. I see no indication that there is any intention on the part of your organization to correct this initial mistake or to make any allowances in your studies for the extraordinary amount of race mixture which has taken place within the so-called Negro group in the United States.

The error might not be fatal if everybody who read these findings understood that by Negro in the United States we did not mean a race at all, but a certain social group.[66]

And for Locke that "extraordinary amount of race mixture" to which Du Bois referred and which Herskovits had documented helped to lift his own vision beyond the narrow perspectives of the "Sociologist," the "Philanthropist," and the "Race-Leader." Beyond the limits of their separate visions, Locke understood that diversity, complexity, and the act and art of imagination constituted the elements of an African American identity. If this identity also offered a "platform of the newer science of social culture," it was an identity that was itself buttressed by the work of that "real scientist" Herskovits and his mentor Franz Boas.[67]

Locke's primary task in *The New Negro* is to present, to interpret, and to celebrate profound changes taking place in the mental and moral outlook of the most recent generation of young black Americans to come of age. To do so, Locke links this generation with the past, to a collective folk spirit or temperament. But Locke's emphasis is on the present, on the creative use of what the past has to offer and what Edward Sapir called "the transforming energies of personalities at once robust and saturated with the cultural values of their time and place."[68] Not only does the younger generation see past and present with new eyes, but in so doing they also see themselves in a new light. As a consequence, others too, whites as well as blacks, are now challenged to reassess (to become aware of) the assumptions or preconceptions that shape and continue to obscure their vision. The "dusty spectacles of controversy," Locke writes, are more real than the reality that is now to be seen:

So for generations in the mind of America, the Negro has been more a formula than a human being—a something to be argued about, condemned or defended, to be "kept down," or "in his place," or "helped up," to be worried with or worried over, harassed or patronized, a social bogey or a social burden. The thinking Negro even has been induced to share this same general attitude, to focus his attention on controversial issues, to see himself in the distorted perspective of a social problem. His shadow, so to speak, has been more real to him than his personality. . . . Little true social or self-understanding has or could come from such a situation.[69]

It is now time for blacks and whites to break out of the "old chrysalis of the Negro problem." To do so it is first necessary to realize the extent to which their lives are still wrapped in the dead skin of their and society's patterned ways of thinking and acting.

Locke broadly accounts for this new spirit in terms of demographic and economic changes taking place in the United States (the migration of blacks from the South and the increased diversity of social life in Northern cities) and nationalistic movements taking place throughout the world. But the center of his attention, the center itself, is Harlem, for it is here that one can most vividly see the transformation of "social fact" into states of mind and the embodiment of this awareness in various forms of creative expression. The essence of this intensity of feeling and expansion of vision is race, a racial consciousness that unifies as well as deepens the meaning of their identity as black Americans. Thus, Harlem is understood to be "the laboratory of a great race-welding." In turn, it is here that race as a "vast spiritual endowment" flowers in the voice and writing of Langston Hughes, Claude McKay, Jean Toomer, Zora Neale Hurston, and many others. Although Harlem as a "race capital" is not typical, it is "prophetic." As the "mainspring of Negro life," it is also prophetic in a broader sense. For just as Harlem has become a Mecca for black Americans, it also functions as "the advance-guard of the African peoples in their contact with Twentieth Century civilization."[70]

In his hopeful, at times joyful, declaration that the "day of 'aunties,' 'uncles,' and 'mammies' " is over, that Harlem surges with a new spirit of racial pride and self-respect, Locke reassures the reader that "the Negro mind reaches out as yet to nothing but American wants, American ideas."[71] Such reassurance reflects Locke's own deep, personal commitment to the ideals and institutions of a democratic society. But he is also extremely fearful that if white Americans respond with hostility to this awakened sense of self-worth, the present optimism could degenerate into cynicism, counter-hatred, and reverse racism—"a defiant superiority feeling." At the same time, Locke also greatly fears that the black masses, once aroused by new yet false hopes, will lash out in their anger and frustration. Clearly, the immediate responsibility for what takes place, whether it be constructive or destructive, lies within the power and reason of white Americans.[72] But the one individual who embodies the negative side of Locke's ambivalence as to the celebration of racial pride is Marcus Garvey, for Locke perceives in Garvey's racial exhortations the voice of the demagogue, the voice of conflict. Clearly, the mid-1920s are for Locke a critical time wherein the dreams of a truly free and democratic society can just as easily become a nightmare of hatred and violence.

The balance that Locke seeks to achieve between racial consciousness and racial conflict distinguishes his thought from that of Boas and Herskovits. Although both Boas and Herskovits repeatedly challenged in scholarly as well as popular writings prevailing racist ideas and institutions, their intellectual and theoretical concerns did not generate the same alarm that Locke felt compelled to voice in *The New Negro*. In this light, as Leonard Harris argues in "Identity: Alain Locke's Atavism," Locke's writings are best understood as polemics, as "weapons in the theoretical battles of the day," and not as "treatises or explicit and definite statements of beliefs."[73] Harris's comments are a helpful reminder that one cannot fully separate even Locke's more abstract intellectual formulations from the racism he personally experienced, saw all around him, and thought deeply about. It is no less important, however, to keep in mind Nathan Huggins's caution that "there is an aspect of [Locke's] thinking in which he is not a politician or a person involved in a program."[74] What Huggins has in mind is Locke's philosophical and aesthetic concern for form, as form both embodies and shapes elemental protean energies. Although Locke is not unmindful of the content of form (especially in its social and cultural content) he is deeply interested in the dynamics of form, the emotional and cognitive energy of form itself. As a consequence, the apprehensions Locke voices in *The New Negro* are no less the result of tensions implicit in the very dynamics of his own intellectual imagination, and it is these tensions that Locke addresses most directly in his 1935 essay "Values and Imperatives."

In "Values and Imperatives" Locke immediately establishes as well as confronts the central challenge, relativism, that grounds his philosophical thought and links his intellectual outlook with that of the twentieth century: "All philosophies, it seems to me, are in ultimate derivation philosophies of life and not of abstract, disembodied 'objective' reality; products of time, place and situation, and thus systems of timed history rather than timeless eternity."[75] Free from the "old intellectualist trinity of Beauty, Truth and Good" and free, as well, from tight "colorless, uniformitarian criterion of logic," one can now experience the world through one's own eyes and one's own feelings. Freedom, not conformity, and diversity, not uniformity, is the potential that relativism promises. At the same time, disorder, a world without boundaries—at least without boundaries so tightly drawn they deny common understanding—is no less the danger of the relativism that Locke so emphatically embraces. How, then, to achieve freedom as well as order and to make one the basis for the other?[76]

Central to Locke's challenge is the question of values. For values, Locke insists, are central to human consciousness and give to experience its form and meaning. Values are not simply moral categories or codes of conduct, but qualities of perception and feeling rooted in the existential nature of man himself. "We must realize," he writes, "that not in every instance is this normative control effected indirectly through judgmental or evaluational processes, but often through primary mechanisms of feeling modes and dispositional attitudes."[77] Not only are values (feeling modes) rooted in elemental states of feeling, but as feelings change so too does the understanding or importance of that which is valued (the content): "We are forced to conclude that the feeling-quality, irrespective of content, makes a value of a given kind, and that a transformation of the attitude effects a change of type in the value situation."[78] To illustrate his point, Locke notes that the artist might find beauty or inspiration in something previously ignored or disparaged. The change in evaluation, however, is not in the object itself, but in the attitude toward the object, a process of perception in which a "feeling-reference or form-quality" molds the "value-mode."[79]

Although Locke's emphasis on the protean nature of feelings suggests freedom and diversity, this emphasis also raises the specter of the tyranny of passions and intolerance toward others. Thus, whereas Locke initially refers to generic types of value as "feeling modes each with its own characteristic form," he also calls them "psychological tribes," absolutes that limit and imprison. As a consequence, whether broadly understood to be the "rationale" of an age or more narrowly the "lineaments of a personality, its temperament and dispositional attitudes," relativism threatened to undercut the very promise it was thought to have.

Locke's answer to the problems that relativism poses are found in relativism itself. At the level of the individual (that which relates to the existential process of constructing reality) and at the level of society (that which relates to the more general understanding that society constitutes diverse areas of meaning and experience) Locke foresees greater tolerance and a heightened awareness of the need for tolerance.

One thing is certain,—whatever change may have occurred in our thinking on the subject, we are still monists and absolutists mainly in our practice of value, individual as well as social. But a theoretical break has come, and seems to have set in simultaneously from several quarters. Panoramically viewed, the convergence of these trends indicates a new center for the thought and insight of our present generation, and that would seem to be a philosophy and a psychology, and perhaps too, a sociology, pivoted around functionalistic relativism.[80]

One's absolutes are made to take their place within a context of other absolutes. Upon this basis, freedom and order are mutually achieved, for diversity and multiplicity sustain as well as qualify the most passionately held beliefs.

Although Locke concludes that "cultural relativism . . . is the culminating phase of relativistic philosophy," the weight of his essay is on the individual "irrespective of context" and psychological categories of value at the root of individual perception. Even his use of the artist to illustrate the psychological dynamics of form speaks of the artist in individual and even universal terms. There is, then, at the heart of Locke's philosophic thought, a central and continuing tension between the individual and the group, a tension Locke not only addresses but seeks to sustain.[81] It is in his discussion of form that is focused the deeper tensions that also mark his social and cultural concerns.

In the introduction to "Values and Imperatives," what he calls his psychograph, Locke notes that he would like to claim "the good-Greek principle—Nothing in excess" as his life motto. Because of circumstance, however, he adds that "all things with a reservation" is probably more descriptive of his life. In the comments that follow, Locke briefly details the paradoxes that framed his life, his self-understanding, and his critical outlook. Seen in the context of these remarks, the reservations Locke voices in "Values and Imperatives" can be understood, to some extent, in terms of his claim that all philosophies "may merely be the lineaments of a personality." But the lineaments of understanding that Locke uses to frame his life-story—"I project my personal history into its inevitable rationalization as cultural pluralism and value relativism"—are themselves part of an intellectual tradition that serves both to configure the projections Locke makes and to make somewhat problematic his relationship and that of the individual to the rationalizations he offers.

In his role as midwife, Locke was committed above all to encouraging expressive forms of black culture and to celebrating their potential to shape a collective black identity. In so doing, however, he joined with other midwives who contributed to his understanding of this role and who, themselves, continued to puzzle tensions in his and their own efforts to relate the one and the many. Until his death in 1942, Franz Boas struggled with questions that addressed not only the problematic relationship of the individual to the culture but also his own problematic relationship to that which he observed.[82] Throughout his life, as well, Melville Herskovits struggled to come to terms with the ethnographic, ethnic, and ethical paradoxes of those who, as Locke phrased it, "feel and hope in the direction of universality, but still think and act particularistically."[83]

NOTES

1. The New Negro (November, 1925) was the expansion of an issue of *Survey Graphic*, "Harlem: Mecca of the New Negro," which appeared on March 1, 1925. In late March (1924), Paul Kellogg, editor of *Survey Graphic*, contacted Locke with the idea of devoting an entire issue of his magazine to black writers and intellectuals. Throughout the year Locke and Kellogg revised and reevaluated their original ideas, made contacts with various black

writers, and criticized and modified the work they had begun to receive. In January, 1925, in a letter to George Peabody (a close friend of Franz Boas's colleague Elsie Clews Parsons), Kellogg explained the vision that he and Locke shared and hoped soon to achieve:

Our number is not built around Du Bois or his long time militant espousals. Neither is it built around Booker T. Washington's or Mr. Moton and their industrial-educational and rural programs. We may be altogether wrong, but we think we sense a new approach—growing out of northward migrations and the city environment—the silver lining of the injurious circumstances you speak of: the Negro expressing himself not against something but for something and so breaking with the Du Bois tradition. . . . It seems to me that the cultural renaissance is in opposition essentially to the rural and vocational and community programs of the Hampton tradition. Near at home, perhaps, it is harder to see it; but I believe it is there and that it does offer a text by which the needs and aspirations of our Negro fellow citizens can be interpreted in a way which will win a fresh hearing. Such at least is our endeavor.

Paul Kellogg to George Peabody, 28 January 1925, University of Minnesota Social Welfare History Archives.

2. Even Marcus Garvey, who was profoundly critical of Locke, initially hailed the Harlem issue of *Survey Graphic* for not being "built around the needs of Negroes and their grievances but their contributions—around talents still half buried in napkins of prejudices and under-privilege." Garvey's comments are in a letter from Paul Kellogg to the trustees of the Kann Traveling Fellowship, wherein Kellogg mentions a telegram he had received from Garvey praising the Harlem issue. (April 19, 1925 University of Minnesota). Years later Nathan Huggins commented in his *Harlem Renaissance* that "Locke's editing of and contribution to this volume [*The New Negro*] and his energetic championing of the intellectual movement of Negroes in the 1920's made him the father of the New Negro and the so-called Harlem Renaissance." Huggins, *Harlem Renaissance* (New York: Oxford University Press, 1971), 56–57.

3. Arna Bontemps vividly recalls the general sense of astonishment and euphoria that black writers experienced:

When acceptances from Harper's; Harcourt, Brace; Viking; Boni and Liveright; Knopf; and other front-line publishers began coming through in quick succession, the excitement among those of us who were writing was almost unbearable. The walls of Jericho were tumbling. When new books by Negro authors were announced—any books by any Negroes—we held our breath till we could get our hands on copies. We gobbled them up, memorizing the poetry and lingering over the prose with such rapt attention that thirty years have not erased it from our minds. We were not too critical. The wonder was that we and our friends could be published at all. Of course, we had all been writing since childhood, and all of us had vaguely hoped to have something published eventually, but I think I am safe in saying we were all surprised—more than surprised. We had never dreamed that it would happen so soon.

Stephen Bronz, *Roots of Negro Racial Consciousness* (New York: Libra, 1964), 95.

4. Alain Locke, "Values and Imperatives," in *American Philosophy, Today and Tomorrow,* eds. Sidney Hook and Horace Kallen (New York: Lee Furman, 1935), 312.

5. Locke's self-defined role as a "mid-wife" to the men and women of the Harlem Renaissance is probably best understood in the more general language of his "life-motto": "I should like to claim as life-motto the good Greek principle—'Nothing in excess,' but I have probably worn instead as the badge of circumstance,—'All things with a reservation.' " Locke, "Values and Imperatives," 312.

6. Alain Locke, "Dark Weather Vane," *Survey Graphic* (August, 1936): 457.

7. Alain Locke, *The New Negro* (New York: Atheneum, 1968), 15. Throughout the 1920s, in such articles as the following, Locke voiced similar encouragement: "Should the Negro

Be Encouraged to Cultural Equality?" *Forum*, 77 (October 1927): 500–519; "A Decade of Negro Self Expression," 26 (compiled by Alain Locke Trustees of the John F. Slater Fund-Occasional Papers, 1928); "Ethics of Culture," *Howard University Record* 17 (January 1923): 178–85; and "Negro Contributions to America," *The World Tomorrow* (June 1929): 255–57.

8. Locke, "Dark Weather Vane," 457–58.

9. Houston A. Baker, *Jr. Modernism and the Harlem Renaissance* (Chicago: University of Chicago Press, 1987), 73.

10. Nathan Huggins, "The Alain L. Locke Symposium," *Harvard Advocate* (December 1, 1973): 10.

11. Russell Linnemann, ed., *Alain Locke: Reflections on a Modern Renaissance Man* (Baton Rouge: Louisiana State University Press, 1982), xiv.

12. In addition to the work of Cruse, Huggins, and S. P. Fullinwider, *The Mind and Mood of Black America* (Homewood, IL: The Dorsey Press, 1969), articles on Locke began to appear in various academic journals.

13. Harris's rationale for this anthology is instructive:

No biography of Locke nor comprehensive collection of his works now exists. Moreover, relatively few articles have been published focusing attention on specific concepts and the use of terms in Locke's work. This anthology functions as an introduction to an emerging appreciation of Locke's philosophy, recognition of a subterranean deconstructive project, acknowledgment of an enigmatic moment that gave rise to a creative praxis, and a praise song for a philosophy that lived in the Harlem Renaissance and lives beyond.

Harris, "Rendering the Subtext: Subterranean Deconstructive Project," in *The Philosophy of Alain Locke: Harlem Renaissance and Beyond*, ed. Leonard Harris (Philadelphia: Temple University Press, 1989), 287.

14. In addition to Johnny Washington, Ernest Mason and Leonard Harris deserve special mention for the attention each has given to Locke's philosophical ideas. See Mason's, "Alain Locke on Race and Race Relations," *Phylon* 4, no.4 (1979): 342–50; his "Black Art and the Configurations of Experience: The Philosophy of the Black Aesthetic," *College Language Association Journal* 27 (1983): 1–17; and his "Deconstruction in the Philosophy of Alain Locke," *Transactions of the Charles S. Peirce Society* 23 no.1 (winter 1988): 85–105; and Harris's "The Legitimation Crisis in American Philosophy: Crisis Resolution from the Standpoint of the Afro-American Tradition of Philosophy," *Social Science Information* 26 (1987): 57–73; and his "Identity: Alain Locke's Atavism," *Transactions of the Charles S. Peirce Society* 24 (winter, 1988): 65–83.

15. Although William B. Harvey considers Locke to be a "philosophical anthropologist" and situates Locke within the "German School" of anthropological thought, he gives no attention to Boas and Herskovits. See Harvey's "The Philosophical Anthropology of Alain Locke," in Linnemann, *Alain Locke*, 17–28. Leonard Harris also links "the anthropological studies of black people as humans" with Locke's *The New Negro*, but he too does not bring Boas and/or Herskovits into the discussion. See Harris, "Rendering the Subtext: Subterranean Deconstructionist Project," 279–89. For this reason George Hutchinson writes, "The connections between Boasian anthropology, pragmatism, and the Harlem Renaissance have never been carefully explored, despite the fact that the confluence of these 'communities of interpretation' offers a model of the sort of effective interdisciplinary and intercultural exchange to which many academic intellectuals today aspire. Among other things, it again exemplifies the crosscurrents of thinking about race, culture, and nation that had such a

profound impact upon American modernism." Hutchinson, *The Harlem Renaissance in Black and White* (Cambridge: Harvard University Press, 1995), 62.

16. Somewhat arbitrarily, I have selected twenty years. Locke's dissertation was the expansion of a paper he had written at Oxford.

17. W.E.B. Du Bois, "The Renaissance of Ethics: A Critical Comparison of Scholastic and Modern Ethics," Harvard University, 51–52.

18. Locke, "Values and Imperatives," 313.

19. W.E.B. Du Bois, *Crisis* 35 (June 1928): 202. Ruthledge M. Dennis provides some perspective on Locke's empiricism. Dennis, "Relativism and Pluralism in the Social Thought of Alain Locke," in Linnemann, *Alain Locke*, 29–49.

20. Ernest D. Mason, "Alain Locke's Philosophy of Value," in Linnemman, *Alain Locke*, 4.

21. Alain Locke, "The Problem of Classification in the Theory of Value," Ph.D. diss., Harvard University, 1918, 4.

22. Locke, "Values and Imperatives," 328.

23. Ezra Pound, *"The New Age"* (May 1, 1913): 9.

24. As Harris writes, "Locke's deconstructive project not only entailed a rejection of metaphysics but an effort (a) to go beyond the illusion that a given group held inherently preferable beliefs or values that in some way cohered with the nature of things, (b) to denude the romanticism of cultural pluralists who believed in the likelihood of a world without regulative value guides or imperatives, and (c) to expose the way pluralism was misguidedly used as a rouge for the perpetuation of the segregated status quo." Harris, "Rendering the Subtext," 281.

25. Ibid., 279–80.

26. Locke, "Values and Imperatives," 330.

27. Michael R. Winston, *Dictionary of American Negro Biography* (New York: Norton, 1982), 394.

28. This text grew from the article "The Mind of Primitive Man" (1901) that captured the attention of Du Bois.

29. Other topics included "Practical and Political Conceptions of Race"; "Phenomena and Laws of Race Contacts"; "Modern Race Creeds and Their Fallacies"; and "Racial Progress and Race Adjustment."

30. In Section 4 of his lectures—"Modern Race Creeds and Their Fallacies"—Locke critiqued "The Biological Fallacy"; "The Fallacy of the Masses"; "The Fallacy of the Permanency of Race Types"; "The Fallacy of Race Ascendancy"; and "The Fallacy of Automatic Adjustment."

31. Jeffrey C. Stewart, *The Critical Temper of Alain Locke—A Selection of His Essays on Art and Culture* (New York: Garland, 1983), 412.

32. Ibid., 413.

33. Alain Locke, "The Problem of Race Classification," in Harris, *Philosophy of Alain Locke*, 168.

34. Ibid., 165.

35. Ibid., 164.

36. Ibid., 164, 168.

37. Ibid., 169.

38. Ibid., 168.

39. For a recent discussion of this enduring question, see Michael Carrithers, "Is Anthropology Art or Science?" *Current Anthropology* 31 (June, 1990): 263–82.

40. Herskovits goes on to say,

the individuals would be examined as to their genealogies, which are considered reliable by competent observers.... Where such definite information would be unobtainable, recourse to skin color, nose form, and other racial characteristics would be had to determine the amount of mixture.... Since the larger portion of the population of this section is of heterozygous composition individuals not only of the first but succeeding filial generations, as well as the children of these, would be available. The Mendelian action of the characters selected would naturally follow as a subject for study, particularly in regard to the F1, F2, and succeeding series.

Melville Herskovits, typescript of proposal, c. 10 April 1923, Melville Herskovits Papers, Northwestern University Archives.

41. "I recall that sometime ago you indicated that you would like at some time to meet Mr. Locke whose review of Dixon's 'Racial History of Man' you liked. Mr. Locke has returned from Europe and is at present back at Howard University where he teaches. He is planning, however, to spend the eleventh and the twelfth in New York and if you are still interested it might be possible for you to see him while he is here." Charles S. Johnson to Melville Herskovits, 8 January 1924, Melville Herskovits Papers, Northwestern University Archives.

42. Wissler was a colleague of Boas at Columbia University and in *Man and Culture* (1923) drew upon Boas's critique of Graebner's *Methode der Ethnologie*, a critique Boas had first voiced in "Scientific Books," *Science* 34 (December 8, 1911): 804–10.

43. Woodson, however, had already suggested to Boas that Washington might be qualified to work with Herskovits and Boas himself. See, Carter G. Woodson to Franz Boas, 13 October 1923, American Philosophical Society.

44. Melville Herskovits to Alain Locke, 22 April 1924, Howard University Archives.

45. On April 24, 1924 Locke wrote to Herskovits that he had revised the *Survey* outline and that "I have tentatively put you down for a short but very important thing on "Has the Negro a Unique Social Pattern?" And I have been bold enough to characterize it as an analysis of the Negro's peculiar social pattern, and an estimate of its capacity in social survival and culture building." Melville Herskovits Papers, Northwestern University Archives. However, Locke's displeasure with Herskovits' emphasis lead to Locke enlisting contributions from Frank Tannenbaum and Walter White: "You will notice from the enclosed how your article finally pairs up. Your theme is the dilemma from the inside—Tannenbaum's the same from the outside.... I think it was only this point of view [the social dilemmas as opposed to the spiritual and psychological] that differentiated the approach of Herskovits. I evidently didn't get the point over. You see I have shifted him back to his main theme in the Survey article,—viz the complete Americanism of the Negro." Locke to Walter White, c. Summer, 1925, Manuscript Division, Library of Congress. Herskovits, however, felt that he had understood Locke all too well—"By the way, did you see the Harlem number of the Survey? You were right, for I won hands down, and they printed my paper quite as I had written it." Herskovits to Horace Kallen, 27 March 1925, Melville Herskovits Papers, Northwestern University Archives.

46. In his annual report to the Board of Fellowships in the Biological Sciences of the National Research Council, Herskovits wrote,

I was fortunate when I came to start work at the Colored Orphan Assylum at Riverdale, New York City, in finding that the records of height and weight for the children who were in the orphanage, and who had passed thru [*sic*] it since 1912, had been kept with sufficient care thru the foresight of the Superintendent Dr. Mason Pittman to allow of very definite work being done on the influence of an orphanage environment on the racial growth curve for this type, which I had gathered or these two traits on the basis of the data gathered from the children of Public School 89, who live at home. Thru the courtsey of Professor Boas, I was afforded assistance in the arduous task of copying the measurements out of the files, and thus saved much time, since it was no small one, there being about 18000 observations on some 1500 children of both sexes.

Herskovits, 28 February 1925, Melville Herskovits Papers, Northwestern University Archives.

47. Herskovits to Alain Locke, 1 February 1924, Howard University Archives.

48. As Herskovits writes,

I am writing to President Durkee by the same mail, telling him of my change in plans and how happy I shall be to accept his very kind offer of cooperation with me in my work. Now, for several things I'd appreciate your doing. First, you might pass the word to your students who are influential among the student body of my coming, and the desirability of supporting my research by allowing themselves to be measured and urging others to do the same. I am going to try for a series of 1000 males, by the way, and I plan to stay until almost June. Again, you might pass the word around among your colleagues, and you might also scout about to see where I might find a convenient nook in which to carry on the actual measuring.

Herskovits to Locke, 5 January 1925, Melville Herskovits Papers, Northwestern University Archives.

49. In his critique of Graebner's *Methode der Ethnologie* Boas notes that

[The] exclusion of the psychological field seems to me to give to the whole "Method" a mechanical character . . . the complete omission of all psychological considerations makes itself keenly felt. The significance of an ethnic phenomenon is not by any means identical with its distribution in space and time, and with its more or less regular associations with other ethnic phenomena. Its historical source may perhaps be determined by geographic-historical considerations, but its gradual development and ethnic significance in a psychological sense, as it occurs in each area, must be studied by means of psychological investigations in which the different interpretations and attitudes of the people themselves toward the phenomenon present the principal material. . . . [T]he more we learn of primitive culture, the clearer it becomes that not only is the participation of each individual in the culture of his tribe of an individual character, or determined by the social grouping of the tribe, but that also in the same mind the most heterogenous complexes of habits, thoughts and actions may lie side by side, without ever coming into conflict.

"Scientific Books," 805, 808.

50. Alain Locke, "The Concept of Race as Applied to Social Culture," *Howard Review* 1 (June 1924): 290.

51. Ibid.

52. Ibid., 296.

53. Ibid.

54. Ibid.

55. Ibid.

56. Walter Jackson, "Melville Herskovits and the Search for Afro-American Culture," in *Malinowski, Rivers, Benedict and Others: History of Anthropology,* ed. George Stocking (Madison: University of Wisconsin Press, 1986), 95. Also, and more generally, David Scott, "That Event, This Memory: Notes on the Anthropology of African Diasporas in the New World," *Diaspora* 1 (winter 1991): 261–84; St. Clair Drake, "Anthropology and the Black Experience," *Black Scholar* 2 (September–October, 1980); Richard Handler, "Boasian Anthropology and the Critique of American Culture," *American Quarterly* 42 (June, 1990): 252–73; William S. Willis, Jr., "Skeletons in the Anthropological Closet," in *Reinventing*

Anthropology, ed. Dell Hymes (New York: Random House, 1974), 121–52; and John F. Szwed, "An American Anthropological Dilemma: The Politics of Afro-American Culture," in Hymes, *Reinventing Anthropology,* 153–81.

57. When Locke first wrote to Herskovits to interest him in the question "Has the Negro A Unique Social Pattern?" Locke's expectations were clearly expressed: "I have been bold enough to characterize it [the question] as an analysis of the Negro's peculiar social pattern, and an estimate of its capacity in social survival and culture building." But when Herskovits wrote that Harlem was "essentially not different from any other American community" Locke felt compelled to add in an accompanying editorial note that "Old folkways may not persist, but they may leave a mental trace, subtly recorded in emotional temper and coloring social reactions." *Survey Graphic* 6 (March, 1925): 676. Not only did Locke challenge Herskovits's image of Harlem but he questioned, as well, the deeper supporting assumptions that Herskovits voiced: "What there is today in Harlem distinct from the white culture which surrounds it, is, as far as I am able to see, merely a remnant from the peasant days in the South. Of African culture, not a trace. Even the spirituals are an expression of the emotion of the Negro playing through the typical religious patterns of white America." Locke, "The Dilemma of Social Pattern," *Survey Graphic* 6 (March 1925): 678.

58. Ibid., 676.

59. Herskovits stated:

My work to date seems to foreshadow the fact that the American Negro is developing a homogenous type, which is being consolidated and the variability of which is, to say the least, no greater than that of White population. And if it be objected that my use of the term "American Negro" be too broad, it can only be asserted that the children studied in New York came from every section of the South as well as from the West Indies and various parts of the North, thus giving a very broad selection. It is hoped that the results of the work now being carried on at Howard University will throw further light on this problem.

Herskovits, Report of Progress to The Board of Fellowships in the Biological Sciences (National Research Council), 28 February 1925, Melville Herskovits Papers, Northwestern University Archives, 5.

60. Herskovits said:

If it is true that the consolidation of the Negro group in this country is occurring, then there must obviously be some factor of social selection at work among these people, which is to account for the fact that breeding within the group takes place. . . . But that there is a smaller amount of this mixture taking place than was the case in earlier times is apparent from the fact that the genealogies I gathered in New York gave, in only a very few instances, accounts of the person measured being a primary cross; while in the genealogical material gathered at Howard University I have not found one instance of a primary cross in over 200 cases. . . . I was given the clue to the social factor which may account to a large degree for the development of a homogeneous type, however, in conversations recently with several members of the faculty of Howard University, who were discussing the social situation within the Negro community.

Ibid.

61. Herskovits, Report of Progress to the Board of Fellowships in the Biological Sciences, 1 March 1925, to 13 February 1926, Melville Herskovits Papers, Northwestern University Archives, 3.

62. Herskovits, Report to Board of Fellowships in the Biological Sciences, 27 January 1926, Melville Herskovits Papers, Northwestern University Archives, 2.

63. Ibid.

64. As Walter Jackson writes, "The book's novelistic format allowed scope to develop in some depth the personalities of several Saramaccans and to give a sense of how each of these individuals functioned in the culture." Jackson, "Melville Herskovits and the Search for Afro-American Culture," 108.

65. Alain Locke, "Who and What Is Negro?" in Harris, *Philosophy of Alain Locke*, 209.

66. W.E.B. Du Bois to A.V. Kidder, 8 January 1927, W.E.B. Du Bois Papers Special Collections and Archives, University of Massachussetts Amherst Library.

67. In "Identity: Alain Locke's Atavism," Leonard Harris calls attention to Locke's sense of the limits of "scientific sociology: "It is not that statistics are of no use in understanding social change for Locke, but that the 'inner life' of the human experience moves forward in advance of statistical research and in ways not capturable by our scientific powers." Harris, *Transactions of the Charles S. Peirce Society* 24 (winter 1988): 73. But Harris misses the irony that the science of Boas and Herskovits helped Locke to come to this understanding.

68. In "Culture, Genuine and Spurious," Sapir writes, "There is no sound and vigorous individual incorporation of a cultured ideal without the soil of a genuine communal culture; and no genuine communal culture without the transforming energies of personalities at once robust and saturated with the cultural values of their time and place." David Mandelbaum, ed. *Selected Writings of Edward Sapir* (Berkeley: University of California Press, 1949), 322. Just as Richard Handler and Jocelyn Linnekin wrote of Sapir and the distinction Sapir made between a "genuine" and a "spurious" culture, Locke sought to "provide individuals . . . with a rich corpus of pre-established (traditional) forms *and* with the opportunity to 'swing-free.' " Handler and Linnekin, "Tradition, Genuine or Spurious," *Journal of American Folklore* 97 (July–September 1984): 287.

69. Locke, *The New Negro*, 3–4.

70. Ibid., 14.

71. As Locke writes,

The racialism of the Negro is no limitation or reservation with respect to American life; it is only a constructive effort to build the obstructions in the stream of his progress into an efficient dam of social energy and power. Democracy itself is obstructed and stagnated to the extent that any of its channels are closed. Indeed they cannot be selectively closed. So the choice is not between one way for the Negro and another for the rest, but between American institutions frustrated on the one hand and American ideals progressively fulfilled and realized on the other.

Locke, *The New Negro*, 12.

And in a personal letter to Paul Kellogg, Locke distinguished what he claimed to be kindred expressions of racial consciousness throughout the world from that which was taking place among black Americans: "It seems to me what they [the Irish Renaissance led by Yeats, Synge, Lady Gregory, etc.] miss is the generic character of such social and cultural awakenings: a more scientific view of culture would give them a more democratic view at the same time." Alain Locke to Paul Kellogg, 19 February 1926, University of Minnesota Social Welfare History Archives.

72. "Whether it [race consciousness] actually brings into being new Armadas of conflict or argosies of cultural exchange and enlightenment can only be decided by the attitude of the dominant races in an era of critical change." Locke, *The New Negro*, 14.

73. Harris, "Identity," 70.

74. Huggins, "Alain L. Locke Symposium," 24.

75. Locke, "Values and Imperatives," 313.

76. "No conception of philosophy, however relativistic, however opposed to absolutism, can afford to ignore the question of ultimates or abandon what has been so aptly though skeptically termed "the quest for certainty." Ibid.

77. Ibid., 314.

78. Ibid., 321.

79. Thus, Locke proceeds to elaborate modalities of feeling (exaltation; tension; acceptance or agreement; repose or equilibrium). If, for example, one thinks a particular painting to be good or successful, the evaluation is essentially a subjective one rooted in the "form feeling" of repose or equilibrium. Although the particular merits of the painting might be defined in the course of discussion, the initial and all important response was of a more elemental nature.

80. Locke, "Values and Imperatives," 332–33.

81. In "Negro Youth Speaks," for example, Locke quoted Jean Toomer to illustrate both a "modernity of style" and a "vital originality of substance—Georgia opened me. And it may well be said that I received my initial impulse to an individual art from my experience there." Locke, *The New Negro*, 51.

82. In "Some Problems of Methodology in the Social Sciences" (1930), Boas writes, "The individual can be understood only as part of the society to which he belongs, and that society can be understood only on the basis of the interrelations of the constituent individuals." Boas, ed., *Race, Language, and Culture* (New York: The Free Press, 1966), 260. In "The Aims of Anthropological Research" (1932) Boas writes, "The problems of the relation of the individual to his culture, to the society in which he lives have received too little attention. The standardized anthropological data that inform us of customary behavior, give no clue to the reaction of the individual to his culture, nor to an understanding of his influence upon it." Boas, *Race, Language, and Culture*, 258. And in a volume that Boas edited entitled *General Anthropology* (Boston: D. C. Heath, 1938), he argues that although "it seems most desirable and worthwhile to understand each culture as a whole and to define its character," he doubted that "it is possible to give a picture of the culture which is at the same time a picture of a personality," 680–81.

83. Alain Locke, "Unity Through Diversity: A Baha'i Principle," (1930), in Harris, *Philosophy of Alain Locke*, 134–38. James W. Fernandez explores in "Tolerance in a Repugnant World and Other Dilemmas in the Cultural Relativism of Melville J. Herskovits" the philosophical, methodological, and practical issues that Herskovits faced in his commitment to cultural relativism. As Fernandez writes, "I have posed the dilemmas, the perplexing choices, which Herskovits struggled with: cultural and/or ethical relativism, tolerance and/or tough-mindedness, practical relativism and/or applied anthropology, universals and/or particulars, world society and/or ethnocentrism—dilemmas he struggled with and, indeed, by the nature of the case, could not ever resolve." Fernandez, *Ethos* 18 (1990): 159.

Chapter 4

"Camels of Obviousness and Gnats of Particularities": Alain Locke, Melville Herskovits, Roger Fry, and Albert C. Barnes

T*he New Negro* both documents and is meant to be a document for the "dramatic flowering of a new race-spirit" taking place on American soil. Although Harlem is understood to be the "mainspring," the "laboratory," the "capital" of this "fresh spiritual and cultural focusing," its roots go deep into "the racy peasant undersoil of the race life." Historically and geographically, the lines of racial consciousness run North and South. At the same time, Harlem also intersects with other lines of awareness that link with Africa and the dispersion of African peoples into the frontiers of the New World. In Locke's striking phrase, Harlem is the "home of the Negro's Zionism," drawing upon as well as expressing the full diversity of "Negro life" (the African, the West Indian, and the Negro American). Not only are black Americans conscious of acting as "the advance-guard of the African peoples in their contact with Twentieth Century civilization," but this awareness is, in turn, an "effort to recapture contact with the scattered peoples of African derivation." Thus, *The New Negro* is meant to symbolize, to celebrate, and to further this dramatic shift in racial consciousness.

Locke was not the first black American to link Africa and America both historically and imaginatively. W.E.B. Du Bois's *The Negro* (1915) was a major effort to establish the cultural importance of Africa and the significance it had for black Americans. And Du Bois's work takes its place alongside that of the many, often anonymous others in the nineteenth century who evoked Africa in song, sermon, political tract, novel, and historical essay. But *The New Negro* seeks to fuse past and present on the level of image and imagination. Whereas Jean Toomer suggests that the Dixie Pike "has grown from a goat path in Africa," Langston Hughes writes of the Negro soul that "has grown deep like rivers"—the Euphrates, the Congo, and the Nile. And river and path open, as well, upon Bruce Nugent's

"Sahdji," Arthur Schomburg's "The Negro Digs Up His Past," Locke's "The Legacy of the Ancestral Arts," trickster stories, Baoule and Bushongo masks, drawings and decorative designs of Aaron Douglas, and Du Bois's "The Negro Mind Reaches Out." In its several parts and as a whole, *The New Negro* represents "a fresh spiritual and cultural focusing."

In recent years, various students of the Harlem Renaissance have taken note of Locke's ambitious claims and have offered their own understanding of what was and was not achieved. Harold Cruse, for example, in *The Crisis of the Negro Intellectual* does not see the "black intelligentsia" of the 1920s as an "advance-guard of the African peoples" but a generation of intellectuals seduced by white attention and the chimera of radicalism voiced by the Communist Party. As a consequence, Cruse argues, the clarifications that should have been made were never achieved and subsequent generations have paid the price.[1] Likewise, Nathan Huggins argues in *Harlem Renaissance* that compelling as it was to identify with Mother Africa, the ultimate results of this identification were ambiguous. Ambiguity, however, was not only in the results per se but in the search itself. For it is Huggins's claim that Americans—black and white—are provincials "forced through condition and education to look elsewhere for the springs of civilization and culture." As a consequence, Huggins writes, "black men yearned, as American provincials, to find meaning and identity in Africa; their frustration was a measure of their Americanization."[2] Although their analysis differs, both of these critics look back to the 1920s as a time when Africa's imagined importance for black Americans only served to reveal the limits and frustrations of the imaginations involved.

Until recently various elements of Cruse's and Huggins's critical concerns have served to frame subsequent interpretations of the Harlem Renaissance. Houston Baker, however, radically challenged the general emphasis on limits and limitations and, in so doing, offered a very different reading of the importance and accomplishments of these earlier figures. As Baker emphatically states in *Modernism and the Harlem* Renaissance, "I disagree entirely with the general problematic I have just suggested, a problematic that judges the Harlem 1920s a 'failure.' In my discussion I offer what is perhaps a *sui generis* definition of modern Afro-American sound as a function of a specifically Afro-American discursive practice."[3] As Baker's title suggests, his revision of the Harlem Renaissance turns on the conceptual term—modernism—that, he argues, has prejudiced understanding and ensured misunderstanding ever since.[4] Better to begin with Booker T. Washington's speech at the Negro exhibit of the Atlanta Cotton States and International Exposition (September 18, 1895) than Virginia Woolf's calendrical musing that "in or about December, 1910 human character changed."[5] Better to root Afro-American modernism in the trickster language of Washington than the "collaged allusiveness of T. S. Eliot's *The Waste Land* and Joyce's *Ulysses*, the cubist reveries of Picasso, the imagism of Pound, or the subversive politics of surrealists."[6]

Although Baker doesn't pursue the issue, implicit in his critique of modernism as a frame of reference is the allied term—"primitivism"—that has long served to link the two concepts and with Africa as well.[7] Listen, for example, to Meyer

Schapiro's ecstatic salute to the Armory Show, which brought modern art to New York City in 1913:

In this love of the primitive as a stronger, purer humanity, the moderns built upon a novel taste of the nineteenth century. But now for the first time the intensity and simplicity of primitive color and drawing were emulated seriously . . . together with this simplicity and intensity, which seemed to revive a primitive layer of the self . . . the painters admitted to their canvases . . . uncensored fancies and associations of thought akin to the world of dreams; and in this double primitivism of the poetic image and the style they joined hands with the moralists, philosophers, and medical psychologists who were exploring hidden regions and resources of human nature in a critical, reforming spirit. The artists' search for a more intense expression corresponded to new values of forthrightness, simplicity, and openness to a joyous vitality in everyday life.[8]

William Rubin's two-volume *Primitivism in 20th Century Art: Affinity of the Tribal and the Modern* (1984) is but one of many efforts to document as well as celebrate the "twin phenomena" of the modern and the primitive.[9]

In the critical literature on the Harlem Renaissance, however, this connection has been central to the ambivalence that has been voiced by various critics. Huggins, for example, linked his comments on Africa and African American provincialism with what he called "the Negro intellectual's fascination with primitivism."[10] Likewise, Robert Bone argued in *Down Home* that in one way or another the writers of the Harlem Renaissance had been victims of this "racist caricature, . . . some black authors embraced the new stereotype, others tried to fend it off, or adapt it to their own ends, but all succumbed in one way or another to its seductive power."[11] For Baker, these critical judgments, however well intended, were essentially self-defeating. Taking his cue from Michel Foucault's *Madness and Civilization*— "if you are in a madhouse, then you must be mad"—Baker abandoned altogether the categories that had "dominate[d] the analytical discourse of Afro-Americans."

Freed from the tyranny of this conceptual mistake, it was now possible, Baker argued, to see that Africa and things African had resonance within a field of discourse distinctly and importantly African American. Countee Cullen might write: "One three centuries removed / From the scenes his fathers loved / Spicy grove and banyan tree, / What is Africa to me?" but the significance of his statement was not its problematic blend of images, its imaginative limits, but the fact that Cullen, along with others of his generation, subverted as well as displaced prevailing assumptions as to what black Americans thought, felt, and were capable of expressing.[12] At the same time, Baker took note of the African masks and statues from Bushongo, Sudan-Niger, the Ivory Coast, Dahomey, and the Congo that graced the pages of *The New Negro*. They serve, he suggested, as "ancestral and culturally specific leitmotivs." Thus, it was clear to Baker, at least, that Locke's inclusion of these "ancestral arts" importantly contributed to *The New Negro's* meaning—"a broadening and enlargement of the field of traditional Afro-American discursive possibilities." Africa was not antithetic to one's sense of *patria* but an element of consciousness within a field of awareness whose boundaries only then were in the process of being formed.[13]

More recently, George Hutchinson also argues in *The Harlem Renaissance in Black and White* that modernism is key to a conceptual understanding of the Harlem Renaissance and key, as well, to the intellectual and institutional dynamics that mark these years—"To enter the history of American modernism by way of an interracial perspective, I believe, can offer a new vision of the period."[14] No less than Baker, Hutchinson was unhappy with previous interpretations that employed "high" modernism in one way or another as if it was a relevant concern. Although Hutchinson took issue with Baker's critical reading of modernism, he shared Baker's critical judgment that the centrality of primitivism in black and white conceptions of African American identity needed to be qualified:

The point I am suggesting here is that the dominant view of the approach of the New Negro—and their white friends—to African identity simply does not square with the documentary evidence. It recognizes only one side of a complex dialectical relation and ignores the real significance of Boasian anthropology, pragmatism, literary realism, and historicism to the New Negro movement—all of which exerted a powerful and salutary counterpressure to the exploitation of "primitive and exotic" projections of the white racial psyche.[15]

For both men Africa, the concern for Africa and African art was important emotionally and symbolically, a key element in the "notion of a renaissance as a recovery of 'a classical heritage heretofore overlooked or ignored.' "[16]

Although Baker's and Hutchinson's emphasis importantly contrasts with other interpretations, they add little to our understanding as to how Locke came to assemble these forms, the specific aesthetic and cultural meaning they were meant to have, and the particular dilemmas he tried to resolve in giving to Africa a visible presence in *The New Negro*. At the same time, these modernist figures cannot easily be dismissed or set aside. Their presence was significant, and no one was more aware of their presence and their significance than Locke himself. In his essay "The Legacy of the Ancestral Arts," Locke called attention to almost every major painter and sculptor in Germany and France to respond to African art in the beginning decades of the twentieth century. Beyond the works of Picasso, Matisse, Marc, Modigliani, Epstein, and Lipschitz, Locke's thoughts also included the poets Guillaume Apollinaire and Blaise Cendrars as well as critics and collectors Paul Guillaume and Roger Fry. Locke's point is that (1) "there would be little hope of an influence of African art upon the western African descendants if there were not at present a growing influence of African art upon European art in general"[17] and (2) that "African sculpture has been for contemporary European painting and sculpture . . . a mine of fresh *motifs*." As a consequence, shouldn't there be, he proposes, no less an influence "upon the blood descendants, bound to it by a sense of direct cultural kinship?"

To answer Locke's challenge, to pursue the aesthetic and cultural considerations he brings to bear, it will be necessary to trace the vein of riches he himself first opened. In so doing, it will become clear, as well, that names not usually associated with the "prospects of [this] rich yield"—Franz Boas, Melville Herskovits, Alfred Stieglitz, Albert C. Barnes, Paul Guillaume, and Roger Fry—were also important contributors to the *communal* project known as *The New Negro*.[18]

Locke's essay, "The Legacy of the Ancestral Arts," is the revision of an earlier article "A Note on African Art" that first appeared in *Opportunity* (May 1924), a special issue on African art that also included Barnes's "The Temple" and Guillaume's "African Art at the Barnes Foundation." Not only does Locke's essay "A Note on African Art" provide a perspective on the second essay, its elaboration and shift in emphasis, but it also serves to suggest a theoretical framework for the evaluation of African art.

Locke begins this essay with the emphatic claim that "The significance of African art is incontestable; at this stage it needs no apologia."[19] In fact, given the range of fantasy and misinformation with which African art has been burdened, Locke suggests that "Its chief need is to be allowed to speak for itself, to be studied and interpreted rather than to be praised or exploited."[20] What he offers, as a consequence, is a brief historical sketch to help trace the altered perception of things African from "dumb, dusty trophies of imperialism" to objects of art. However, what seems most significant to Locke is that African art has both an aesthetic and a cultural meaning: "What it is as a thing of beauty ranges it with the absolute standards of art and makes it a pure art form capable of universal appreciation and comparison; what it is as an expression of African life and thought makes it an equally precious cultural document, perhaps the ultimate key for the interpretation of the African mind."[21] Ideally, these two considerations, the universality of a pure art form and the formal particularity of African expressions, would be related. But for the present, they represented two important but as of yet separate understandings.

Locke's thoughts were partly an act of clarification, an effort to sort out present concerns from past assumptions and misconceptions. Beyond this, however, he also looked forward to "the construction of a new broadly comparative and scientific aesthetics" to help answer such basic questions as the origin and function of art. For this reason, he singled out the work of Emile Torday and J. A. Joyce on the Bushongo and A. A. Goldenweiser's *Early Civilization* (1922) as especially promising ethnographic "lines of interpretation."[22] At the same time, he anticipated that the comparative study of such "culture elements as art, folk-lore and language" would eventually provide "the most reliable clues and tests for African values" as well as the sense of a cultural past for black Americans as they "struggle for a racial idiom of expression" all their own.

Although Locke singled out Goldenweiser and his work *Early Civilization* as a hopeful beginning for comparative study, it was Melville Herskovits, not Goldenweiser, who most nearly fulfilled this role. Whereas Goldenweiser did most of his work among the native peoples of North America, as did Boas and almost all of his students, it was Herskovits, soon to be a close friend and colleague of Locke, who would devote his life to the study of African culture and its spread into the western hemisphere. More important, however, than attempting to distinguish the particular impact of any one individual on Locke's understanding of African art were the broad lines of analysis that students and colleagues of Boas all shared with their common mentor. In his praise of *Early Civilization*, for example, Locke called attention to Goldenweiser's "rejection of the evolutionary formula which would make all African art originate from crude representationalism" and his emphasis on abstract principles of design and aesthetic form as "determinants of its stylistic technique and conventions." These concerns and this emphasis, however, were rooted in Boas's groundbreaking work, *The Mind of Primitive Man*, which appeared in 1911.

In his revolt against the evolutionary racial science of the nineteenth century (what George Stocking calls "the critique of racial formalism"), Boas challenged the fundamental presumption, "a lack of originality," that supposedly distinguished Europeans and non-Europeans and justified the world's peoples being ranked in stages of ascending superiority. In so doing, Boas offered an alternative formalism in which the "rational forms" evident in the cultural objects of non-Europeans (basketry, carvings, architecture, pottery, metal work, and spinning) revealed both technical skill and the play of individual imaginations. To be creative, quite simply, was intrinsically a human phenomenon and "the evaluation of actions from [an] ethical and aesthetic viewpoint" something "peculiar" to mankind as a species. However, more than universality was being argued here. For Boas's emphasis on a shared "aesthetic impulse" was cast within an intellectual framework that stressed diversity and the plurality of standards necessary to evaluate the success and meaning of a people's aesthetic achievements. Art, like culture, had its own intrinsic integrity. As a consequence, the problematics of history, not the uniformities of science, were best suited to help reveal their shared integrity. Herein was the matrix of ideas that Boas would more fully develop in his later work *Primitive Art* (1929).

Primitive Art is built on the premise that "in one way or another esthetic pleasure is felt by all members of mankind" and that "no matter how diverse the ideals of beauty may be, the general character of the enjoyment of beauty is of the same order everywhere."[23] Beauty, however, is only knowable by its form, and form, in turn, is directly related to technique, the technical skills and traditions carried within a people's cultural experience. Thus, in making form ("fundamental forms"; "fixity of form"; and "fixity of design") and not content the essential critical consideration, Boas argued for both the universality of human consciousness and the diversity of human expression.[24] In isolating the formal properties of art, however, Boas introduced a tension in his argument that he, as well as Locke, would struggle to resolve. For in validating the arts of other peoples and with form the theoretical centerpiece, the relationship between art and culture became increasingly strained.

The immediate problem Boas sought to address, how best to contextualize or arrange the available artifactual evidence, was central to his life-long challenge to 19th-century evolutionary anthropology. In his earlier disputes with the principal authorities of the Smithsonian, for example, Boas argued with John Wesley Powell and Otis T. Mason for displays that grouped objects so as to suggest the "whole way of life" of a particular people. "Life-groups," not man in the abstract, was Boas's intellectual focus. But no matter how grouped, once objects were removed from their original context, their meaning became increasingly unclear. As George Stocking notes, "Removed . . . from their original contexts in space and time, and recontextualized in others that may or may not seek to recreate them, the meaning of the material forms preserved in a museum must always be acutely problematic."[25] Although speaking more generally of the museum movement in anthropology, Stocking's comments are no less appropriate for judging Boas's efforts in *Primitive Art* to provide a context for the art he presented.

Boas introduces *Primitive Art* with the comment that "our object is . . . an attempt to determine the dynamic conditions under which art styles grow up."[26] He immediately notes, however, that the historical record is woefully inadequate to accomplish this goal: "the specific historical problem requires much fuller material than what we now possess. There are very few parts of the world in which we can trace, by archaeological or comparative geographical study, the growth of art styles."[27] As a consequence, Boas's efforts to contextualize form(s) so as to suggest its meaning, the meaning to those who authored it, is severely compromised. To help fill this gap in space and in time, he inserted into his text a carefully detailed, descriptive analysis of the style of the decorative art of the Coast Indians of the Pacific Northwest. His analysis, anchored in the continuity of "fixed formal elements found in this art," is meant to show that "this art style can be fully understood only as an integral part of the structure of Northwest coast culture."[28] But the leaves of this book, much like the ethnographic exhibits Boas battled to change, do not echo with the voices of those whose work we try to understand. Instead, the interpretive logic of Franz Boas fills the void that history and research fails to provide. Since, as he recognized, this strategy might not be entirely satisfactory, we the readers are asked to draw upon our own thoughts and feelings. Thus encouraged, it is presumed that we can now see not only ourselves in others but others within ourselves.

Context was one challenge. Art or artifact was another. In his concluding remarks, Boas asks, "Do they [primitive people's] possess the same keenness of esthetic appreciation that is found at least in part of our population?"[29] By now, given the detail and documentation of his work, the question is clearly rhetorical. The answer is yes. But the question has other implications. In making form central to the question posed, has Boas now undercut the problem of context from another direction? As Marianna Torgovnick writes, "The tension between the designations 'art' and 'functional object' permeates the politics of art theory and museum exhibitions when they pertain to primitive societies. In turn, that tension forms part of this century's most characteristic intellectual debates between contextual and formal approaches, between differentiating via historical and cultural backgrounds and universalizing via the study of deep structures and continuing forms."[30] Although the tensions Torgovnick refers to are rooted in a deeper and more general intellectual tradition than Boas's immediate concern for primitive art, these tensions serve to frame his thinking. Perhaps, as James Clifford suggests, "the separation of ethnography and art has not been watertight."[31] But, as Clifford concludes, "generally speaking, the ethnographic museum and the art museum have developed fundamentally different modes of classification."[32]

Boas's remarks made in 1929 have no direct bearing on the ideas Locke put forth in "A Note on African Art." However, Locke was a careful student of *The Mind of Primitive Man*. As Herskovits's class notes from 1922–23 reveal, these ideas were first introduced in Boas's teaching at Columbia University and became part of the intellectual heritage his students took with them as they embarked on their own scholarly careers.[33] At the same time, a major strand of the friendship that developed between Locke and Herskovits was their shared interest in Africa and African culture. Six months after they first met in January 1924 and prior to teaching with Locke at Howard University, Herskovits made an extensive tour of the principal European anthropological and African ethnological collections.[34] One year later, he outlined to the National Research Council his hopes to trace the cultural roots of African Americans: "I wish to continue my work on the Negro in Africa as well as in this country, on both the physical make-up of the African peoples in the region from which the ancestors of the American Negroes have come, and the cultural background which characterized these ancestors. . . . Although I have felt that the behavior of the American Negro is, in the main, quite like that of the Whites in this country, I must confess that there is a possibility of there being something of a differing temperamental base which has not been studied."[35] To do this, Herskovits proposed returning to "the great African collections of the major European ethnological museums."[36] Later, with the help of Boas and Elsie Clews Parsons, he would do research in Suriname, West Africa (Dahomey, Nigeria, and the Gold Coast), and the Caribbean (Trinidad and Haiti). Throughout these years, Herskovits kept in touch with Locke. In 1931 he wrote,

I am forwarding to you . . . something that you asked me for when I saw you before we left on our field trip. It comes from Nigeria and is a figure that is used by twins. When one of a pair of twins dies the other will always carry one figure such as this about with him and anything that happens to the living twin must also happen to the effigy or the spirit of the dead one will come to take away that of his brother or sister thus causing the death of the remaining one of the pair. . . . This was made by the grandfather of the present woodcarver, who also does beautiful things, and comes from the city of Abeokuta in Nigeria. Incidentally, don't let anyone talk to you about the extinction of African wood-carving or any other form of West African culturization. The cultures over there are very vital and are thoroughly integrated and resistant to European influences.[37]

Locke was delighted with the gift, "it is doubly precious for itself, and as a gift from you." "I don't suppose," he added, "it can affect me, except aesthetically."[38]

Important as the anthropological concerns of Boas and Herskovits were, the tensions Boas confronted in relating the part to the whole were compounded by Locke's effort to bridge the gap between Africa and America. At the same time, given the understanding that African art was "pure form," the gap Locke sought to bridge between Africa and America included that between "culture meaning" and "aesthetic meaning." Perhaps, it was not yet possible to place African art within a meaningful historical or cultural framework.[39] As a consequence, one could only speculate as to what a particular carving or casting meant to its anonymous creator or to those for whom it was meant to be used. Aesthetically, however, as the embodiment of elemental form and as a catalyst for the European imagination, to Locke African art was at least knowable: "It follows that this art must first be evaluated as a pure form of art and in terms of the marked influences upon modern art which it has already exerted, and then that it must be finally interpreted historically to explain its cultural meaning and derivation. What the cubists and post-expressionists have seen in it intuitively must be reinterpreted in scientific terms, for we realize now that the study of exotic art holds for us a serious and important message in aesthetics."[40] The place to begin, then, was to pay close attention to its influence upon contemporary French art. As Locke claimed, in contrast to the English and the Germans, the French had been most sensitive to the aesthetic values of African art, language, and music.[41] To help chart the way aesthetically, Locke singled out Paul Guillaume and Roger Fry as having provided the most "authentic interpretations."

In 1933 Fry was awarded the prestigious Slade Professorship of Fine Arts at Cambridge University. Although many thought the recognition unconscionably late, it did acknowledge Fry's long reign (perhaps along with Clive Bell) as the preeminent art historian and critic in English intellectual life. In Stephen Spender's estimation, at least, Fry was "the most constructive and creative influence on England between the two wars." In 1910, Fry organized the first Postimpressionist exhibition "Manet and the Post-Impressionists," and two years later followed this *"succes d'estime"* with a second Postimpressionist exhibition. Thus, under Fry's continuing inspiration and goading, France, in general, and names all but unknown in England—Cezanne, van Gogh, Gaugin, Vlaminck, Derain, and Picasso—soon became the center of a new consciousness called modern. At the same time, beginning with his essay "The Art of the Bushmen" (1910), Fry initiated a line of argument that linked the arts of non-Western peoples with the cultural ferment he sought to inspire. In his important volume of essays, *Vision and Design* (1920), Fry combined such diverse essays as "Negro Sculpture," "Ancient American Art," "The Ottoman and the Whatnot," "The Munich Exhibition of Mohammdean Art" and "The Art of the Bushmen" together with essays on Paul Cezanne, Renoir, and the French Postimpressionists.

In an important sense Fry was a midwife in his own right, seeking to free his contemporaries from the "comfortable mental furniture" of the Greco-Roman tradition and the emphasis on content (or subject matter) as the essence of artistic accomplishment. To do this, he initiated a new vocabulary and a new sensibility to accompany as well explain the art he challenged others to accept. What distinguished Fry's theoretical efforts to define "the re-establishment of purely aesthetic criterion in place of the criterion of conformity to appearance" was form ("significant form")—the essential elements (line, mass, space, light, and shade; color; and the inclination of the eye of the plane) that constituted the separate but related elements of the total configuration.[42] As Beverly H. Twitchell suggests, "Though manifesting some diversity and incorporating shifts over a period of many years, Roger Fry's formalism was a broad but consistent feature unifying his massive work."[43] Here, then, was a voice to be heeded, one that importantly contributed to the profound changes taking place in "aesthetic sensibility" and the linking of this sensibility with a challenge as clear as it was astonishing: "The artist of to-day has therefore to some extent a choice before him of whether he will *think* form like the early artists of European races or merely *see* it like the Bushman."[44]

In his "A Note on African Art" and then in *The New Negro*, Locke quoted directly from Fry's essay "Negro Sculpture." Most important, Locke claimed, Fry established the terms in which one could understand the historic and aesthetic importance of African art—"Some of these things are great sculpture—greater, I think, than anything we produced even in the Middle Ages."[45] What made this sculpture so great was "its complete plastic freedom." In contrast with Western notions of plasticity, burdened with concerns for representation, these "African artists really can see form in three dimensions."[46] As a result, these forms were not "mere echoes of actual figures" but possessed an "inner life of their own." Not only did Locke use Fry to provide perspective, but the question of perspective itself was for Locke no less important. As he pointedly remarked, "the problems raised by African art are now recognized at the very core of art theory and art history."[47] Thus, in the context of Fry's response to modern art and the problems Fry sought to resolve, Locke understood African art to be an imaginative awakening to the prevailing limitations of his and his people's cultural identity. However, within the configuration of modernism itself, that defined by Fry as vision and design, there was a complex inner tension that rendered problematic the connections that Locke sought to achieve.

As Marianna Torgovnick has forcefully argued, Fry clearly had little to offer regarding the cultural meaning of the sculpture he praised so highly[48]:

Quite strikingly, Fry makes no attempt to distinguish between different parts and different peoples in Africa. Hundreds of distinctions must be made; Fry makes only two—Bushman and "Negro"—the breadth of the second category creating an overlap. More important, Fry shows no recognition that the objects discussed as museum pieces were often functional items, and sometimes sacred objects, in the daily life or special rituals of a people. . . . But even if we grant the validity of sometimes giving aesthetic considerations priority over ethnographic ones, the latter do not lose all relevance. Fry's discussion of African objects is analogous to a discussion of medieval chalices and reliquaries that proceeds without reference to Christianity or to the organization of the medieval church, indeed which neither knows nor cares that such things existed.[49]

But Locke did not seek this in Fry nor did he comment on Fry's failure to integrate these "significant forms" into a cultural setting. Perhaps Locke was disappointed. More likely he did not expect this from someone like Fry. Instead, Fry offered something theoretically important, the possibility of conceptualizing art in such a way as to answer some of the questions Locke had already explored philosophically and psychologically. Integration would be the work of others, individuals like Locke himself.

Locke wanted, as he writes in "A Note on African Art," a "scientific aesthetics" and Fry, in his effort to identify the "specifically aesthetic emotion by means of which the necessity of relations is apprehended," had drawn important analogies between art and science.[50] Both men, in effect, shared a common desire to link the aesthetic with elemental states of emotion and to translate this emotion into a synthesis that was more than the sum of its parts. How to proceed, however, was not entirely clear. Form was the key. At a certain level, Fry argued, form and content became inextricably fused. But translating "the chaotic and accidental conjunction of forms and colours" into "the whole mosaic of vision" would prove to be elusive.

Fry never completely accepted Clive Bell's contention that "significant form" was some elemental quality completely independent of time and space. What Fry called "the emotional elements of design" also included the artist's intentions and the observer's responses.[51] But, as Fry's biographers have noted, Fry was never fully able to pin-point the meaning of form or its relationship to the meaning of its structured whole.[52] In 1914 he wrote, "is it not the fusion of this something with form that makes the difference between the finest pattern-making and a real design?"[53] Six years later, in the "Retrospect" to *Vision and Design*, he simply referred to "this vague adumbration of the nature of significant form."[54] Now, rather than slide into "the depths of mysticism," he preferred to leave the problem "on the edge of that gulf."[55] But the challenge remained, to be taken up by Albert C. Barnes. In his hands, the dilemmas Fry faced would be directly passed to Locke.

Highly opinionated and abrasive, Barnes dedicated his life to the collecting and teaching of art. In 1922 he established the Barnes Foundation in Merion, Pennsylvania, having amassed the largest private collection of modern art (Matisse, Monet, Picasso, Cezanne, Renoir, and Degas) and African art in the world.[56] Although Barnes's valuable collection of paintings has recently been made available for public viewing, he remains, for most Americans, an obscure and/or mysterious figure.[57] In December, 1923 Barnes and Locke met in Paris. In the following month Barnes sought his assistance for an article, "Contribution to the Study of Negro Art in America," to be published in *Ex Libris*, the journal of the American Library in Paris.[58] Three months later, Barnes informed Locke that his article would also appear in Paul Guillaume's *Les Arts à Paris* and hoped that if he thought "Contribution" had any merit he would send it to an American journal so as to reach "the most sympathetic and intelligent attention."[59] One week later, Locke invited Barnes, who was now in Pennsylvania, to meet with several friends in New York City.[60] Thus began a friendship of uncertain complexity that would include, as well, Barnes's close and often strained involvement with several of the most prominent figures of the Harlem Renaissance.

Through Locke, Barnes was introduced to Walter White and Charles S. Johnson, who would both marvel at his formidable energy and quickly tire of his explosive temper and heavy-handed sense of self-importance. Upon their first meeting, White immediately asked for Barnes's assistance with an article, "If White Had Been Black," which he felt exceeded his own specific knowledge.[61] Barnes advised him that what he had written was "trash and shouldn't be published" and virtually overwhelmed him with a slashing critique of all whom White had used to make his argument: "[Stuart] Culin nice guy but a mental cripple, a hopeless doddering old ignoramus in anything which relates to art. Einstein is a mental giant and a connoisseur compare to him—that doesn't detract any thing of truth of statement from my public assertion the other night that Einstein is a colossal bluff. De Zayas is in somewhat the same class as Einstein with dullness substituted for Einstein's Clive Bell-like counterfeit thinking in smooth, slick language."[62] According to Barnes, the only individual of stature was Roger Fry: "let the sole reference to Negro plastic art be what Roger Fry has written." All the rest, Barnes advised, were "the literary equivalents of prostitution."[63]

With Johnson, there was less acrimony. As editor of *Opportunity*, Johnson was in a position to be of use to Barnes and was generally receptive to Barnes's ideas.[64] In March, while abusing White both to his face and to others, Barnes asked Johnson if he would be interested in publishing his article on Guillaume, "The Temple," and coupled this inquiry with a prospectus for a future issue of *Opportunity* to be devoted to African art and the special role he and Guillaume had played in giving recognition to Africa's rich cultural heritage:

1. Paul Guillaume is potentially the most influential white friend the Negro has today . . . that debt should be acknowledged.
2. The Barnes Foundation has ready a crack between the eyes for the so-called authorities in antique art . . . consists in showing the masterpieces of Negro sculpture side by side with finer pieces of ancient Greek and Egyptian sculpture than can be found in the Metropolitan Museum of Art. It may be left to us to apply scientific method to make known that Negro art is in just that highest class of creations.
3. Nobody competent has ever studied Negro art according to the modern conceptions of the psychology of aesthetics utilized according to the scientific method.[65]

Johnson was especially eager to pursue Barnes's idea and promised that "this suggestion of yours should bear fruit and you may depend upon me to push it to the limit."[66] In May, *Opportunity* offered a special issue on African art. The cover, provided by the Barnes Foundation, was a reproduction of a ceremonial mask from the Ivory Coast and the lead editorial was a very complimentary introduction to Barnes and the work he was doing.[67] In addition to the article by Barnes, and Guillaume's "African Art at the Barnes Foundation," Locke's "A Note on African Art" comprised the content of this special issue.

Although Johnson had expressed interest in Barnes's "Contributions to the Study of Negro Art," he used "The Temple," Barnes's special tribute to the electricity of French intellectual life and Paul Guillaume's early and influential appreciation of African art. Now, however, Locke wanted "Contributions" for the special Harlem issue of *Survey Graphic* (retitled "Negro Art and America"), and this was soon followed by Locke's use of the same article in *The New Negro*. In fact, Locke had been reluctant to use Barnes's article in *The New Negro*. He would like to have had Carl Van Vechten, the novelist and friend of most every black cultural figure in the 1920s, write an article on "The Negro in American Art," but Van Vechten was committed to writing an article for *Vanity Fair* and pleaded lack of time. As a consequence, Locke had to settle for what he called the "kindly but vague assertions" of Dr Barnes. Although Locke did not fully explain to Van Vechten his dissatisfaction with Barnes, it seems clear that Barnes had offered little to help resolve some of the questions Locke had raised in "A Note on African Art."

Barnes's essay is an uneven blend of historical and cultural analysis. His various generalizations, however, are grouped and somewhat unified by the sharp dichotomy he makes between the cultural and historical experience of whites and blacks: "That there should have developed a distinctively Negro art in America was natural and inevitable. A primitive race, transported into an Anglo-Saxon environment and held in subjection to that fundamentally alien influence, was bound to undergo the soul-stirring experiences which always find their expression in great art."[68] In these terms, Barnes spoke forcefully of what "the cultured white race owes to the soul-expressions of its black brother" and singled out "the renascence of Negro art" as not only something of great beauty but "as characteristically Negro as are the primitive African sculptures."[69] Barnes, however, no less than Fry, sent mixed messages. In this essay, Africa is little more than a timeless and placeless expanse of energy, its primary significance being its contrast to the aimless and devitalized ways of modern life. And in "Negro Art, Past and Present," an essay that appeared one year later in *Opportunity*, Barnes celebrates the achievements of black Americans, a people "torn from their native environment and from their carefree, irresponsible life."[70] Clearly, Barnes was of marginal help to Locke in his effort to provide a cultural context for the art he so greatly valued.

Barnes, like Fry, was essentially uninterested in the historical complexities of Africa and the myriad of cultural distinctions that distinguished peoples from one another who lived on the African continent. In fact, the concern for this kind of detail in various ethnographic museums of the world was understood to be a problem that had to be overcome.[71] For this reason Barnes praised Guillaume as one who "had rescued the obscure ancient Negro art from its mere ethnological significance."[72] What mattered was art, not artifact, and as art these objects were understood to have a formal significance independent of their social and material context. Thus, Barnes notes that "ancient Negro sculpture" reveals in "the Negro race" an "entirely unsuspected wealth of plastic endowments" and "an ability to arrange forms in varied, rhythmic, harmonious, moving designs which do not suffer by comparison with the most distinguished classic achievements of any of the other races."[73] Barnes's response to African art, sustained in great part by Fry's critical authority, was itself an extension of the more general modernist concerns that Fry articulated in *Vision and Design*, *Transformations* (1926), and *Cezanne: A Study of His Development* (1927). Thus, Barnes's own work, *The Art of Painting* (1925) as well as his *The Art of Cezanne*, *The Art of Matisse*, and *The Art of Renoir*, all reflect, in Beverly Twitchell's words, Fry's "distinctive imprint."[74]

Barnes lacked Fry's sophistication and Fry's awareness that theoretically formalism remained an ongoing intellectual and aesthetic challenge. For Barnes, in contrast, art was simply a self-contained dynamic of intrinsically meaningful elements (color, light, line, and space). And he applied his formula as if it were a stamp. As a result, his books are "lengthy, leaden, and often redundant."[75] In his own mind, at least, Barnes saw himself as "stripping [art] of the emotional bunk which the long-haired phonies and that fading class of egoists, the art patrons, have encumbered it."[76] As he confided to Locke, he thought of himself as one of the few white friends of black Americans, a friend constantly beleaguered by misinformed and racist others.[77] From the point of view of Walter White and Charles S. Johnson, however, Barnes's presence was decidedly a mixed blessing. As for Locke, Barnes's "Negro Art in America" was only acceptable by default. He wanted "something more suggestive and concrete." Unable to find a suitable alternative, Locke offered his own interpretation of the past, "The Legacy of the Ancestral Arts," both to supplement and to extend Barnes's inadequate sketch.[78]

Much of "Legacy" is a rewording of material brought forward from his *Opportunity* article, "A Note on African Art." At that point, however, Locke's intention was to explore more directly the implications that African art might have for the social and cultural identity of black Americans. At the very least, Barnes, Guillaume, and Fry had helped to make visible African art as a vital and invaluable cultural heritage. But beyond the importance of this recognition, there remained for black Americans an inner psychic landscape to be explored and revealed—"hints of a new technique, enlightening and interpretative revelations of the mysterious substrata of feeling under our characteristically intense emotionality."[79] But again the conundrum: Blacks no less than the "average European Westerner" seemed to confront an enigma, strange forms from the void of time and distance. As Locke expressed it, "Except then in his remarkable carry-over of the rhythmic gift, there is little evidence of any direct connection of the American Negro with his ancestral arts."[80] What, then, to make of these compelling yet alien objects?

One answer Locke offered was to turn the alienation and incomprehension of the viewer into the very significance of what one observed. Thus, Locke argued that the inability to make sense of these unfamiliar objects was the result of a cultural conditioning that had imprisoned both whites and blacks within a limited range of increasingly meaningless forms and sterile conventions. Blacks, however, had been the more insidiously circumscribed in that the prevailing conventions had promoted little self-recognition beyond "caricature and genre study." Thus, African art functioned as a revelation through which to achieve new forms of self-expression and self-awareness. Such an answer, however, did little more than re-word the problem which Locke had intended to answer.

More promising was his definition of African art as the expression of a folk temperament and a folk tradition. Now, more directly and inwardly racial, Locke here assumed an emotional bond between peoples of African origin, a bond foreign to those whose cultural roots traced back to Europe. And yet, Locke immediately confronted an impasse of even greater complexity than the limbo of past neglect he initially addressed:

The characteristic African art expressions are rigid, controlled, disciplined, abstract, heavily conventionalized; those of Aframerican—free, exuberant, emotional, sentimental and human. Only by the misinterpretation of the African spirit, can one claim any emotional kinship between them—for the spirit of African expression, by and large, is disciplined, sophisticated, laconic and fatalistic. The emotional temper of the American Negro is exactly the opposite.[81]

Black Americans were Americans, a people separated from their geographic and cultural origins and molded within the "peculiar experience [of] America and the emotional upheaval of its trials and ordeals." If, then, one could not expect from "the arts of the forefathers" either "cultural inspiration" or "technical innovations," perhaps it was possible to learn "the lesson of discipline, of style, of technical control pushed to the limits of technical mastery."[82] However, whether such abstraction led to a "racial art" or rendered such an idea problematic remained to be seen.

Although Locke sought to improve upon Barnes's contribution to *Survey Graphic*, his argument was not strikingly different. Each defined and accounted for the creative vitality of black Americans in a similar way. Each celebrated the "pure-plasticity" of African art and its impact on the intellectual and artistic imagination of Europeans. If Locke was more concerned than Barnes to relate the formal aesthetic properties of African art to an underlying racial and emotional temperament, his success advanced little beyond Barnes's declared intent to restrict himself to the "psychology of aesthetics."[83] Locke's dilemma was to discover in African art the very meaning(s) his aesthetic understanding and his critical vocabulary seemed to deny. At the conclusion of "Legacy," Locke was cautious yet hopeful that he had singled out a minimal basis upon which to proceed: "The African spirit is at its best in abstract decorative forms. Design, and to a lesser degree, color, are its original fortes." But Locke himself was not fully satisfied with this minimal answer.

Aware that a synthesis of the aesthetic and the cultural significance of African art remained to be achieved, Locke eagerly responded one year later to Carter G. Woodson's suggestion that he propose a plan of study of African art for possible funding by the Association for the Study of Negro Life and History. Locke indicated that what he proposed would be a study of "African art as an Expression (or index) of African culture." He submitted, as well, a bibliography of readings as well as a list of the principal collections of African art that would constitute the initial research needed to be done.[84] Upon receipt of Locke's proposal, Woodson consulted with Boas as to the potential value of such a study:

Dr. Alain Leroy Locke, the author of a recent book entitled *The New Negro*, has suggested that the Association make him an allowance for the study of African art. His study will be partly research and partly interpretation. He has outlined it as the memorandum herewith enclosed will show. Kindly inform me frankly whether you feel that this study properly comes within the purview of what we planned to do in Anthropology or whether we can justly use our Anthropology fund to finance a study of this sort. I feel that such a work as Prof. Locke would produce should be very informing. I am in doubt, however, as to whether he can produce anything original on this side of the Atlantic and the fund will not be sufficient to finance him in Europe. I shall be governed by whatever you and Prof. Hooton may have to say.[85]

However, Boas, though he knew Locke personally and admired his work, regretted that he was unable to endorse his plan.[86] In a follow-up letter to a second inquiry from Woodson, Boas expressed doubt that Locke had sufficient "ethnological knowledge . . . to carry through a plan of this kind."[87] As a consequence, Locke's proposal was rejected, and the research he hoped to do was set aside.

For the remainder of the decade and into the next, Locke played a role similar to the one he voiced in "A Note on African Art," championing African art and its potential to help configure the cultural identity of black Americans. In "To Certain of Our Philistines," *Opportunity* (May 1925), "Art Lessons From the Congo," *Survey Graphic* (February 1927), "A Collection of Congo Art," *The Arts* (February 1927), "Beauty Instead of Ashes," *Nation* (April 1928), and "The American Negro As Artist," *American Magazine of Art* (September 1931) Locke kept his audience informed as to the impact African art had and continued to have on Europe's "leading modernists"—Picasso, Modigliani, Matisse, Epstein, Lipschitz, and Brancusi. He coupled this ongoing instruction with the recognition of young black sculptors and painters ("the younger modernists") who had "begun to reflect African influences" in their work.[88] However, by the middle of the next decade, Locke's emphasis had dramatically shifted.

"African Art: Classic Style" is Locke's response to the exhibition of African art organized by James Sweeney for the Museum of Modern Art in 1935. Locke was extremely impressed, stating that of the seven major exhibitions since Alfred Stieglitz first showed African art at Gallery 291 in 1914 this was clearly "the definitive exhibition of African classics." Not only did Sweeney draw from seventy-two European and American collections (the Barnes Foundation being a conspicuous oversight), but most important Sweeney provided "a master lesson in the classic idioms of at least fourteen of the great regional art styles of the African continent."[89] Although Locke still associated "classic" with the "art object" itself, his emphasis now was on context (fourteen regional styles) and the historical "phase" when this art came to fruition.

African art, Locke now argued, was "best understood directly, and in terms of its own historical development." To look at Africa through modernist eyes was, in effect, to see African art "through a glass darkly." Not only were analogies with the classic art of Greece and Rome misleading but so too was it a distortion to see this art in terms of "its correlation with modern art or its admitted influence upon modern art."[90] To do so was to dilute its strength and simplicity. Locke even accepted Sweeney's suggestion that (1) "the new appreciation of African art" and the "Negro plastic tradition" and (2) "the working out of the new aesthetic in European art" were "coincidental rather than cause and effect."[91] Nowhere in this essay does Locke encourage his reader to see Africa as a mirror. Nowhere does form hold promise for an African American identity. Africa expresses Africa, and we, together with Locke, stand on the margins—"Apart from texture and feel," Locke notes, "I fancy there can be little appreciation of it [African art] in anything approaching native terms."[92] Differences, not similarities, are what one must now learn and learn to accept. The Museum of Modern Art, Locke concludes, has rendered a great service, for what we now learn is that African art is "really too great for imitation or superficial transcription."

Ernest D. Mason and Leonard Harris have addressed Locke's cultural and aesthetic concerns and in so doing provide a complement to the general argument that Houston A. Baker, Jr. made in *Modernism and the Harlem Renaissance*. In "Black Art and the Configurations of Experience: The Philosophy of the Black Aesthetic," Mason links the etymological sense of the term aesthetic ("perceptible by the senses") together with Locke's understanding of experience as "form-quality." In so doing, the boundaries of experience are understood to be extremely elastic and the province of the "aesthetic attitude" is neither provincial nor limited to the formal properties of art: "perceptual recognition is, as Locke tells us, the act of experiencing figures (objects, events, situations, persons) not in isolation but contextualized with a reciprocating movement of perception, conception and valuation."[93] Thus, Mason argues, Locke provided an important theoretical foundation for a black aesthetic, one that included "the experiences and perceptions that black people [had] of themselves and others."[94] Likewise, Harris, in "Identity: Alain Locke's Atavism," also argues that much of what Locke wrote was an effort to broaden the political and cultural identity of black Americans, "weapons in the theoretical battles of the day."[95] In particular, so as to counter the critical views of Nathan Huggins and Harold Cruse, Harris understands Locke's intellectual concerns to be a serious effort to shift attention away from essentialist ("atavistic") explanations of cultural identity to cultural and historical forms of explanation. It is in the context of this argument, then, that Harris pays special attention to Locke's need to confront "the anthropological status of black people as humans" and his interest in Africa and African art.

Both points of view situate Locke within the mainstream of concerns black intellectuals addressed in the 1920s. Importantly, Mason and Harris relate these concerns to Locke's intellectual and theoretical imagination. What we don't see, however, is what Locke shared with others—most notably Franz Boas and Melville Herskovits, Roger Fry, Paul Guillaume, and Albert C. Barnes.[96] To paraphrase Mason, the "experience" Locke sought to configure included a range of critical opinion that linked New York with London and Paris.[97] At the same time, this shared understanding posed problems for Locke he was unable to resolve. Leonard Harris is quite right to emphasize that context and contingency, not "innate temperaments and quintessential cultural traits," distinguish Locke's philosophic and cultural discourse. But Locke did share with others the "essential" understanding that African art was form. However, as Jean Laude has argued, such appreciation is highly selective, uniquely modern, and gives to African art an abstract significance it rarely possesses for those who create it.[98] As a consequence, providing a context for these "rigid, controlled, disciplined, abstract, heavily conventionalized" figures proved difficult to achieve. No less difficult was the effort to construct an "emotional kinship." Ultimately, Locke had to question the adequacy of the intellectual resources he had drawn upon. No less problematic were the emotional qualities of form that Locke derived from epistemology as well as experience.

At a recent showing of African art objects at the Guggenheim, "Africa: The Art of a Continent," considerations that Locke struggled to resolve sixty to seventy years earlier continued to challenge informed opinion. Most notably, Cornel West, Kwame Anthony Appiah, and Henry Louis Gates all addressed the Western response to things African (Africa itself) so as to free the present from this limited and limiting intellectual heritage. West, for example, declares,

Gone are the old intellectual frameworks predicated on crude white supremacy and subtle Eurocentricism. The once popular categories of "barbarism," "primitivism," and "exoticism" have been cast by the academic wayside. The homogeneous definitions and monolithic formulations of "African-art" have been shattered. The Whiggish historiographical paradigms of cultural "evolution" and political "modernization" have been discarded.[99]

Appiah offers an even more fundamental challenge, addressing his reader as well as the exhibition itself: "So we might as well face up to the obvious problem: neither *African* nor *art*—the two animating principles of this exhibition—played a role as *ideas* in the creation of the objects in this spectacular show."[100] In their critique of the Western response to African art, both West and Appiah made no effort to establish a particular need or concern that African Americans might have in the exhibition's brilliant presence. For both men, the exhibition simply challenged "our prevailing views of reality" and, as Appiah suggested, these magnificent pieces "should be a potent reminder of the humanity you share with the men and women that made them."

Gates, too, critiqued "the court of judgment that is Western art," focusing on the European modernists for whom African art was so important and whose response to this art so deeply shaped future understanding.[101] Although Gates is no less intent than West and Appiah to insist on the intrinsic beauty of African art, he is more explicitly concerned with the interpretive response of African Americans.[102] In this context, he calls attention to Locke's essay "The Legacy of the Ancestral Arts" that appeared in *The New Negro*:

Locke's solution to this quandary . . . is as curious as Picasso's waffling about influences upon him: by imitating the European modernists who so clearly have been influenced by African art . . . African Americans will become African by becoming modern.[103]

However, if Locke's attitudes toward African art, and by extension the attitudes of other African Americans, are to be addressed, his ideas must be given a fuller reading. Clearly, there is an argument to be made that the ambivalence individuals such as Picasso had toward Africans—"this assembly of degenerate and feeble-minded posterity"—contributed to the ambivalence African Americans also felt regarding the beauty of African art. But this was a consideration that Locke himself had already voiced (though not directed at Picasso per se) in his ambivalence toward the writing of Albert C. Barnes and in his efforts to encourage an awakened black consciousness. At the same time, Locke did not argue that "African Americans will become African by becoming modern." His thinking was more complex than that. In fact, he came to understand that modernism was not so much a universal that subsumed the particular but itself a particular understanding or conception no less partial than the diversity it was thought to transcend.

It is unfortunate that the only reference to Locke that appears in this entire volume is to suggest that, at best, his efforts only fostered a kind of "Afro-Kitsch." Ironically, however, Locke's struggle to make sense of African art anticipates many of the same critical considerations later made by West, Appiah and Gates in their response to "Africa: The Art of a Continent." Although he draws upon the critical opinions of James Sweeney and other non-African sources in his essay "African Art: Classic Style" (1935), Locke, as seen, now distinguishes African and modernist concerns as well as the concerns of Africans and African Americans. Above all, he concludes (sounding very much like these later commentators) "It [this exhibit] presents African art as really too great for imitation or superficial transcription. Its result must surely be to engender respect for the native insight and amazement for the native technique."[104] It is time that Locke's pioneering interests be placed not only in his own time but in ours as well.

NOTES

1. Harold Cruse, *The Crisis of the Negro Intellectual* (New York: William Morris, 1967), 21–22.

2. Nathan Huggins, *Harlem Renaissance* (New York: Oxford University Press, 1971), 83.

3. Houston A. Baker, Jr., *Modernism and the Harlem Renaissance* (Chicago: University of Chicago Press, 1987), xiv.

4. Baker writes,

I would suggest that judgments on Afro-American "modernity" and the "Harlem Renaissance" that begin with notions of British, Anglo-American, and Irish "modernism" as "successful" object, projects, and processes to be emulated by Afro-Americans are misguided. It seems to me that Africans and Afro-Americans—through conscious and unconscious designs of various Western "modernisms"—have little in common with Joycean or Eliotic projects. Further, it seems to me that the very *histories* that are assumed in the chronologies of British, Anglo-American, and Irish modernisms are radically opposed to any adequate and accurate account of the history of Afro-American modernism, especially the *discursive* history of such modernism.

Ibid., xv–xvi.

5. Virginia Woolf, "Modern Fiction," in *The Common Reader*, ed. Andrew McNeillie (New York: Harcourt Brace Jovanovich, 1984).

6. Baker, *Modernism and the Harlem Renaissance*, xiii.

7. It is interesting to note that Woolf dated the shift in human character in response to the first Postimpressionist exhibition in England, "Manet and the Post-Impressionists," organized by Roger Fry. In the same year, Fry, in turn, had published his essay "The Art of the Bushmen" in the journal *Atheneum*.

8. Meyer Schapiro, "Rebellion in Art," in *America in Crisis,* ed. Daniel Aaron (New York: Alfred Knopf, 1952), 214–15.

9. Other important books in this celebratory tradition are Robert Goldwater, *Primitivism in Modern Art* (New York: Vintage Books, 1967); Carl Einstein, *Negerplastik* (Berlin: E. Wasmuth, 1923); Paul Guillaume and Thomas Munro, *Primitive Negro Sculpture* (New York: Harcourt Brace, 1926); and Marius de Zayas, *African Negro Art: Its Influence on Modern Art* (New York, 1916).

10. Huggins, *Harlem Renaissance*, 187.

11. Robert Bone, *Down Home* (New York: G. P. Putnam's Sons, 1975), 125. Beyond the immediate focus of this ambivalence there has flowered an immense literature that has critically addressed a larger ambivalence—Western conceptions of "others" and the political and social consequences of these conceptions. Marianna Torgovnick, *Gone Primitive: Savage Intellects, Modern Lives* (Chicago: University of Chicago Press, 1990); Adam Kuper, *The Invention of Primitive Society* (London: Routledge, 1988); and Susan Hiller, *The Myth of Primitivism* (London: Routledge, 1991) are but three recent studies that have critiqued the limitations of Western conceptions of non-Western peoples. Also, see Michael North's, *The Dialect of Modernism: Race, Language and Twentieth Century Literature* (New York: Oxford University Press, 1994).

12. As Baker writes, "Certainly Countee Cullen, for example, served a national need in a time of 'forced' institution building and national projection. He gained white American recognition for 'Negro poetry' at a moment when there was little encouraging recognition in the United States for *anything* Negro. And Cullen gained such recognition by means of a mastery of form pleasing *to Afro-Americans* as well as Anglo-Americans." Baker, *Modernism and the Harlem Renaissance,* 86.

13. Although Arnold Rampersad addresses the Harlem Renaissance from a different perspective than Baker and with a specific focus on the imagination and poetry of Langston Hughes, he also addresses the "question of modernism" and suggests that "Hughes's place in it, needs to be seen in the context not merely of Harlem but of international cultural change in the twentieth century." See Rampersad, "Langston Hughes and Approaches to Modernism," in *The Harlem Renaissance Revaluations* ed. Amritjit Singh (New York: Garland, 1989), 67.

14. George Hutchinson, *The Harlem Renaissance in Black and White* (Cambridge: Harvard University Press, 1995), 31.

15. Ibid., 185.

16. Ibid., 428.

17. Alain Locke, "The Legacy of the Ancestral Arts," in *The New Negro* (New York: Atheneum, 1992), 255–56.

18. Also see, Malgorzata Irek, "From Berlin to Harlem: Felix von Luschan, Alain Locke, and the New Negro" in *The Black Columbiad* ed. Werner Sollors and Maria Diedrich (Cambridge: Harvard University Press, 1994), 174–84. Hutchinson has given extended attention to Locke's relationship with Barnes and John Dewey, Dewey's and Barnes's close

relationship, and their common interest in African art and the "asethetics of experience." Hutchinson's comments on Dewey help to clarify Locke's intellectual focus. And, as Hutchinson writes, "It was in dialogue with Guillaume and Barnes that Locke developed his chief orientation to African art." Hutchinson, *Harlem Renaissance*, 427. Locke, however, did not, as Hutchinson claims, borrow Barnes's views of African art "wholesale."

19. Alain Locke, "A Note on African Art," in *The Critical Temper of Alain Locke—A Selection of His Essays on Art and Culture,* ed. Jeffrey Stewart (New York: Garland, 1983), 131.

20. Ibid., 131.

21. Ibid.

22. As Locke writes,

It is most encouraging therefore to see an emancipated type of scientific treatment appearing, with Torday and Joyce's historical interpretation of art in terms of its corresponding culture values, and in Goldenweiser's rejection of the evolutionary formula which would make all African art originate from crude representationalism, that is to say, naive and non-aesthetic realism. For Goldenweiser, primitive art has in it both the decorative and the realistic motives, and often as not it is the abstract principles of design and aesthetic form which are the determinants of its stylistic technique and conventions.

Ibid., 133.

23. Franz Boas, *Primitive Art* (New York: Dover Publications, 1955), 9.

24. In addressing the question of style, whether the "purely decorative" or the "idea of representation," Boas concludes, "In every case . . . the formal element that characterizes the style, is older than the particular type of representation. This does not signify that early representations do not occur, it means that the method of representation was always controlled by formal elements of distinctive origin." Ibid., 354.

25. George Stocking, *Objects and Others—Essays on Museums and Material Culture* (Madison: University of Wisconsin Press, 1985), 4. Also see in this same volume, Elizabeth Williams, "Art and Artifact at the Trocadero: Ars Americana and the Primitivist Revolution," 146–66; Ira Jacknis, "Franz Boas and Exhibits: On the Limitations of the Museum Method of Anthropology," 75–111; and Edwin L. Wade, "The Ethnic Art Market in the American Southwest, 1880–1980," 167–91.

26. Boas, *Primitive Art*, 7.

27. Ibid.

28. Ibid., 280.

29. Ibid., 356.

30. Torgovnick, *Gone Primitive: Savage Intellects, Modern Lives*, 81.

31. Clifford, "Objects and Selves—An Afterword," in *Objects and Others: Essays on Museums and Material Culture,* 242. John Dewey's comment in *Art as Experience* remains pertinent,

Suppose, for the sake of illustration, that a finely wrought object, one whose texture and proportions are highly pleasing in perception, has been believed to be a product of some primitive people. Then there is discovered evidence that proves it to be an accidental product. As an external thing, it is now precisely what it was before. Yet at once it ceases to be a work of art and becomes a natural "curiosity." It now belongs in a museum of natural history, not in a museum of art. And the extraordinary thing is that the difference that is thus made is not one of just intellectual classification. A difference is made in appreciative perception and in a direct way.

Dewey, *Art as Experience* (New York: Capricorn Books, 1958), 48–49.

32. Clifford, "Objects and Selves—An Afterward," 242.

33. These are Herskovits's class notes taken in January 17, 1923:

Thus the case of representative and interpretive art we must see that the psychological attitude toward the two on the part of the artist is different—in the case of the latter there is the lively aesthetic-techno-logical feeling, while in the case of representation the motive is very different—merely as a reminder or play or what not. The aesthetic motive is absent and the artist only has representation in view. When the artist gets virtuosity in technique the representation takes on an aesthetic element. This virtuosity can be highly developed in technical processes—basketry in California, tying in Polynesia, or trades (iron-working, weaving, pottery-making) in Africa—and technical excellence has an aesthetic value—e.g., a basket made with a regularity of stitch we call beautiful. Also, there is the tendency of the virtuoso to make his own task difficult. As soon as specialization occurs and the worker plays with his technique, pattern and design are bound to appear—as twilling in basketry. Similarly with the handling of planks with edges, geometrical patterns result from the playing with technique. Similarly with African iron-work.

Thus, in art there are two unrelated sources of development—representative art, which may or may not have aesthetic value, and geometrical or conventional design, which develops from the play with technique. These may affect each other reciprocally but to arrange designs in series from representative to geometric art is a naive disregarding of the psychological background of art.

Melville Herskovits Papers, Northwestern University Archives. Importantly, Boas argues for the universality of the creative impulse. Herskovits and Locke, however, would both make efforts to give "the psychological background of art" a cultural meaning.

34. In his report to the Board of Fellowships in the Biological Sciences, National Research Council, Herskovits detailed his travels: England, France, Germany, Belgium, Netherlands, Denmark, Sweden, and Italy. Herskovits, 28 February, 1925, Melville Herskovits Papers, Northwestern University Archives.

35. Melville Herskovits to Edith L. Elliot, 21 January 1926, National Research Council, Melville Herskovits Papers, Northwestern University Archives, 2.

36. Herskovits reported:

A study of such a problem as wood-carving of these people, an outstanding characteristic of their cultures, of their designs, or of some other cultural trait would at the same time give us an idea toward connecting the culture of the African with whatever vestiges of it might be observable in the American Negroes, and give me the most excellent possible preparation for the African field work I hope later to do. The problem of the West African wood-carving is of particular significance in the light of my particular problem, since it is in the realm of the artistic products manifested in this country particularly through the Negro spiritual that any innate connection with the African temperament might most easily be seen.

Ibid.

37. Herskovits concludes, "I hope you will be getting out here [Evanston] this winter as I should like nothing better than to show you some of the things that I brought back from this trip. My bush-Negro specimens are also out where they can at least be looked at and I would like you to see those, too." Melville Herskovits to Alain Locke, 29 October 1931, Melville Herskovits Papers, Northwestern University Archives.

38. Alain Locke to Melville Herskovits, 30 November 1931, Melville Herskovits Papers, Northwestern University Archives.

39. At least, Locke drew upon Guillaume Apollinaire's comments in *Apropos de l'Arts des Noirs* (1917) to make this point: "In the present condition of anthropology one cannot without unwarranted temerity advance definite and final assertions, either from the point of view of archeology or that of aesthetics, concerning these African images that have aroused enthusiastic appreciation from their admirers in spite of a lack of definite information as to

their origin and use and as to their definite authorship." Locke, "A Note on African Art," in *Critical Temper*, 131.

40. Ibid.

41. As Locke writes, "Roughly speaking, one may say that the French have been pioneers in the appreciation of the aesthetic values of African languages, their poetry, idiom and rhythm." Ibid., 134–35.

42. Although the term "significant form" is generally attributed to Clive Bell in his work *Art* (1914), the inspiration and its more complex elaboration is understood to be Fry's. See Frances Spalding, *Roger Fry: Art and Life* (Berkeley : University California Press, 1980).

43. Beverly H. Twitchell, *Cezanne and Formalism in Bloomsbury* (Ann Arbor: University of Michigan Research Press, 1987), 78.

44. Roger Fry, "The Art of the Bushmen," in *Vision and Design* (New York: Meridian Books, 1966), 97.

45. Locke, "A Note on African Art," 132.

46. Ibid., 133.

47. Ibid., 132.

48. Torgovnick, "The Politics of Roger Fry's Vision and Design," in *Gone Primitive*, 85–104.

49. Ibid., 97.

50. Fry writes, for example,

None the less, perhaps, the highest pleasure in art is identical with the highest pleasure in scientific theory. The emotion which accompanies the clear recognition of unity in a complex seems to be so similar in art and in science that it is difficult not to suppose that they are psychologically the same. It is, as it were, the final stage of both processes. This unity-emotion in science supervenes upon a process of pure mechanical reasoning; in art it supervenes upon a process of which emotion has all along been an essential concomitant.

Fry, "Art and Science," in *Vision and Design,* 83.

51. Fry wrote,

It may be that in the complete apprehension of art there occurs more than one kind of feeling. There is generally a basis of purely physiological pleasure, as in seeing pure colours or hearing pure sounds; then there is the specifically aesthetic emotion by means of which the necessity of relations is apprehended, and which corresponds in science to the purely logical process; and finally there is the unity-emotion, which may not improbably be of an identical kind in both art and science.

Ibid.

52. See Spalding, "Significant Form," in *Roger Fry—Art and Life*, 153–73.

53. Ibid., 165.

54. Fry, "Retrospect," in *Vision and Design*, 302.

55. Ibid.

56. See *The Harlem Renaissance: A Historical Dictionary for the Era*, ed. Bruce Kellner (Westport, CT: Greenwood Press, 1984), 24–25.

57. Recently, the Barnes collection made its first appearance outside the carefully guarded walls of Barnes's private estate. As reported in the *International Herald Tribune*,

It was the first time the *Haus der Kunst* had ever stayed open all night. Then again, it was also the first time a museum show in Munich had drawn more than 400,000 people. . . . The exhibition, 'From Cezanne to Matisse: Great French Paintings From the Barnes Foundation,' was on the last day of its last stop on a two-and-a-half-year international tour. . . . Barnes had amassed about 800 paintings and 200 sculptures, including some 170 Renoirs, 55 Cezannes and 20 Picassos, which he liked to display in crowded, quirky arrangements that included Gothic hardware, African sculpture, furniture and porcelains. . . . [T]he mystery of seeing these hidden treasures, major masterpieces by major artists that would never been [*sic*] shown outside Pennsylvania again, gave it serious news value.

International Herald Tribune (October 22, 1996).

58. Barnes wrote:

Thanks for your letter and your kind promise to send me the data requested. I want to glean only a summary of what the best-known Negro artists have done, not to worship them but to show their relation to what the ordinary, unknown, Negro lives every day in spiritual things. . . . I am interested in Negro art which is too commonly unrecognized or overlooked.

Albert C. Barnes to Alain Locke, 8 February 1924, Howard University.

59. More gentle and more talented, Guillaume served as the Foreign Secretary for the Barnes Foundation. In his own right, he was an early collector of African art and a great admirer and friend of modernist painters who appeared at his doorstep and in the pages of his journal *Les Arts à Paris*.

60. Although eager to make the trip, Barnes was not sure it would be safe. The following letter to Locke well serves to reveal Barnes's raw and overbearing personality: At present if I went to New York I would run the risk of being arrested for criminal libel because of my public reprisals of the dirty trick the *Dial* pulled on Buermeyer in the March issue. Craven is just a propagandist for some ignorant, academic painters who announced their intention to "wipe up the ring with me." Thayer knows that, but is sore at me for what Paul Guillaume can tell you I did last summer to him and his then managing editor when I balked their project to do other dirty tricks on two people, one of whom was the honest Paul Guillaume. . . . [T]he Craven article is a mixture of lies and innuendos, while the statements of objective facts about paintings are sheer moonshine, and the cheapest bluffs. Albert C. Barnes to Alain Locke, 11 March 1924, Howard University.

61. Walter White to Albert C. Barnes, 24 March 1924, Howard University.

62. Albert C. Barnes to Walter White, 25 March 1924, Howard University.

63. Unsure what to make of Barnes's tirades, White forwarded his correspondence with Barnes to Locke, asking Locke to read the letters and "advise me what is the matter with your friend in Philadelphia." Walter White to Alain Locke, April 12, 1924, Manuscript Division, Library of Congress. Barnes, in the meantime, had been confiding to Locke that White's article was "ridiculous," that White was a "light-weight," and that his "manuscript has revealed a cheapness which I hardly suspected . . . the whole mess is a sloppy offensive mess." Albert C. Barnes to Alain Locke, 25 March 1924, Howard University.

64. As did White, however, Johnson also found Barnes to be difficult to take. In a letter to Locke, Johnson confided his feelings: "No, I did not attend the Philadelphia meeting and for several good reasons—one of them the folder which Dr. Barnes had published and distributed. I couldn't face Philadelphia after that. I like his enthusiasm and his extraordinary energy, and without doubt he has given a tremendous impetus to interest in *Opportunity*, but the personal exaggerations are absolutely devastating." Charles S. Johnson to Alain Locke, 16 May 1924, Howard University.

65. Albert C. Barnes to Charles S. Johnson, 22 March 1924, Howard University.

66. Charles S. Johnson to Albert C. Barnes, 26 March 1924, Howard University.

67. As Locke wrote,

Those who know Dr. Albert C. Barnes treat him as a valuable secret. In the heart of Philadelphia he has in successful operation one of the most astounding experiments in human relations in industry yet tried; in his home in Merion, Montgomery County, Pennsylvania, he has the most complete and valuable collection of modern art in this country, and one of the best in the world. He was the first and is distinctly the last word in Primitive African Art and his pieces, the rarest of their kind—exquisite, exotic, distinctive,—once casually valued at fifty thousand dollars, are becoming invaluable. This is primitive art, and there are limits to discovery. And there are yet Philadelphians who ask "Who is Dr. Barnes?" And there are "sophisticates" who sense the forcible entry of the primitive African motif into modern art, who take their wisdom from Clive Bell's clever vagaries and de Zayas' outlandish speculations. It is perhaps pardonable if this ritual of silence is broken, if only for a moment, on one who has known the native art of Negroes longer and who still knows it better than any one in the United States, and who ranks close to Paul Guillaume as one of the foremost authorities on it in the world.

Alain Locke, "Dr. Barnes," *Opportunity,* (May 1924): 133.

68. Albert C. Barnes, "Negro Art and America," *Survey Graphic* (March 1925): 668.

69. Ibid.

70. Albert C. Barnes, "Negro Art, Past and Present," *Opportunity* (May 5, 1926): 149.

71. See Elizabeth A. Williams, "Art and Artifact at the Trocadero: Ars Americana and the Primitivist Revolution," in Stocking, *Objects and Others*, 146–66.

72. Albert C. Barnes, "The Temple," *Opportunity* (May, 1924): 139.

73. Barnes, "Negro Art, Past and Present," 168.

74. As Beverly H. Twitchell writes,

Barnes imitated Fry's objective aspirations in both formal analysis and explanation of techniques, as in his notion of taking an "experimental attitude." When he analyzed works, Barnes discussed their "components" and "distinctive organization," which united as "plastic form." Indeed, Barnes so condensed and simplified the views of Fry and Bell that he concluded that style, form, and expression were identical and inseparable from the artist's life and temperament.

Twitchell, *Cezanne and Formalism in Bloomsbury,* 195.

75. In discussing Picasso's response to African sculpture, for example, Barnes writes,

About 1909 the sculptural influence began to be paramount, and naturalistic rendering gave place almost completely to the rendering of abstract forms. In his still-lifes of this period several objects are often placed so close together that the whole group functions as a single mass. His former suave, curved lines have become sharp and heavy, and the objects outlined are angular and blocklike. The pinks, blues and yellows of his earlier work have changed into a somber combination of slate, drab green, and dull brownish red. These new shapes and colors are the distinctive mark of Picasso's form at that period and constituted the point of departure for cubism.

Albert C. Barnes, *The Art of Painting* (New York: Harcourt Brace, 1925), 390. For a more appreciative view of Barnes and his response to modern and African art, see Mark Meigs, "The Barnes Foundation and the Philadelphia Museum of Art: Bifurcated Loci of Cultural Memory, *Annales: Lieux de Mémoire aux* États-Unis 18 (1995): 37–64.

76. Carl McCardle, "The Terrible Tempered Barnes," *Saturday Evening Post* (March 21, 1942): 93.

77. Albert C. Barnes to Alain Locke, 7 May 1924, Howard University.

78. Clearly, Hutchinson has overstated the case when he claims that "Barnes [was] the person upon whom Locke and *Opportunity* relied as their house expert on African aesthetics and its relation to European modernism . . . and [that] he borrowed his views of African art wholesale from the irascible manufacturer." Hutchinson, *The Harlem Renaissance in Black and White,* 45.

79. In a letter to Walter White, Locke confirmed his own concern for "race temperament" in telling of a conversation he had with Paul Guillaume: "There is every indication, here and abroad of increasing interest in the artistic possibilities of our race material and of our race

temperament. Discussing the vogue of African Art in Paris and elsewhere on the Continent, M. Paul Guillaume told me that in his judgment merely the surface values had been exploited up to the present, and that in his view final interpretation and development of its possibilities could only conceivably come from within the race group." Alain Locke to Walter White, c. 1924, Manuscript Division, Library of Congress.

80. Alain Locke, "The Legacy of the Ancestral Arts," 254.

81. Ibid.

82. Ibid., 256.

83. It is to be noted that Barnes also envisioned something more than an exclusively formal analysis. As Locke quotes Barnes, "Negro art is so big, so loaded with possibilities for a transfer of its value to other spheres where Negro life must be raised to higher levels, that it should be handled with the utmost care by everybody. . . . It involves intellectual, ethical, social, psychological, aesthetic values of inseparable interactions." Alain Locke, "Research For Primitive Art," *Opportunity* (June 1924): 165.

84. Locke wrote,

My plan would be to undertake directly a study of AFRICAN ART AS AN EXPRESSION (or INDEX) of AFRICAN CULTURE, but in reading through the quite voluminous literature . . . to take notes and citations covering the broader field of the cultural values of the African civilizations in so far as social customs or social philosophy reflected in folk-lore, religious or social beliefs, or institutional practice might give clues to these values. Especially in the field of art symbols and their closely related religious conceptions, I believe we have the only available clues left to the moot question of the antiquity and indigenous character of certain supposedly African contributions to early civilization.

The collections Locke listed were the following—Brussels, London, the Pitt-Rivers private Museum; Berlin Institute of Ethnology; Hamburg, Dresden, Frankfort on Main, British Museum, Barnes Foundation Collection; University of Pennsylvania Museum; Ward Collection (Smithsonian); and the Blondiau Collection of Bushongo and Congo Art, which formed the Harlem Museum of African Art installed in 1927 in the Harlem Library on 135th Street. Alain Locke to Carter G. Woodson, November 16, 1926, American Philosophical Society.

85. Woodson went on to say,

I am taking it for granted that you know Prof. Locke is a well educated man of unusual ability. He is a Doctor of Philosophy of Harvard University. He studied at Oxford and in Germany. He can use both French and German in his researches. His advanced work in school, however, was in Philosophy rather than in History or in Anthropology. For some time he has been making a study of the background of the Negro in Africa. He has a keen appreciation of African art. My impression of him, however, is that he is a literary man rather than a research student willing to do drudgery.

Carter G. Woodson to Franz Boas, 16 November 1926, American Philosophical Society.

86. Franz Boas to Carter G. Woodson, 18 November 1926, American Philosophical Society.

87. Franz Boas to Carter G. Woodson, 22 November 1926, American Philosophical Society.

88. Those Locke called "the younger modernists" included Archibald Motley; Lillian Dorsey; William H. Johnson; Hale Woodruff; Richmond Barthé; Sargent Johnson; James Lesesne Wells; and Aaron Douglas. This recognition was coupled with Locke's continuing encouragement to black Americans to see in Africa the locus of a new aesthetic and a new consciousness:

However, the constructive lessons of African art are among the soundest and most needed of art creeds today. They offset with equal force the banalities of sterile, imitative classicism and the empty superficialities of literal realism. They emphasize intellectually significant form, abstract design, formal simplicity, restrained dignity, and the unsentimental approach to the emotions. And more important still, since Africa's art creed is beauty in use, they call for an art vitally rooted in the crafts, uncontaminated with the blight of the machine, and soundly integrated with life.

Alain Locke, "The American Negro as Artist," *American Magazine of Art* 23 (September, 1931): 210–20.

89. Alain Locke, "African Art: Classic Style," *American Magazine of Art* 28, no. 5 (May 1935): 271.

90. Ibid.

91. Ibid., 271–72.

92. Ibid.

93. Ernest D. Mason, "Black Art and the Configurations of Experience: The Philosophy of the Black Aesthetic," *College Language Association* 27 (September 9, 1983): 3.

94. Ibid., 2.

95. Leonard Harris, "Identity: Alain Locke's Atavism," *Transactions of the Charles S. Peirce Society,* 24, no. 1 (winter 1988): 70.

96. Hutchinson has helped to clarify Locke's intellectual focus by giving extended attention to Locke's relationship with John Dewey and Albert C. Barnes, Dewey's and Barnes's close relationship, and their common interest in African art and the "aesthetics of experience." However, Locke, as seen, had severe misgivings about Barnes and did not borrow, as Hutchinson claims, "his views of African art wholesale from the irascible manufacturer." Also, Hutchinson gives no attention to the formalist concerns of Roger Fry and his importance for both Barnes and Locke and too little attention to the significance of form in Franz Boas's discussion of culture and aesthetics. Hutchinson, *The Harlem Renaissance in Black and White*, 42–50, 62–77.

97. In reply to a critique of *The New Negro*, Locke wrote to the literary editor of *The New York Sun*,

Now as to details, Mr. Seligmann balks both at camels of obviousness and gnats of particularities. When I say "of one colored writer," who happens to be Rudolph Fisher, that he combines the terseness and emotional raciness of Uncle Remus with the art of Maupassant and O. Henry, it ought to be obvious that I mean to say he combines the naive and the sophisticated arts of narrative,—and I think he does. If , again, I include in a list of American music influenced by Negro idioms French works that on good authority of Darius Milhaud in The Living Age, June, 1925, were direct experimental limitations [imitations] by the French modernists of music they heard played by Negro musicians at the Casino de Paris and elsewhere, it ought to be obvious that I am not "slipping," but trailing—and a pretty obvious track. Coming to the other end of the scale with Mr. Seligmann, I don't see how it was particularly incumbent upon me to mention the Stieglitz exhibition as the first exhibit of African sculpture in America, when I didn't mention any. Had I, I would have cited the de Zayas exhibition of 1916, of which the pamphlet catalogue is listed in my bibliography. As to the contention that this or any other American exhibit was the "first exhibition in the world to relate that (African) sculpture to modern French and American painting, sculpture and other modes of expression", Mr. Seligmann has made a statement more foolish and unsupported than any he accuses me of making: page Picasso, or if not in the lobby, M. Paul Gullaume [*sic*]!

Alain Locke to the Literary Editor of the *New York Sun*, 1926, Manuscript Division, Library of Congress.

98. As Laude writes,

Each African statue has a religious or, in the broad sense, a social purpose. It is an instrument or tool that has at the outset no emotional or aesthetic intent. Very few arts are so unconcerned as African art about the effect produced on viewers. Even the Bini bronze heads and statues, long thought of as products of secular art, were arranged on altars. Some Tellem, Dogon, and Bambara statuettes are covered over with a sacrificial coating of dried blood or millet gruel or with adventitious elements such as cloth, nails, or shells, which blur or mask the sculpted forms.

Jean Laude, *The Arts of Black Africa,* trans. Jean Decock (Berkeley: 1971), 195–96.

99. Cornel West, "Introduction," in *Africa: The Art of a Continent* (New York: Guggenheim Museum, 1996), 1.

100. Appiah, *Africa: The Art of a Continent,* 6.

101. Gates wondered "whether or not without black African art, modernism, as it assumed its various forms in European and American art, literature and music and dance in the first three decades of the twentieth century would possibly have existed as well," Gates, *Africa: The Art of a Continent,* 22.

102. As Gates concludes, "And if the resurrection of African art, in the court of judgment that is Western art, came about as a result of its modernist variations, this exhibition is testament to the fact, if there need be one, that African art at the end of the century needs no such mediation. It articulates its own sublimity most eloquently. For centuries, it has articulated its own silent sublimity most eloquently." Ibid., 25.

103. Ibid.

104. Locke, "African Art: Classic Style," 151.

Chapter 5

"Universality of Life under the Different Colors and Patterns": Claude McKay

Like a sunken galleon, the Harlem Renaissance continues to attract the attention of those eager to explore its precious cargo. Divers, in the form of witnesses and scholars, have been carefully assembling its varied contents while generally charting its course through American waters. As participant and as scholar, Arna Bontemps was one of the first. In his charming memoir, "The Awakening: A Memoir," (1972) Bontemps recalled the year 1922 to be of special significance. While browsing that summer in the library of the University of California at Los Angeles, he chanced upon Claude McKay's *Harlem Shadows*. Galvanized by the first sentence he read—"These poems have a special interest for the races of man because they are sung by a pure blooded Negro"—Bontemps immediately borrowed the book and shared its contents with his friends. Two years later, with McKay's poetry and his friends responses "in my consciousness," Bontemps packed his suitcase and bought a one-way ticket to New York City. Then and now, we continue to trace McKay's footsteps. With Bontemps's help and that of others, Claude McKay has become increasingly visible to those curious to fathom what took place nearly seventy years ago.[1]

As with all treasure ships, pieces of the past keep floating to the surface despite the most diligent collecting. Bontemps, for example, was unaware that McKay had written *Negry v Amerike* (*The Negroes in America*) while attending the Fourth Congress of the Third Communist International in Moscow, 1922–23. Also unaware of McKay's effort to explain America to Russia's revolutionary avant-garde, were Harold Cruse, who discussed McKay's radical politics in *The Crisis of the Negro Intellectual* (1968), Nathan Huggins, who included McKay in *Harlem Renaissance* (1971), and James R. Giles in his biographical work *Claude McKay* (1976).[2]

Discovered by Wayne Cooper in the New York Public Library, *The Negroes in America* was not translated into English until 1979.

Even if available, it is not clear that this thin volume would have significantly altered these critics' understanding of McKay or their more general understanding that McKay mirrored what they perceived to be the essential aimlessness of the Harlem Renaissance itself. For both Cruse and Huggins, McKay represented the vulnerability of the talented black intellectual falling prey to the corrupting flattery and influence of the larger white society. As Cruse writes, "the essentially original and native creative element of the 1920s was the Negro ingredient—as all the whites who were running to Harlem actually knew. But the Harlem intellectuals were so overwhelmed at being "discovered" and courted, that they allowed a bona fide cultural movement . . . to degenerate into a pampered and paternalized vogue."[3] Central to this pampering (or pandering), as Huggins argued, was "the white vogue in black primitivism."[4] For both men, as a consequence, McKay's autobiographical title *A Long Way from Home* perfectly captured his own personal dilemma and his larger symbolic importance. And for Cruse, at least, McKay was never further from home than when he left Russia in 1923 and, after a brief stay in Berlin, settled in Paris in the fall of that same year.[5]

Although McKay would not return to America until 1934, he was never completely absent from the creative activity taking place in Harlem or forgotten by those whom he left behind. Likewise, as the criticism of Cruse and Huggins suggests, McKay has never completely been forgotten by scholars who have turned their attention to the Harlem Renaissance.[6] But McKay has not been a figure who has gained the attention of a large body of scholars. Wayne Cooper, for example, introduced his *The Passion of Claude McKay: Selected Prose and Poetry 1912– 1948* (1973) with the announcement that "This volume brings together for the first time a comprehensive selection of poetry and prose of Claude McKay."[7] Fourteen years later Cooper followed this collection with the first comprehensive study of McKay: *Claude McKay; Rebel Soujourner in the Harlem Renaissance* (1987). More recently, Tyrone Tillery completed a second major study: *Claude McKay: A Black Poet's Struggle for Identity* (1992). Sandwiched between these two works, an academic conference primarily devoted to McKay was held in Mysore, India: "Claude McKay, the Harlem Renaissance and Caribbean Literature" (January 1980). In both of these biographies, and in the conference papers edited by A. L. McLeod, (*Claude McKay—Centennial Studies—1992*), McKay's *The Negroes in America* finally surfaced.[8]

As McLeod suggests, *The Negroes in America* is neither "a literary nor a sociological landmark," but it is an important document. Written after McKay had been in the United States for ten years and on the threshold of twelve expatriate years in France, Spain, and Morocco, it provides "a means of understanding much of his [McKay's] later writing and the wherewithal for a more complete appreciation of his creative personality."[9] McLeod, however, makes little effort to explore his suggestive remark. Instead, McKay is discovered to be a near contemporary, one whose shrewd social and political observations "were penned a half-century before the heady days of Black Power in the United States."[10] In these terms, McKay, presumably, is most important to later generations.

In the recent attention given to McKay and to *The Negroes in America,* it is Wayne Cooper who has made the greatest effort to follow McLeod's lead. To do this, his strategy, for the most part, is to follow and expand upon McKay's introductory remarks:

It was not my intention to please my Russian comrades: I have written with the aim of letting them know the truth about the American Negro, his place in the worker's movement, and his relationship to that movement; about his place in American society, and about the relationship of organized labor and American society to him. I have written in the spirit of a critic imbued with class consciousness, exactly as one would write in America in order to be heard by both whites and blacks.[11]

In particular, Cooper details McKay's critical "class consciousness" and his effort to sustain a Marxian analysis while centering his critique on the question of race, a question that cut across ideological and national boundaries.[12] Next, Cooper briefly extends his analysis to encompass McKay's bitter differences with Max Eastman and others with whom McKay worked on the radical literary journal the *Liberator,* differences that centered on the tension between race and radical politics. And finally, Cooper informs us that McKay "managed to include several important cultural phenomena within his Marxist framework."[13]

Unfortunately, Cooper's remarks relating to "cultural phenomena" are little more than a listing of McKay's three central chapter headings: "Negroes in Sports," "Negroes in Art and Music," and "Negroes in Literature." He does note, however, that in McKay's concluding remarks on "Art and Music" that McKay comments on the recent attention given by European artists and intellectuals to African art: "Our age is the age of the Negro in art. The slogan of the aesthetic art world is 'Return to the Primitive.' The Futurists and Impressionists are agreed in turning everything upside down in an attempt to achieve the wisdom of the primitive Negro."[14] Cooper's only comment, however, is to conclude that in these remarks one can see McKay's future direction as a writer: "Such an effort appealed enormously to McKay's romantic nature, and in his novels and short stories he would within the next decade confound the conservative critics of black art and literature by extolling the apparently aimless existence of 'primitive' black drifters who existed on the fringes of urban life in America, Europe, and the Caribbean."[15] Although Cooper links McKay's response to the interest in African art with what he takes to be McKay's own imaginative vision, Cooper's remarks are barely more suggestive than A. L. McLeod's initial comments. The need here, however, is not simply to further develop this thematic link. For taken out of the context of these three chapters, Cooper's emphasis seriously truncates McKay's more complex vision. At the same time, this larger textual context is itself more suggestive of McKay's "creative personality" and the path his writing will take than Cooper's hasty conclusion acknowledges.

In these three central chapters, McKay addressed three key critical concerns: (1) issues of race within and across national and geographical boundaries (in particular France, the United States, and Africa; (2) issues of race as they relate to the politics of cultural appropriation and production (elite and popular); and (3) issues of racial and cultural identity and the role(s) of intellectuals in constructing that identity. In so doing, McKay not only provides insight into his own imaginative and intellectual self-understanding but also his imaginative and intellectual self-positioning. Although Cooper correctly emphasized McKay's Marxist critical perspective, it is important to keep in mind McKay's later comments to James Weldon Johnson, "I went to Russia as a writer and a free spirit and left the same."[16]

In the chapter "Negroes in Art and Music," McKay focused on the exploitation of Africa by the colonial powers of Europe. The African Hall of the British Museum, for example, wherein one could gaze at delicate ivory carvings and intricate bronze sculptures, stood, above all, as a monument to the British annexation and plundering of Benin (West Africa).[17] To document the destructiveness of this cultural ransacking as well as to substantiate the worth of the objects taken, McKay drew upon the "brilliant essays and books" of the German anthropologist Leo Frobenius[18] together with the shrewd insights of Roger Fry who "lavish[ed] praise on the unknown Negro artists and their complete mastery of the form of the fourth dimension" in *Vision and Design*[19] McKay's judgments, however, did not serve to extol the "wisdom of the primitive Negro," but to highlight both the loss that Africans had endured and the continued ignorance and contempt that most Europeans had for Africa and Africans. As a consequence, the "Return to the Primitive," what McKay referred to as "the slogan of the aesthetic art world," was a double-sided and bitter irony. On the one hand, those who embarked on this culture hunt, "the ultra-civilized," were "too civilized" to understand what they had found. On the other hand, their efforts, however futile, came at the expense of Africans and descendants of Africans still very much alive: "Homage is rendered to dead Negro artists, while the living must struggle for the recognition of a just place for Negroes in the industrial society of the modern world."[20]

In the second half of this short chapter, McKay turned his attention to Anglo-Saxon America, a people and a city (New York) which, McKay argued, was even "less receptive . . . to the artistic works of Negroes than London [and the English]."[21] Critical as he was of white Americans, McKay was especially critical of African American intellectuals who he felt were only too eager to prove themselves in ways that were no less debasing than the stereotypes they sought to disprove: "Why, among contemporary American Negroes, is there this tendency (which always ends unsuccessfully) to improve composers' works which are as finished and complete as spirituals or the melodies of Negro plantation songs? Simply because the Anglo-Saxon critic . . . takes as a model the classical works of the period of slavery and thrusts this model onto the contemporary Negro artist."[22] Not only did this effort to please create a false sense of accomplishment, a false sense of acceptance, but most seriously it undermined any possibility of developing a true sense of cultural identity—"They would replace genuine Negro folk songs and jazz songs with mediocre Negro singers performing Italian arias, German songs, and Chopin waltzes in decorous drawing rooms."[23] Thus, to avoid what McKay called "spiritual impotence," it was necessary for the "Negro intelligentsia" to fully accept their and their people's historical and cultural experience. Only in this way, could they help forge a sense of collective identity through the conscious realization of "its ideals as a group."

In contrast to the Anglo-Saxon critic ("hypocritical, incompetent, filled with racial prejudices, and stupid"), McKay singled out the sensitivity of European critics and the freedom of self-expression allowed in Germany, France, Italy, and Russia. To make his point, and with France as his focus, McKay wrote of the African American painter Henry [Ossawa] Tanner,[24] who "has made himself one of the idols of the Parisian salons," and René Maran, whose novel *Batouala* received the highest literary award France had to offer, the *Prix Goncourt* (1921).[25] The public fortune of both of these men, one an expatriate from America and the other a Martiniqan living in France, contrasted with the personal fate of the eminent W.E.B. Du Bois, author of *The Souls of Black Folk*, who remained an "outcast" in his own land.[26] These striking contrasts were embedded in more general observations McKay had to make regarding the greater degree of personal comfort individuals with black skin experienced in France.[27] These observations, in turn, were anchored in the memory of the recent war wherein black American troops were lionized by the French public and decorated by the French government while slandered and segregated by their fellow Americans.[28]

In using France to help define the racial and class boundaries of Anglo Saxon culture, and the psychological damage that resulted, McKay did not want to be misinterpreted. As he wrote in "Negroes in Sports," "The good treatment of individuals from those whom they meet in France is valued so highly by Negroes that they are beginning to forget about the vile exploitation of Africans by the French."[29] The use of African troops as canon fodder against the Germans, for example, served to suggest the illusionary quality of much that had passed for respect. At the same time, McKay emphasized that racial tensions were evident as well in the dynamics of present day life. Events such as the light-heavy weight fight between the Senegalese fighter, Louis Phal Siki, and the French boxer, Georges Carpentier (September 24, 1922), revealed with dramatic clarity, McKay argued, the racial passions latent in French society.[30] France and the reputation of France now appeared, when not used to critique American intellectual and cultural life, to be no less insidious and seductive than the siren appeal of "Italian arias, German songs and Chopin waltzes."

McKay never fully reconciled his double vision of France—France the friend and France the oppressor of black-skinned peoples. But, in his role as the clear-sighted outsider he cautioned that it was necessary to translate the meaning of Liberté, Égalité, Fraternité. It was also necessary not to be misled by the translations of others. In particular, McKay singled out the commentary of Blaise Diagne (deputy from Senegal in the French parliament), who declared "that French Negroes must first of all look at themselves as Frenchmen and not as colored internationalists."[31] On the other side of the Atlantic, McKay cautioned against the American black intelligentsia who "look[ed] upon France as the foremost cultured nation of the world."[32] In this light, Du Bois's "outcast" status was now seen somewhat advantageously, a vantage point that others had forfeited or failed to exploit: "But for the Negro masses and for America, it is better that Dr. Du Bois cannot be swallowed by the bourgeoisie. For the Negro masses it is good that even black-skinned servants of the oppressor of these masses like Deputy Diagne, who is so proud of his French origin, be forced to recognize that Negroes have to carry on a difficult and unequal struggle for existence in the conditions of contemporary civilization."[33] To some extent, McKay identified his own situation with that of Du Bois. Although he addressed important differences between the two of them, McKay called attention to Du Bois's courage, his vigorous intellect, and his marginal status vis-á-vis whites and blacks. Thus, from his own vantage point in distant Moscow, McKay was also one not to be "swallowed" by the enthusiasms or politics of others.

In the final chapter of this centrally located triptych, "Negroes in Literature," McKay shifted his attention to Haiti, to the slave revolt led by Toussaint L'Ouverture and L'Ouverture's stunning victory over the powerful forces of Napoleon. In so doing, McKay both reaffirmed the revolutionary capabilities of the oppressed peoples of African origin and reconfigured, historically and geographically, the moral and political center of the French Revolution. At the same time, McKay argued that slavery was the matrix for a more general transformation of the consciousness and culture of African slaves:

The exploitation of Negroes by Western peoples has given birth among black-skinned people transplanted to a foreign soil to a folklore very distinct from the folklore of the various African tribes, although the influence of the latter can be traced in Negro folksongs and epics in the United States and in the islands of the West Indies. . . . As a result, an altered English was created, which the Negro masses of America now usually speak. This dialect, however, still contains a few words of native African origin, especially in the islands. But thanks to the great development and influence of modern American industry, the Negro dialect of the United States quickly lost its peculiarities and acquired those of the folk dialect of the proletariat.[34]

McKay's effort, here, to radicalize folk culture, to turn dialect into the language and consciousness of the proletariat, served to carry the revolutionary spirit of L'Ouverture into the urban landscape of industrial America. It also challenged the critical response of white critics who "have declared this Negro folklore to be a distinctive contribution of Negroes in the artistic world of the West," and, on this basis, would condemn those writers who transformed or ignored this "exotic flower."[35] Thus, not unlike the false counsel of those who encouraged blacks to write in the style of "Pope, Dryden, Goldsmith, and Longfellow," McKay saw this celebration of dialect as itself another trap that only ensured slavish imitation to an ideal that had little to do with creating a black consciousness and that neutralized any desire or effort to change the status quo. As a consequence, McKay suggested, "there are only two paths by which American Negro writers can go to attain their aim." The first choice, clearly a dead end, was to write in dialect, "to follow the directions of the decadent school of old critics."[36] The second choice was to follow the "directions of the new school of critics, chiefly Jews," who had a "great heritage of racial community expression in literature."[37]

Although McKay cautioned against writing in the style of Pope, Dryden, Goldsmith, and Longfellow, he nevertheless argued that "In the end, Negroes find sufficient expression for their feelings with the aid of the difficult and aristocratic English language."[38] To some extent, these remarks, as well as the perspective in which McKay had cast African American writing, derived from his own experience as a writer. McKay's first collections of poetry, *Constab Ballads* (1912) and *Songs of Jamaica* (1912), were written in the dialect of the Jamaican peasantry. But his next two books, written after he had left Jamaica for the United States, *Spring in New Hampshire and Other Poems* (1920) and *Harlem Shadows* (1922), were written in sonnet form. And with the appearance of *Harlem Shadows,* McKay was immediately hailed as the most important black poet writing in America. As James Weldon Johnson enthused,

Mr. McKay is a real poet and a great poet. . . . No Negro has sung more beautifully of his race than McKay and no poet has ever equaled the power with which he expresses the bitterness that so often rises in the heart of the race. . . . The race ought to be proud of a poet capable of voicing it so fully. Such a voice is not found every day. . . . What he has achieved in this little volume sheds honor upon the whole race.[39]

However, if the trajectory of his own imaginative writing served to chart the somewhat obscure path that led from Toussaint L'Ouverture to the use of "aristocratic English language" and the "clear, pure . . . elevated and colorful language" of Du Bois, McKay was not drawing upon personal experience only to create an historical perspective. Biography was also a measure of self, a way to situate as well as chart his own personal destiny.

McKay's underlying intellectual concern throughout this chapter is to highlight the power of the poetic imagination and the role of the intellectual. This emphasis includes an assessment of his own place within this concern. As a consequence, we first encounter Toussaint L'Ouverture in McKay's quoting William Wordsworth's poem, "To Toussaint L'Ouverture," and not directly as an historical figure.

Toussaint, the most unhappy man of men!
Whether the whistling Rustic tend his plough
Within thy hearing, or thy head be now
Pillowed in some deep dungeon's earless den;—
O miserable Chieftain! where and when
Wilt thou find patience! Let die not; do thou
Wear rather in thy bonds a cheerful brow:
Though fallen thyself, never to rise again,

Live, and take comfort. Thou hast left behind
Powers that will work for thee; air, earth, and skies;
There's not a breathing of the common wind
That will forget thee; thou hast great allies;
Thy friends are exaltations, agonies,
And love, and man's unconquerable mind.[40]

As McKay phrased it, " 'Toussaint L'Ouverture' found a response in the heart of Wordsworth, who respected his memory." But Wordsworth's heart concluded with a resounding emphasis on "man's unconquerable mind." This emphasis on heart and mind, as well as a tension between the two, would also be McKay's, serving to frame both his understanding of the world and his own self-understanding. Although issues of race and class remained central to his literary imagination, these issues intersected with and even took form as an existential tension between emotion and intellect. For this reason, McKay's two central characters in *Home to Harlem* and *Banjo*, Jake/Banjo and Ray, reflect in their separate yet related identities the deep attraction McKay felt both for D. H. Lawrence and Julian Benda.[41]

As Wayne Cooper has argued there is a direct connection between *The Negroes in America* and the two novels McKay would soon write while living in France, *Home to Harlem* (1928) and *Banjo* (1929). As seen, however, the connection Cooper had in mind was the primitivist influence of European intellectuals and artists who turned to African art for inspiration. Thus, Cooper, as well as most critics who have discussed McKay, made primitivism the distinctive focus of McKay's literary imagination. It is a mistake, however, to link McKay's inspiration too narrowly with the aesthetic interests of European artists. McKay, after all, mocked the efforts of the Futurists and Impressionists and gave no indication that he could or would follow in their footsteps. More importantly, the substantive content of Cooper's claim, the celebration of "the apparently aimless existence of 'primitive' black drifters," should be significantly broadened in meaning and linked with McKay's understanding of race and racial consciousness together with the context in which he located this consciousness. Finally, one should also take note of the awareness that McKay had of himself as an outsider and the political and symbolic importance he gave to this role.

As the title of *The Negroes in America* suggests, McKay's focus is America, though he situates this focus in the larger context of Europe's colonial presence in the world. Within this panoramic vision, however, it is not easy to locate McKay. He writes of America, but he is not American. He briefly alludes to his Jamaican origins but writes most tellingly of Haiti and Toussaint L'Ouverture. He refers to his childhood among English missionaries and the intellectual influence of an English aristocrat but devotes most of his attention to the politics and mystique of France. Finally, although McKay states emphatically that "the Negro question is at bottom a question of the working class," he sees himself as a "free spirit" whose destiny is to do something "significantly creative as a Negro." In part, then, McKay assumed the role of the outsider and used this role to complement the critique he was making, the marginalization and exploitation of peoples of African descent.[42] In this light, Adam Lively has recently argued that McKay had a "sophisticated appreciation of the political implications of primitivism" precisely because it served to challenge the dominant white culture.[43] Lively might have added as well that from this vantage point McKay also challenged African American intellectuals and the renaissance focused in Harlem.

Marginalization, however, could also be a consciousness of being as much as a predicament of being. Just as marginality served as a "site of resistance," it also served to ground a racial consciousness free of the constraints that others had imposed.[44] As McKay would later write in *A Long Way from Home*,

What, then, was my main psychological problem? It was the problem of color. Color-consciousness was the fundamental of my restlessness. And it was something with which my white fellow-expatriates could sympathize but which they could not altogether understand. . . . Not being black and unable to see deep into the profundity of blackness some even thought that I might have preferred to be white like them. They couldn't imagine that I had no desire merely to exchange my black problem for their white problem. For all their knowledge and sophistication, they couldn't understand the instinctive and animal and purely physical pride of a black person resolute in being himself and yet living a simple, civilized life like themselves.[45]

Not unlike Alain Locke, who distinguished between one's shadow self and one's real self, McKay made primitivism a vital center of consciousness while challenging the presumption that whites (French, English, American) represented a center of consciousness for others to calibrate their separate individual and collective identities. For this reason, McKay's poetry and his novel *Banjo* were eagerly read by the young French-speaking African and West Indian intellectuals—most prominently Léopold Senghor, Aimé Césaire, and Léon Damas—who were beginning to formulate a cultural and racial ideology of blackness, Négritude.[46]

At the same time, however, McKay's emphasis on a distinctive consciousness ("the instinctive and animal and purely physical"), though racially centered, was not limited to race. In the following poem, written in Paris in 1925, McKay addressed the question of consciousness itself as central to his own self-understanding:

My House

For this peculiar tint that paints my house
Peculiar in an alien atmosphere,
Where other houses wear a different hue,
I have a stirring always very rare
And romance-making in my ardent blood,
That channels through my body like a flood.

I know the dark delight of being strange,

The penalty of difference in the crowd,
The loneliness of wisdom among fools.
Yet never have I felt but very proud,
Though I have suffered agonies of hell,
Of living in my own peculiar cell.

There is an exaltation of man's life,
His hidden life, that he alone can feel.
The blended fires that heat his veins within,
Shaping his metals into finest steel,
Are elements from his own native earth,
That the wise gods bestowed on him at birth.

Oh each man's mind contains an unknown realm
Walled in from other men however near,
And unimagined in their highest flights
Of comprehension or of vision clear;
A realm where he withdraws to contemplate
Infinity and his own finite state.

There he may sometimes catch a god-like glimpse
Of mysteries that seem beyond life's bar;
Thence he may hurl his little shaft at heaven
And bring down accidentally a star,
And drink its foamy dust like sparkling wine
And echo accents of the laugh divine.

Then he may fall into a drunken sleep
And make [*sic*] up in his same house painted blue
Or white or green or red or brown or black—
His house, his own, whatever be the hue.
But things for him will not be what they seem
To average men since he has dreamt his dream![47]

Significantly, in McKay's metaphor of a house no one else lives there. The experience is singular. It is also universal, representing the estrangement that others—blue, white, green, red, brown, and black—experience as well. Thus, whereas the narrator initially offsets feelings of alienation and loneliness by deeper emotions of identification intrinsic to his natural being (his "ardent blood" and "elements from his own native earth"), these thoughts lead to more general thoughts as to the alienation that all men experience regardless of color or social identity. In so doing, the narrator's attention shifts from social self-consciousness to consciousness itself—"Oh each man's mind contains an unknown realm / Walled in from other men however near." However, in contrast with Wordsworth's ringing celebration of "man's unconquerable mind," McKay appeals to a transcendent level of mystery and makes of consciousness ultimately something both private and privately experienced. Free to imagine the world and oneself in new and unfamiliar ways, one nevertheless remains a stranger to all but a few. As a consequence, when writing of and championing the strength of group identity, there is in McKay's vision both space for and a deep inner tension between group and self-identity.

Although McKay had a lot to say about France in *The Negroes in America*, he had never been there until after he had left Moscow.[48] But once in France, he was a most discerning observer. As Michel Fabre writes, "because of his deeper political awareness McKay proved to be more discriminating than [Countee] Cullen in his likes and dislikes, less superficial than [Langston] Hughes in rendering French ways of life and the Paris atmosphere, and more sophisticated than either in his views about the colonial situation and the black diaspora."[49] What distinguished McKay's response to France from most others, whites and blacks, was that he simply did not rush to Paris to embrace culture, to stand in awe of Notre Dame or to prowl the great corridors of the Louvre.[50] As he wrote in his poem "Paris,"

Paris has never stormed my stubborn heart
And rushed like champagne sparkling to my head
Whirling me round and round till I am spent
To fall down like a drunkard at her feet.[51]

McKay even kept the Paris of the avant-garde at a circumspect distance. Although he had contact with some of the most celebrated individuals then living in Paris, their enthusiasms were not fully his own.[52] Toward the French, as well as toward those who crowded into Paris, McKay was always most conscious of himself as an outsider, as the observer of those whose interests were marginally his own. As McKay wrote to Walter White, the most important thing about France was that the French left you alone.[53]

As Fabre's remarks suggest, McKay's discerning eye reflected an ambivalence toward France that he had already expressed in *The Negroes in America*. However, if McKay's years in France reinforced prior political convictions, they also exposed him to an intellectual climate that deepened and enriched these earlier convictions. McKay, for example, had singled out René Maran for his attack in *Batouala* of the French presence in Africa.[54] But then they would soon meet. Fifteen months after having received the *Prix Goncourd*, Maran was forced to resign his administrative duties in Oubangui-Shari (present-day Chad) and returned to Paris in 1923. There, together with Kojo Touvalou Houénou of Dahomey, Maran established *Les Continents*, the first black newspaper founded in Paris and the precursor to several journals that would also challenge French colonial policy, attack the politics of Blaise Diagne, and formulate in various ways the ideological elements of Négritude.[55] Equally important, Maran began to write of the renaissance taking place in Harlem, and his salon became a meeting place for African Americans as well as the French speaking blacks who made their way to Paris[56] Both in print and in person, McKay figured in events he could hardly imagine prior to his crossing the border into France.

McKay also discovered in the port city of Marseilles an even more compelling strata of social life than he had found elsewhere in France. As he wrote to Langston Hughes,

I am now in Nice but I don't care much for the Riviera landscape. Marseilles I really love more than any place in France. It is the most vivid port I ever touched. Wonderful, dirty, unbeautiful, rolling in slime and color and hourly interest. There all the scum of the sea seems to drift on to natural soil. I love it more than any of the English, American or German ports.[57]

This "scum" included men from Martinique, Guadeloupe, Senegal, Dahomey, Madagascar, Morocco, and Algeria. Thus, not only had Africa come to Paris and Marseilles, but France was itself a gateway to Africa. These discoveries, ranging from René Maran to the vagabond life of the Marseilles waterfront, all found their way into McKay's novel of the black diaspora, *Banjo*.[58]

McKay's letter to Hughes is part of an extensive correspondence he exchanged with several individuals in the Harlem Renaissance throughout his years in Europe and Morocco. In particular, in addition to Hughes, McKay was in contact with Arthur Schomburg, Walter White, Alain Locke, and James Weldon Johnson.[59] As such, these letters are a valuable source to help piece together McKay's life once he left Russia. And his two biographers, Wayne Cooper and Tyrone Tillery, have made good use of this material. Surprisingly, however, little attention has been given to the letters McKay exchanged with Hughes. Although the two men would not actually meet until McKay's return to the United States in 1934, theirs was a special relationship. At least, both understood their relationship to be special, and this understanding helped to sustain the confidences they exchanged.

McKay valued Hughes's opinion "above any of the Negro intellectuals," and Hughes, in turn, praised McKay as "still the best of the colored poets."[60] This appreciation rested upon the conviction that each shared the other's literary sensibilities. As McKay wrote, "Again, I am glad you like *Home to Harlem*. My characters are the people you sing about, the people I really love and significantly they were the people I sang about when I was your age."[61] Not only did they recognize in one another a shared artistic vision, but they both saw themselves outside the understanding of mainstream black intellectual criticism: "You should [not] be bothered about the whims and prejudices of the Negro intelligentsia. They are death to any would be Negro artist. A plague on them and however hard hit and down I am they wont [*sic*] get their claws on me [McKay]."[62] Although each expressed a general hostility to the taste of the "masses," the black middle class, and the black intelligentsia (the "Niggerati"), the names of Alain Locke and Du Bois drew the most frequent criticism. These feelings of mutual esteem and a shared sense of common purpose prompted the exchange of critical ideas regarding questions of form and the techniques of writing.

After one year in France, and now in the port city of Toulon, McKay wrote to Hughes, "I want to talk to you about your writing. Your stuff seems the most sincere and earnest to me of any that young Afro-America is doing."[63] After a brief critical glance at the poetry of Countee Cullen—a poetry McKay judged to be more facile and more fluent but lacking in depth—McKay offered the following advice: "You ought to pay more attention to technique I think. That blues thing for instance I thought remarkably good but you should have made the whole of it more colloquial. You bring in some literary words which appear strange in such an atmosphere."[64] One month later, and now in Bordeaux, McKay added detail to his earlier remarks,

"Night came [sic] tenderly / Black like Me" is exquisite with beauty but to me you spoil it with that quote prose line in the first stanza—"That is my dream." I have not the poem here therefore I am not sure if I quote you write [sic]. But my point is that the poem is enough a dream by itself without your breaking the artistic unity and *telling* us that it is.[65]

Six months later, and back in Toulon after a winter in Paris, McKay gave his opinion of Locke's Harlem issue of the *Survey Graphic* and coupled these brief remarks with an analysis of Hughes's contributions:

I received copies of the Harlem *Survey Graphic* which is an excellent number except for (to me) the fictions. They're poor, lacking in individuality. I liked the language of your poems. I did not like the *sentiment* of "I Two" nor the form. "Our Land," I love; for it is lovely. You've got a great gift of poetry color, clear vision, and simplicity, but you have a tendency to jam in an absolute prose line among your most beautiful lyric lines. That spoils a poem, of course. It is strange that you do it. Countee Cullen whose work I consider quite inferior to yours never does it. He's a born rhymster. What I loath in Cullen is his richly religious twist. It's ugly. Your Jazzonia is a lovely word thing, but "In a Harlem cabaret / Six long-headed jazzers play" is a bald prosaic statement of fact. Perhaps though you could not feel as lyrical about the players as of the girl. Dream Variation is also very beautiful. But in the very midst of that lilting loveliness you bring in the prose fact, "That is my dream." Why Langston? We know it is a dream without your telling us. You ought to leave something to our imaginations and intelligence. Take that line and you have a very perfect lyric. The two last lines classic in their beautiful simplicity.[66]

On occasion, McKay offered critical judgments of his own writing. In April 1925, for example, he noted to Hughes that he had completely rewritten his novel *Color Scheme*. "It was," he explained, "bad as a novel—no form to it."[67] Four years later, he explained to Hughes the differences he felt in the writing of *Home to Harlem* and *Banjo*: "*Banjo* grew differently than *Home to Harlem* [in which] the writing flowed out of a perfect emotional state of unbalanced love. . . . Briefly *Banjo* is objective, *Home to Harlem* subjective."[68]

Although McKay was clearly not an experimentalist in form, questions of form were clearly important.[69] Not only did he understand that aesthetic criteria were the province of the artist but that for art to be successful it had to be aesthetically successful. As he wrote to Hughes, the great remembered phrases in poetic literature (even the anonymous folk things that fall from the tongues of the people) are those phrases that combine the most perfect marriage of words, rhythm, movement and atmosphere. A dead, flat stock phrase may manage to hold in the regular rhythm of strong vigorous verse without falling to pieces from dry rot and over work, but the fine, keen eye or the soul that is moved by color will not find any color in that dead stock phrase and to such a poetry lover, the rhythm is more than broken it is murdered.[70]

However, in order for art to have its own integrity—to achieve "the most perfect marriage of words, rhythm, movement and atmosphere"—a primary consideration was the integrity of the artist. In this respect, McKay shared with Jean Toomer an emphasis on the character and strength of the individual, though McKay was fully aware how much they differed.[71]

Above all, one had to have "a daring independence of mind and spirit." This strength, perhaps a gift with which only some were blessed, was, nevertheless, a gift easily squandered or not fully realized. McKay proceeded to instruct Hughes regarding the pressures that threatened intellectual independence. Racial considerations were important and appeared in forms ranging from intimidation and exploitation to more subtle influences that shaped critical judgment.[72] However, McKay spoke most forcefully, and most personally, of the perils of friendship:

Friendship is certainly the most exacting and selfish sentiment in the world—I at least have found it so. We make friends because certain individuals have something of value to contribute to one's life, mental, social, physical, intellectual, bestial, enervating, as one's bent may be. I myself have found friendship possible only by instinctively and heavily appraising my friends and weighing just how much of my mind and my time I can give to them and letting them comprehend intuitively just how much of their vagaries and other things I could possibly stand.[73]

Now that Hughes had become "somewhat of a public character," it was more important than ever that he not be forced into friendships because of "race or professional sympathy." Above all, McKay counseled vigilance, the need to guard one's integrity. To secure this integrity, it was best to keep one's distance.

At the end of the decade, McKay again wrote to Hughes, this time from Madrid: "I like to live my own life and observe theirs [the Spanish] without going too far into it. I have never liked going too far into other people's lives. I make a few acquaintances and enjoy the spectacle quietly."[74] From the margin, McKay enjoyed the spectacle, and as a spectator he felt sufficiently involved. However, as McKay's letter suggests, his comments regarding the Spanish and his presence as an observer were more generally a coda for his own life and his own self understanding.[75] His comments also served to suggest tensions he felt as a writer, his commitment, for example, to racial expression and his simultaneous desire to be published for reasons other than race.

Every work of art is in reality personal propaganda. It is the way in which the artist sees life and wants to present it but there is a vast chasm between the artist's personal expression of himself and his making himself the instrument of a group or a body of opinion. The first is art the last is prostitution and that is the sole difference between art and propaganda whether the field be that of conservative or radical politics, national or racial questions.[76]

As McKay suggests, however, these tensions were not simply imposed from without and were not only an aesthetic concern but sprang from deeper levels of self that he experienced and sought to voice. *Home to Harlem* and his follow-up novel *Banjo* were that voice.

Home to Harlem is a novel of motion, of men who briefly realize a degree of "sex solidarity" and then drift apart and of women whose lives intersect with as well as orbit the men who come and go. Although individuals seek one another's company, relationships are temporary. More permanent arrangements represent constraint, obstacles to freedom. Harlem is what they all share. Its rhythms are their rhythms. At the same time, these rhythms intersect with the more general rhythms of the trains and the men who work them as they circle through Philadelphia, Baltimore, Pittsburgh, Washington, DC, and back to New York.[77] At novel's end the two central characters flee, Jake goes to Chicago and Ray leaves for the sea. Thus, the principal actors disappear and in so doing establish an ironic counterpoint to the title of the novel. However, if Harlem is a dynamic, its dynamics are stirred, in part, from sources beyond its immediate boundaries.

When the novel begins, Jake deserts that "white folks' war" and returns to Harlem from "that theah white folks' country." In so doing, he enters a world filled with color—individuals described as "putty-skinned," "chocolate to the bone," "crust-yellow," "copper-hued," and "ravishing chestnut" appear against a backdrop of "fascinating new layers of brown, low-brown, high-brown, nut-brown, lemon, maroon, olive, mauve, [and] gold."[78] But Harlem is not simply a refuge, for "white folks" enter directly and indirectly, personally and psychologically, into Harlem life. As a consequence, color is not only a chromatic spectacle delightful to the eye but a highly charged scale of emotion calibrated to measure one's own and another's self worth. Gin-head Susy, for example, "lived with a yellow complex at the core of her heart."[79] Her parties, as a result, were as "yellow as she could make them" and only rarely did "chocolates" make an appearance. As for Susy herself, she had no illusions, "I knowed that I was black and ugly and not class and unejucated."[80] All of these various and conflicting judgments mirror the attitudes of the males whose preferences for women run the spectrum of skin colors but for whom black is "plug-ugly," a last resort. But color is not simply an issue that unites and divides men and women. Color also influences one's choice of professional help, whether, for example, to dare choose a "chocolate-complexioned" doctor rather than one who is Jewish. When color is not the immediate consideration, the voice of white prejudice alienates in equally elemental ways. Thus, for some, food is no less problematic, as individuals avoid "things that 'coons' [are] supposed to like: pork chops, corn pone, chicken or watermelons (what white people called the 'niggers' ice-cream)."[81] When mixed with distinctions of class and differences of ethnicity (West Indian), color adds to the volatility and fracture of this urban life.[82]

Thus, one perspective of Harlem that McKay develops is of a people for whom "white folks" are deeply embedded in their most intimate notions of self. And when moral judgments are made or actions rationalized, white society often functions as a point of reference or a point of rebuke. However, if Harlem is not a sanctuary, it is not simply an extension, an appendage to "that theah white folks' country." Harlem is a culture, a dynamic that includes conflict as well as a deeply felt energy and resourcefulness evident in the music (notably the blues and jazz), the language, the color, and the sexuality of its people. And in moments like the following, Harlem and its people lyrically flow together: "Twilight was enveloping the Belt, merging its life into a soft blue-black symphony. . . . The animation subsided into a moments's pause, a muffled, tremulous soul-stealing note . . . then electric lights flared everywhere, flooding the scene with dazzling gold."[83]

Just as McKay wanted his characters to "yarn and backbite and fuck like people the world over," so too did he seek to be equally frank as a writer. As a consequence, it is not easy to fit McKay's Harlem into the various abstractions Locke offered in *The New Negro*. Locke's generalization, for example, that "the Negro mind reaches out as yet to nothing but American wants, American ideas," only obscured the vitality and exuberance McKay sought to reveal. At the same time, McKay's sense of a folk past—what Locke called the "racy peasant undersoil of the race life"—was expressed in musical forms (jazz and the blues) with which Locke didn't identify. Although Ray had momentary "home-thoughts" of Haiti, this nostalgia for "a green grandeur in the heart of space" fed thoughts of condescension toward Africans and feelings of superiority toward "ten millions of suppressed Yankee 'coons.' "[84] In addition, McKay qualified what Locke called "the laboratory of a great race-welding." Not only did epithets like "monkey-chaser" and "coon" fracture this world but ancestry itself was more than problematic. McKay's people were little aware that they were "the advance-guard of the African peoples." Africa entered Harlem most directly in neon, as the cabaret Congo where one could hear and dance to the "drag blues," the favorite of all the low-down dance halls:

> And it is ashes to ashes and dust to dust,
> Can you show me a woman that a man can trust?
> > Oh, baby, how are you?
> > Oh, baby, what are you?
> > Oh, can I have you now,
> > Or have I got to wait?
> > Oh, let me have a date,
> > Why do you hesitate?
> And there is two things in Harlem I don't understan'
> It is a bulldycking woman and a faggotty man.
> > Oh, baby how are you?
> > Oh, baby, what are you?[85]

Thus, just as Ray thought of leaving Harlem, he weighed its double meaning,

Going away from Harlem . . . Harlem! How terribly Ray could hate it some times. Its brutality, gang rowdyism, promiscuous thickness. Its hot desires. But, oh the rich blood-red color of it! The warm accent of its composite voice, the fruitiness of its laughter, the trailing rhythm of its "blues" and the improvised surprises of its jazz.[86]

In his challenge to Locke (perhaps one should say in his indifference to Locke) and in his inclusion of drug addicts, labor scabs, pimps, alcoholics, women fighting one another nude, venereal disease, and prostitutes, McKay incurred the wrath of those who saw in *Home to Harlem* the heavy shadow of the old negro and not the radiant personality of the new.[87] McKay, however, had his own opinions as to what constituted personality, the ways in which personality was manifested, and what judgments, if any, one should make. Harlem served to frame the discussion, but Harlem itself was primarily experienced through the two principal characters, Jake and Ray.

In *Vicious Modernism: Black Harlem and the Literary Imagination*, James De Jongh claims that the friendship of Ray and Jake is based on "a common longing for heroic cultural and mythic ideals of which the landscapes of Harlem and Haiti are their respective personal analogs."[88] De Jongh contrasts this emphasis on "spiritual kinship" with the over worked emphasis on "personality differences" that, he asserts, most other scholars have made. In making this shift from an emphasis on differences to that of kinship, one can now appreciate, De Jongh argues, McKay's real accomplishment, the effort "to evoke a sense of Harlem's authentic inner life, frame black selfhood in positive terms and elevate personal, cultural, and ethnic self-esteem." Which is to say, McKay was neither a prisoner of, nor out to capitalize on, the image the white writer Carl Van Vechten had established of "Harlem's atavism and bizarre primitivism" in his sensational novel *Nigger Heaven*.[89] De Jongh's reading, however, is made at the expense of including differences in Jake's and Ray's personalities which are important to note because it is in these terms that McKay raises the question of perspective, how to view the racial landscape of Harlem as well as the question of personality itself. In other words, one can read *Home to Harlem* as a serious work together with an emphasis on differences of personality without limiting the significance of these differences to the terms alleged to be Van Vechten's, the tension between primitivism and civilization.[90]

Both Ray and Jake are resourceful individuals whose strengths complement the other's limitations. Jake, for example, explains to Ray that "I runs around all right, but Ise lak a sailor that don't know nothing about using a compass, but him always hits a safe port."[91] But Ray, fearful for Jake's safety, becomes the compass that Jake so cavalierly dismisses, charting the deep seas of history and imagination beyond his limited intellectual horizons—Greek poetry, Haitian history and Toussaint L'Ouverture, Wordsworth's sonnet, and the kingdoms and cultures of West Africa. In contrast, Ray questions his own emotional bearings, "Why don't you [Jake] ever feel those sensations that just turn you back in on yourself and make you isolated and helpless?"[92] Jake, port-oriented as he is, helps Ray to understand the emotional landscape of Harlem, the class and status distinctions among various social groupings of African Americans, and the street and cabaret language of Harlem's people.[93] Thus, each possesses information as well as personal qualities the other lacks. Symbolically, at least, their friendship suggests, as De Jongh claims, the potential as well as the need for "spiritual kinship." And yet, they remain strangers to one another, separated by their profoundly different sensibilities.

Although we are meant to see in Ray and Jake the link as well as the tension between the "head and the heart," this perspective is itself placed in perspective. For ironically what ultimately distances Ray from Jake is Jake's domestic consciousness, not his alleged primitivism. Jake's sense of place, his ability to function within the social and psychological boundaries of Harlem, is for Ray intellectually and emotionally impossible. Whereas Jake feels free to be himself, Ray feels imprisoned, unsure exactly how or where to be himself. Of one thing he was sure, "the things you call fine human traits don't belong to any special class or nation or race of people."[94] For this reason, he felt drawn to Henri Barbusse's novel *Le Feu*, "such a grand anti-romantic presentation of mind and behavior in that hell-pit of life."[95] And yet, Ray's dream—"dreams of patterns of words achieving form"—was meant to answer the need for forms of racial expression that were neither derivative nor obsolete: "We ought to get something new, we Negroes. But we get our education like—like our houses. When the whites move out, we move in and take possession of the old dead stuff. Dead stuff that this age has no use for."[96] Ray's dilemma, however, was McKay's just as Ray was McKay's dilemma. In a letter to Walter White, written after completing his novel *Color Scheme*, McKay argued that personal expression was art, whereas making oneself "the instrument of a group" was prostitution.[97] Although Ray, who first appeared in this soon to be destroyed novel, eventually found his way into *Home to Harlem*, it was, as seen, a temporary stay. When Ray next appeared, he was once again with McKay in the port city of Marseilles in southern France.

Banjo is both a story to be told and a series of stories within stories, some told by individual characters and others the telling of one's personal history. Although the voices to be heard exceed in number and nationality those in *Home to Harlem*, McKay uses a similar strategy to structure as well as frame his material.[98] Thus, Lincoln Agrippa, born in the American South and better known as Banjo, functions as a spirited cicerone, presenting in pungent detail the sordid yet vibrant inner world of the Vieux Port of Marseilles, the city that so fascinated McKay. Once again Ray, with Banjo's assistance, learns to cope with new circumstances as well as to bring an intellectual perspective to this warren of fetid alleyways, bars, outdoor hangouts, and make-shift living quarters. In broadest terms, Ray addresses the global impact of colonialism and capitalism on African peoples, their displacement and alienation (the diaspora), and the continuing importance of Africa culturally and spiritually.[99] Related issues include comments on the relative oppressiveness of French and American racism, the phenomenon of Marcus Garvey, African cultural and political movements in France, and the problematic efforts of African American intellectuals (the renaissance in Harlem). Thus, much like Harlem, though more densely as well as expansively imagined, Marseilles served to frame McKay's own experience living (surviving) and writing in southern France. It also served to focus, as symbol and as platform, issues McKay addressed in *The Negroes in America* and briefly alluded to in *Home to Harlem*.

Although Ray, as well as others, condemns the racist sinew of European and American national cultures and institutions, the ultimate critique is not so much political as psychological.[100] As a consequence, throughout the novel there is an emphasis on pride, self-esteem, and human dignity. Ray, for example, claims to be a proletarian but for reasons both aesthetic and personal.[101] It is his understanding that "some people are born menial-minded and they are not limited to any one class of society."[102] Partly for this reason, he has never "confused faith with politics" and finds in Confucius, as opposed to Western religions, what is most needed, "to rid [the world] of false moralities and cultivate decent manners—not society manners, but man-to-man decency and tolerance."[103] To some extent, Banjo's community of present-minded vagabonds, with their communitarian ethic of sharing all they are able to beg, earn, or steal is a model for Ray's vision of human brotherhood. But, a community of vagabonds proves to be a contradiction in terms. In any event, Ray's deepest commitment is to a personal vision of self that cuts against ties to communal values and even "group life"—"Ray refused to accept the idea of the Negro simply as a 'problem.' All of life was a problem. White people, like red and brown people, had their problems. And of the highest importance was the problem of the individual, from which some people thought they could escape by joining movements."[104] At novel's end, Ray and Banjo leave Marseilles. McKay left as well, completing the novel in Barcelona (1927-28). Two years later McKay took up residence in Morocco and began the writing of his final novel *Banana Bottom*.

For many, *Banana Bottom* is McKay's *tour de force*, representing, symbolically at least, the recovery of his native culture and his native landscape.[105] Set in Jamaica the novel centers on the person of the Bita Plant, the English educated "brown beauty," and culminates in her marriage to the dark-skinned peasant Jubban: "Her music, her reading, her thinking were the flowers of her intelligence and he the root in the earth upon which she was grafted, both nourished by the same soil."[106] In breaking with the picaresque form of *Home to Harlem* and *Banjo*, McKay is understood to have imaginatively achieved what he so forcefully voiced four years later in *A Long Way from Home* (1937): "Well, whatever the white folks do and say, the Negro race will finally have to face the need to save itself. The whites have done the blacks some great wrongs, but also they have done some good. They have brought to them the benefits of modern civilization. They can still do a lot more, but one thing they cannot do: they cannot give Negroes the gift of a soul—a group soul."[107] Thus, for several of McKay's critics the 1930s represent an important shift in his intellectual focus, one that successfully grounded and brought to ground the "free spirit" who left Russia in 1923, lived for the next eleven years in Europe and North Africa, and returned to the United States in February, 1934.[108]

Others, however, contemporary as well as later critics of McKay, see in McKay's intellectual vision a greater continuity with the past than do those who emphasize the new directions his thought has taken. Alain Locke, for example, used the occasion of the appearance of *A Long Way from Home* to denounce McKay as a charlatan, a "prodigal racialist" who remained committed to a "style and philosophy of aesthetic individualism."[109] Not only had McKay not changed but he continued to represent what Locke now saw as the canker at the heart of the Harlem Renaissance itself, "its exhibitionist flair." More recently, however, Michael G. Cooke has argued that McKay neither abandoned nor simply repeated concerns he earlier had voiced in *The Negroes in America* and further explored in *Home to Harlem* and *Banjo*. This continuity, according to Cooke, highlights McKay's true concern, "the ideal of freedom and its need in human relations." However, since "freedom ha[d] no social form or communal status in [*Banana Bottom*],"[110] Bita Plant represents neither a selfish individualism nor a vehicle to celebrate communal values but an individuality that both draws upon and is distinct from the larger folk landscape.

In great part, critical opinion, divided as it is, reflects tensions that McKay himself experienced and voiced throughout his private and public writing. But McKay was not one to provide resolutions that others have either demanded or sought to supply. The final scene of *Banana Bottom* is not the marriage of Bita and Jubban but that of Bita perusing pages of her college text, Blaise Pascal's *Pensées*. She first reads in the twenty-fourth entry, in the section titled "*Les Regles du Jugement, Diversité et Unité,*" that "*la vraie morale se moque de la morale; la morale du jugement se moque de la morale de l'esprit.*"[111] After further reading she falls asleep, only to awaken to the voice of her son as he, covered with the juice of a ripe mango, squirmed in the arms of Anty Nommy—"Showin' you' strengt' a'ready mi li't' man. Soon you'll be l'arnin' fer square you' fist them off at me."[112] However, to make this transition from the intellectual language of Pascal to the heartfelt dialect of Anty Nommy, McKay carefully structured the context, failing to complete Pascal's final line—"*la morale du jugement se moque de la morale de l'esprit, qui est sans règles.*"[113] That Bita is inspired by her reading and unencumbered by this distinction ("*qui est sans règles*"), reflects that "clear thinking was the most beautiful of all things. Love and music were divine things but none so rare as the pure flight of the mind into the upper realms of thought."[114] McKay's editing, in effect, mediates Bita's reading of Pascal and makes possible her expansive reflections. As a consequence, mind and heart are held in tension, a dialectic that favors both, not one at the expense of the other. Bita, in turn, mediates the scene that takes place in her yard. We see what she sees and hear what she hears. But we are also aware that she remains in her house looking out through the window, a spectator as well as a participant.

One year later, upon publication of James Weldon Johnson's *Negro Americans, What Now?* (1934), McKay wrote to Johnson to suggest "that you might have been more positive about two items at least," the appeal and relevance of Communism and/or Labor for black Americans. Although McKay clearly favored the labor movement, his central concern was to support the racial consciousness and group strength of African Americans:

It seems logical to me that a minority people should use every form of group pressure and organization to wrest privileges from the majority. That is precisely what the Jews, Italians, Germans and Irish in this country have done. The Irish would not be so powerful in N.Y.City's civic life if they did not have such a unique social group unity.[115]

McKay's thoughts spilled over into a second letter written at the end of the month. Again, the Labor movement is discussed, McKay less sanguine than Johnson as to what to expect: "We disagree about Labor. I think that so long as the White unins [*sic*] remain selfish and chauvinist, colored workers should organize in separate unions to fight for greater economic advantages, even if they have to pass through the scabbing phase to obtain same. They will surely not win economic justice if they are waiting for white labor to hand it to them as a gift."[116] But, in this same letter, McKay also seeks Johnson's help to secure funds that will allow him "to write the book I want to write [*A Long Way from Home*]." Unable to find work and in need of money, McKay offered Max Eastman's opinion that he lacked support because "from *Home to Harlem* on put the liberals and radicals against me." McKay, however, qualified the implications of Eastman's suggestion: "But creatively I never felt that I was writing particularly for liberals and radicals, not Negroes only as such, because I have been always obsessed with the idea of the universality of life under the different patterns and colors and felt it was altogether too grand to be distorted creatively in the interest of any one group. And so I have always striven to obtain a certain objective balance in my creative work."[117] McKay's notion of objectivity reads like a signature that marks his earliest writings once he left Kansas and traveled north. In an introductory letter to W. S. Braithwaite, McKay told of his difficulties getting published: "When I was in New York I sent a sonnet on the race problem to a prominent newspaper Editor who answered that he would like to print it and asked for more of my work."[118] Subsequent poems, however, were turned down because they did not "contain anything about race": "This has set me wondering whether Fine Art is not beyond nation or race—if one's mind can be limited to one's race and its problems when Art is as sublime as He who gave it to man."[119] But, within a few years, Braithwaite symbolized for McKay all that was wrong with African American writing and criticism. No longer did he think in terms of "Fine Art" and the "sublime." The tension between the individual and the group, however, remained central to his life and his imagination.[120]

NOTES

1. Michael B. Stoff, "Claude McKay and the Cult of Primitivism," in Arna Bontemps, *The Harlem Renaissance Remembered* (New York: Dodd Mead, 1972), 103–26.
    2. As Cruse writes,

McKay saw the problem clearly enough, but he did not tell the Russians his views. Despite the fact that the Russians had accepted him as a bona fide representative of American Negroes, he kept insisting that he was not qualified to represent the American Negro group. McKay should have enlightened the Russians while he was in a position to do so. He should have told them that the Communists in America were about to make serious blunders in handling the national group question.

Harold Cruse, *The Crisis of the Negro Intellectual* (New York: William Morrow, 1967), 57.

3. Ibid., 52. As Nathan Huggins writes,

In the 1920s, except for some earlier individual writers, Negroes were new—self consciously new—to the commercialized arts. They needed supporters and advocates, defense and encouragement from those who were supposed to know. The fact that whites became interested in the Negro would seem fortunate from this point of view. Yet, the question had to be asked in time: whose sensibilities; tastes, and interests were being served by such art, the patron or the patronized?

Huggins, *Harlem Renaissance* (New York: Oxford University Press, 1971), 128.

4. Huggins, *Harlem Renaissance*, 126.

5. "Paris was symbolic of the fate of the Village movement and Claude McKay and Louise Bryant made it all the more so. . . . For all intents and purposes this ended Louise Bryant's career in the radical movement. For her, as for McKay, Paris became the turning point." Cruse, *The Crisis of the Negro Intellectual*, 59.

6. See, for example, S. P. Fullinwider, *The Mind and Mood of Black America* (Homewood, IL: The Dorsey Press, 1969); Jean Wagner, *Black Poets of the United States* (Urbana: University of Illinois Press, 1973); Robert Bone, *The Negro Novel in America* (New Haven: Yale University Press, 1966; *Down Home—A History of Afro-American Short Fiction from Its Beginnings to the End of the Harlem Renaissance* (New York: G. P. Putnams' Sons, 1975); and Amritjit Singh, *The Novels of the Harlem Renaissance—Twelve Black Writers 1923–1933* (University Park: Pennsylvania State University Press, 1976).

7. Wayne Cooper, *The Passion of Claude McKay: Selected Prose and Poetry 1912–1948* (New York: Schocken, 1973), 1.

8. *Claude* McKay—Centennial *Studies—1992,* ed. A. L. McLeod (New Delhi: Sterling Publ. Private Ltd., 1992).

9. Claude McKay, *The Negroes in America*, ed. A. L. McLeod (Port Washington, NY: Kennikat Press, 1979), xiii.

10. Ibid., xii.

11. Ibid., 4.

12. Thus, whereas McKay argued that blacks must be organized along class conscious lines so as to create a strong labor movement, it was no less imperative that white labor and white radicals, for their own self interest, fully accepted blacks as equals. However, except for the Industrial Workers of the World, McKay presented an America wherein the Communist Party and the labor movement had yet to come to terms with the racism within their own ranks.

13. Wayne Cooper, *Claude McKay: Rebel Sojourner in the Harlem Renaissance* (Baton Rouge: Louisiana State University Press, 1987), 187.

14. Ibid.

15. Ibid.

16. As McKay later wrote to James Weldon Johnson, "I went into Russia as a writer and a free spirit and left the same, because I was convinced that however far I was advanced in social ideas, if I could do something significantly creative as a Negro it would mean more to my group and the world than being merely a social agitator." Tyrone Tillery, *Claude McKay—A Black Poet's Struggle for Identity* (Amherst: University of Massachusetts Press, 1992), 71.

17. In 1892 the kingdom of Benin was brought under British protection, and in 1897 the British occupied Benin by force. In 1914 present day Nigeria formed, incorporating Benin

within its boundaries. See Michael Crowder, *The Story of Nigeria* (Boston: Faber and Faber, 1978).

18. As McKay writes, "Frobenius, who told about his explorations and excavations in the territories of various African tribes in brilliant essays and books, gives a remarkable picture of the culture, institutions, and customs of the natives and of their pottery, weaving, architecture, and sculpture, which undoubtedly were destroyed by the European trade in the black body from the fifteenth to the nineteenth centuries." McKay, *The Negroes in America*, 57.

18. Ibid., 59.

20. Ibid., 64.

21. Ibid., 59.

22. Ibid., 62.

23. Ibid., 61.

24. In 1891, Tanner left America for a life of painting in France. Several of his paintings were purchased by the French government—most notably "The Disciples of Emmaus" and "The Resurrection of Lazarus"—and put on display in the Musée du Luxembourg. Tanner was awarded the French Legion of Honor in 1923.

25. *Batouala* was highly praised by black Americans who marveled at the evidence Maran provided of Africa's artistic potential. In turn, Maran took notice of the Harlem Renaissance writers, bringing the New Negro movement to the attention of the French public through his essay "Le Mouvement Negro—Litteraire aux États-Unis." He also began to appear in *Opportunity*. In addition to several articles celebrating black American writers, Maran helped to have Walter White's *Fire in the Flint* translated into French and made several unsuccessful efforts to have Locke's *The New Negro* translated as well. Locke, in turn, attempted (equally unsuccessfully) to interest Alfred A. Knopf in Maran's work. Also see, Michael Fabre, "'René Maran, The New Negro and Négritude," *Phylon* (September, 1975): 340–51.

26. "Dr. Du Bois writes a surprisingly moving work, *The Souls of Black Folk*, written in splendid English; nevertheless he remains up to the present an outcast in American society—if one doesn't count a small part of the American bourgeoisie which is using him for propaganda." McKay, *The Negroes in America*, 52.

27. "The separate, individual black-skinned man from the West Indies or America receives much better treatment in London or Berlin than in New York or in Kingston, Jamaica. He responds more quickly to the cordial atmosphere of Paris than to London. He undoubtedly also feels well in Rome, Vienna, or Madrid." Ibid., 50.

28. "In reality, a large percentage of American Negroes feel rather favorably disposed to this government; American Negro soldiers who were subjected to humiliations from white American officers during the last war noted that in France the French government did not make any distinctions between white and colored soldiers." Ibid., 51–52.

29. Ibid., 50.

30. Siki knocked out Carpentier for the light-heavy-weight championship of the world. McKay drew a parallel with the career of Jack Johnson and the flash of hostility he experienced upon winning the title in 1908.

31. McKay, *The Negroes in America,* 49–50.

32. Ibid., 49. McKay went on further to write,

Thus, the sympathy of the Negro intelligentsia is completely on the side of France. It is well informed about the barbarous acts of the Belgians in the Congo, but it knows nothing at all about the barbarous acts of the French in Senegal, about the organized robbery of native workers, about the forced enlistment of recruits, or about the fact that the population is reduced to extreme poverty and hunger, or about the total annihilation of whole tribes. It is possible that the Negro intelligentsia does not want to know about this, in as much as now it can loosely generalize about the differences in the treatment of Negroes in bourgeois France and in plutocratic America.

Ibid., 52.

    33. Ibid., 50.

    34. Ibid., 52.

    35. Ibid., 68. McKay also notes that,

Stories from the world of animals in the West Indies, field songs and house servants' games, the folktales of Brer Rabbit, and the spirituals and slave songs of the southern states represent a rich treasure house of Negro folklore in the New World. Various proverbs and sayings in which the native wisdom and wit are contained are a characteristic feature of this folklore, but at the same time it is filled with grief, marked by a spirit of primitive Christian submission, giving oneself to the will of God, and hoping for the future life, which is a reward for suffering in this life.

Ibid., 68–69.

    36. Although McKay generally applauded the dialect poetry of Paul Lawrence Dunbar, he saw him as an individual whose writing was no longer relevant to the present, "The poems of Paul Lawrence Dunbar (1872–1906), a pure-blooded American Negro poet, written in dialect, represent the very soul of the Negro during the period of emancipation from personal slavery and the period right after Emancipation. They are full of optimism and contain more joyful notes than the plantation melodies of the slaves." Ibid.

    37. Ibid., 75.

    38. Ibid., 74.

    39. Tyrone Tillery, *Claude McKay—A Black Poet's Struggle for Identity*, 54.

    40. McKay, *The Negroes in America*, 65.

    41. In his biography, McKay writes, "I thought *Ulysses* a bigger book than any one of Lawrence's books, but I preferred Lawrence as a whole. I thought D. H. Lawrence was more modern than James Joyce. In D. H. Lawrence I found confusion—all of the ferment and torment and turmoil, the hesitation and hate and alarm, the sexual inquietude and the incertitude of this age, and the psychic and romantic groping for a way out." McKay, *A Long Way from Home* (New York: Arno Press and The New York Times, 1969): 247.

    And in a letter to Max Eastman (April 25, 1932) McKay writes,

I am convinced that intellect and a real one is absolutely necessary for the making of a literary masterpiece. Therefore I believe M. Benda rests upon sound ground when he demands that artists make "an attempt to comprehend life." They should and only so far as they do comprehend life in its universal aspects will their work have more than a contemporary interest and take rank to stand the test of time.

Cooper, *The Passion of Claude McKay: Selected Prose and Poetry 1912–1948* (New York: Schocken, 1973), 155. Edward Said writes of Benda, "deep in the combative rhetoric of Benda's basically very conservative work [*The Treason of the Intellectuals*] is to be found this figure of the intellectual as a being set apart, someone able to speak the truth to power" Said goes on to say, "Benda proposed that intellectuals should stop thinking in terms of collective passions and should concentrate instead on transcendental values, those that were universally applicable to all nations and peoples." Said, *Representations of the Intellectual* (New York: Pantheon Books, 1994), 8, 30.

    42. Importantly, each of these three chapters centers on a figure or event (Toussaint L'Ouverture; Louis Phal Siki; African Art) that suddenly breaks into the conscious awareness of the white world and challenges its deepest assumptions of superiority and mastery.

43. Adam Lively, "Continuity and Radicalism in American Black Nationalist Thought, 1914–1929," *Journal of American Studies* 18 (1984): 210. And to highlight the emphasis on protest as opposed to the exoticism of primitivism, Lively notes that in *Banjo* [and *Home to Harlem*] the "substance—structure and a sense of a rooted social setting—is deliberately thin." 232.

44. bell hooks writes in "marginality as site of resistance" of marginality as "a position and a place of resistance . . . crucial for oppressed, exploited, colonized people." *Out There: Marginalization and Contemporary Cultures,* ed. Russell Ferguson, Martha Gever, Trinh. T. Minh-ha, and Cornel West (Cambridge: The MIT Press, 1990), 342.

45. McKay, *A Long Way from Home,* 245.

46. Based on a remark of Léopold Senghor's, Carl Pedersen has argued that McKay was the true source of Négritude. See, "Claude McKay: The True Inventor of Négritude," in ed. A. L. McLeod, *Claude McKay—Centennial Studies,* 114–22. Also, Michel Fabre, "From the New Negro to Négritude," in *From Harlem to Paris—Black American Writers in France, 1840–1980* (Urbana: University of Illinois Press, 1991), 146–59; and "Du mouvement nouveau noir a la négritude césairiénne," *Soleil éclate,* ed. Jacqueline Leiner (Tubingen: Gunther Grass Verlag, 1984), 149–59.

47. Claude McKay, "My House," NAACP Files, Manuscript Division, Library of Congress (1925).

48. McKay's years in France are best documented in his autobiography, *A Long Way from Home*; in the letters he wrote to various friends and prominent figures in the Harlem Renaissance—in particular, Arthur Schomburg, Alain Locke, Walter White, James Ivy, Max Eastman, W.E.B. Du Bois, and Langston Hughes; and in several works of fiction—most notably *Banjo*, his short story "Dinner at Douarnenez," and his unpublished novel, *Romance in Marseilles*. The most detailed study of McKay's response to France, "Claude McKay and the Two Faces of France," is to be found in Fabre, *From Harlem to Paris: Black American Writers in France, 1840–1980*.

49. Ibid., 92.

50. McKay's most immediate reason for going to Paris was to find a cure for syphilis, and his poem "The Desolate City" as well as "The Shadow-Ring" reflect his thoughts at that time. But, as his writing in *The Negroes in America* suggests, McKay was extremely skeptical of the French and the mystique of France as an open society. He first voiced criticism of France while in England. See Wayne Cooper, "McKay in England, 1919–1921," in *Claude McKay: Rebel Sojourner in the Harlem Renaissance*, 103–33.

51. Fabre, *From Harlem to Paris—Black American Writers in France, 1840–1980, 96.*

52. "I believe that I understood more about the expatriates than they understood of me, as I went along in the rhythm of their caravan; yet, although our goal was not the same, I was always overwhelmingly in sympathy with its purpose. . . . As I have indicated before, I was aware that if there were problems specifically black, also there were problems specifically white." McKay, *A Long Way from Home,* 245–46.

53. "But I do like the immense elbow room that French civilization gives the individual. You're left alone. You can do as much as you like within the wide limits. You can take the country and ignore the people if you want—and I don't think that is possible in any other country. France has them all beat." McKay to Walter White, 4 December 1924, NAACP Files, Manuscript Division, Library of Congress.

Nine years later (July 31, 1933), in a letter to Arthur Spingarn, McKay voiced a similar opinion: "What is the secret of the French attraction for most strangers? Why do foreign colonies flourish so easily in France? The secret is France's aloofness; they tolerate strangers and allow them to do as they please as long as they don't meddle in French national affairs or do anything to hurt their pride." Fabre, *From Harlem to Paris—Black American Writers in France, 1840–1980*, 109.

54. It was the preface that provoked rage and threats to Maran's life. Speaking as a witness to events too disturbing fully to reveal—men and women turning the dung of horses searching for bits of undigested corn; whole tribes—Dacpas, M'bis Maroukas, La'mbassis, Sabangas, and N'gapous—displaced and forced to scatter—Maran ridiculed official reports portraying an Africa flourishing under French rule. Maran's immediate challenge was to France, but, as he made clear, the deeper challenge was to the moral conscience of the West, to those for whom civilization was a "torch" and not an "inferno."

55. In "Hommage to René Maran," Léopold Sénghor stated that Maran was "the guiding light from whom the Négritude school was born but also a true link between the different continents." Léopold Sénghor, "René Maran, The New Negro and Négritude," *Phylon* (September, 1975): 340–51.

Other journals to appear throughout the 1920s were *L'Action Coloniale, Le Paria, La Dépeche Africaine, La Revue du Monde Noir, Légitime Défense*, and *L'Étudiant Noir*. In addition to these journals, several important political organizations came to life: Ligue universelle pour la défense de la race noire; Comité de la défense de la race nègre; Ligue de la défense de la race nègre; Union intercoloniale; Étoile nord-africaine; Comité universel de l'institut nègre de Paris.

56. See J. Ayo Langley, "Pan-Africanism in Paris, 1924–36," *The Journal of African Studies* (1969): 69–94. Also, Lilyan Kesteloot, *Écrivains noirs de langue française: naissance d'une litterature* (Bruxelles: Institut de Sociologie de l'Université libre de Bruxelles, 1963).

57. Claude McKay to Langston Hughes, 30 April 1926, Claude McKay Papers, James Weldon Johnson Collection, Yale University.

58. Geographical landmarks—the Quartier Reserve (the Ditch), Place Victor Gelu (Bum Square), Boody Lane, Place de la Joliette—are complemented by commercial and communal landmarks, themselves complex social worlds drawn primarily from near and distant countries of the French Colonial Empire. The Cafe African, for example, is the center of the "Negro-Negroid" population of the town—Senegalese, Martiniquans, Guadeloupans, Madagascans, and North African Negroes are often joined by "British West African blacks, Portuguese blacks, and American blacks." Others, as well, from America and Europe—drifters, drop-outs, tourists, and prostitutes—fill this already crowded place.

59. McKay also corresponded with Max Eastman, H. L. Mencken, and the former wife of John Reed, Louise Bullit.

60. "I value your [Hughes] opinion above any of the Negro intellectuals—next Wallace Thurman in whom I find some real independent thinking and strength." McKay to Langston Hughes, 30 March 1928; Claude McKay papers, James Weldon Johnson Collection, Yale University. And Hughes to Claude McKay, 25 July 1925, Claude McKay Papers, James Weldon Johnson Collection, Yale University.

61. McKay to Langston Hughes, 30 March 1928, Claude McKay papers, James Weldon Johnson Collection, Yale University.

62. Claude McKay to Langston Hughes, 24 April 1926, Claude McKay Papers, James Weldon Johnson Collection, Yale University. Hughes wrote, after reading McKay's *Home to Harlem*,

Lord I love the whole thing. Its so damned real! . . . Has there ever been another party anywhere in literature like Gin-Head Susy's. I thought that was marvelously well-done. . . . It's going to be amusing reading what the colored papers will say about it. They will want to tear you to pieces, I'm sure, but since they used up all their bad words on *Nigger Heaven* and the rest on me, I don't know what vocabulary they have left for you. . . . Didn't Keats say "Beauty is truth?" . . . But I don't suppose a one of the Negro editors will see [at] all that *Home to Harlem* is Beauty.

Langston Hughes to Claude McKay, 5 March 1928, Claude McKay Papers, Yale University). Two years later, Hughes wrote to McKay:

You're more or less right about the Negro intellectuals. (After all these months, I could hardly expect you to remember just what you said in that last letter, but anyhow much of it concerned your reputation after it had gone through the mouths of the nigeratti and back to earth again). Sure, they say bad things about you. They say bad things about anybody unless you're right there when they're talking. But who cares? Certainly there are a lot of half-baked beans in the intellectual pot, but they don't make me sick any more like they used to.

Hughes to McKay, 30 September 1930, Claude McKay Papers, James Weldon Johnson Collection, Yale University.

63. McKay to Langston Hughes, 22 September 1924, Claude McKay Papers, James Weldon Johnson Collection, Yale University.

64. Ibid.

65. McKay to Langston Hughes, 28 October 1924, Claude McKay Papers, James Weldon Johnson Collection, Yale University.

66. McKay to Langston Hughes, 8 April 1925, Claude McKay Papers, James Weldon Johnson Collection, Yale University.

67. Ibid.

68. McKay to Langston Hughes, 14 May 1929, Claude McKay Papers, James Weldon Johnson Collection, Yale University.

69. As Arnold Rampersad writes, "With McKay and 'If We Must Die,' we come not only directed to the Harlem school but also to one of its principal tensions—that between radicalism of political and racial thought, on the one hand, and, on the other, a bone-deep commitment to conservatism of form." Rampersad, "Langston Hughes and Approaches to Modernism," in *The Harlem Renaissance: Revaluations,* ed. Amritjit Singh, William S. Shiver, Stanley Brodwin (New York: Garland, 1989), 55. Also, Huggins, "Art the Ethnic Province" in *Harlem Renaissance,* 190–243.

70. McKay to Langston Hughes, 7 May 1925, Claude McKay Papers, James Weldon Johnson Collection, Yale University.

71. In a letter to Walter White, McKay commented on meeting Toomer in Paris,

I met Toomer here for 10 minutes and felt something of that evasion and confusion in his talk too which I see so clearly in his book. He could really do wonderful things if he would be simple and clean and not confuse the reality of Negro life in the purple patches of mysticism. If we're going to do anything in literature and art we've got to stand good straight-out criticism and not allow ourselves to be patronised as Negro artists of America. Another thing that might hurt Negro writers is too much indiscriminating praise from Negro journals. Braithwaite's "scholarly" article some time back could not have been worse. He is a nice man, appreciates literature, but as a critic of high discriminating taste he's futile and hopeless.

McKay to Walter White, 4 December 1924, Manuscript Collections, Library of Congress.

72. McKay warned, for example, that Braithwaite, "the Booker T. Washington of American literature," was frightened by the aggressiveness of whites and was a "warning to every young Negro of artistic aspirations of what he should never emulate." McKay to

Langston Hughes, 22 September 1924, Claude McKay Papers, James Weldon Johnson Collection, Yale University. When speaking more generally of Negro intellectuals, McKay condemned them for "merely second[ing] the leading whites' piddle." McKay to Langston Hughes, 30 March 1928, Claude McKay Papers, James Weldon Johnson Collection, Yale University.

73. McKay to Langston Hughes, 7 May 1925, Claude McKay Papers, James Weldon Johnson Collection, Yale University.

74. McKay to Langston Hughes, 12 December 1929, Claude McKay Papers, James Weldon Johnson Collection, Yale University.

75. Even when suggesting to Hughes how "wonderful" it would be if Hughes might join him in France, McKay was quick to alert him as to how it might work. He didn't want Hughes to have to intuit the "vagaries and other things" that McKay could possibly withstand—"I'm a born bastard of moods, but I am sure you are too and we could adjust ourselves for a holiday together. I am a good fellow in the mood, but when I am out I don't torture and vex my friends—I run away from them like a cat and hide." McKay to Langston Hughes, 30 March 1928, McKay Papers, James Weldon Johnson Collection, Yale University.

76. Claude McKay to Walter White, 7 September 1925, Manuscript Division, Library of Congress.

77. McKay wrote: "Men working on a train have something of the spirit of men working on a ship. They are, perforce, bound together in comradeship of a sort in that close atmosphere. In the stopover cities they go about in pairs or groups. But the camaraderie breaks up on the platform in New York as soon as the dining-car returns there. Every man goes his own way unknown to his comrades. Wife or sweetheart or some other magnet of the great magic city draws each off separately." Claude McKay, *Home to Harlem* (Boston: Northeastern University Press, 1987), 207–8.

78. Ibid., 57.

79. Ibid.

80. Ibid., 85.

81. Ibid., 161–62.

82. Two West Indian women fighting one another, for example, were admonished by a third "can't you act like decent English people?" In reply, one countered, "she come boxing me up ovah a dutty-black 'Merican coon." Ibid., 97.

83. Ibid., 290–91.

84. Ibid., 155.

85. Ibid., 36–37.

86. Ibid., 267.

87. Du Bois was immediately angered with McKay. Du Bois, "The Browsing Reader," *Crisis* 35, no. 6 (June 1928): 202. Locke expressed his strong reservations in "Spiritual truancy," *New Challenge* (fall 1937), in Huggins, *Voices From the Harlem Renaissance* (New York: Oxford University Press, 1976), 404–6.

88. James De Jongh, *Vicious Modernism: Black Harlem and the Literary Imagination* (New York: Cambridge University Press, 1991), 31.

89. This charge goes back to Du Bois's criticism of *Home to Harlem* that McKay had set out "to cater to that prurient demand on the part of white folk for a portrayal in Negroes of that utter licentiousness which convention holds white folk back from enjoying." In De Jongh, *Vicious Modernism*, 31. Van Vechten, however, offered a more complex vision of Harlem (one that made primitivism problematic as a point of view) than either De Jongh or

Du Bois allows. See my "Carl Van Vechten and the Harlem Renaissance," in *Negro American Literature Forum* 10, no. 2 (summer 1976): 39–47.

90. See Bruce Kellner, "Carl Van Vechten's Black Renaissance," in *The Harlem Renaissance: Revaluations* , ed. Amritjit Singh (New York : Garland, 1989), 23–33.

91. McKay, *Home to Harlem,* 206–7.

92. Ibid., 200.

93. The following is a good example of Jake's attitude as well as what he has to offer:

Youse crazy, chappie. You ain't got no experience about it. There's all kinds a difference in that theah life. Sometimes it's the people make the difference and sometimes it's the place. And as foh them sweet marchants, there's as much difference between them as you find in any other class a people. There is them slap-up private-apartmant ones, and there is them of the dickty buffet flats; then the low-down speakeasy customers; the cabaret babies, the family-entrance clients, and the street fliers.

Ibid., 202.

94. Ibid., 242.

95. Ibid., 227.

96. Ibid., 243.

97. Tillery, *Claude McKay—A Black Poet's Struggle for Identity*, 96.

98. As McKay wrote to Hughes upon learning from Hughes that *Banjo* had been published, "Like *Home to Harlem* the bite comes in the second part. Of course I am merely painting scenes as they exist and using my brains to link them up with a story." McKay to Langston Hughes, 30 March 1928, Claude McKay Papers, James Weldon Johnson Collection, Yale University.

99. "Business! Prejudice and business. In Europe, Asia, Australia, Africa, America, those were the two united terrors confronting the colored man." McKay, *Banjo* (New York: Harcourt Brace Jovanovich, 1957), 193.

The Africans gave him a positive feeling of wholesome contact with racial roots. They made him feel that he was not merely an unfortunate accident of birth, but that he belonged definitely to a race weighed, tested, and poised in the universal scheme. They inspired him with confidence in them. Short of extermination by the Europeans, they were a safe people, protected by their own indigenous culture. Even though they stood bewildered before the imposing bigness of white things, apparently unaware of the invaluable worth of their own, they were naturally defended by the richness of their fundamental racial values.

Ibid., 320.

100. As Ray muses, " He hated civilization because its general attitude toward the colored man was such as to rob him of his warm human instincts and make him inhuman. Under it the thinking colored man could not function normally like his white brother, responsive and reacting spontaneously to the emotions of pleasure or pain, joy or forgiveness. Only within the confines of his own world of color could he be his true self." Ibid., 163–64.

Ray looked deeper than the noise for the truth, and what he really found was a fundamental contempt for black people quite as pronounced as in the Anglo-Saxon lands. The common idea of the Negro did not differ from that of the civilized world in general. There was, if anything, an unveiled condescension in it that was gall to a Negro who wanted to live his life free of the demoralizing effect of being pitied and patronized. Here [France], like anywhere . . . . one black villain made all black villains as one black tout made all black touts, one black nigger made all black niggers, and one black failure made all black failures.

Ibid., 275.

Although Huggins offers a generally critical reading of *Banjo*, he notes that

Reading *Banjo* today [1971], one cannot help but be struck by the contemporaneity of its argument. It might well be the work of a present-day black militant or nationalist—racialist, aggressive, rhetorical, and provocative. One thing, of course, has changed; Africa is no longer a generality, an abstraction. There are particular black nations struggling with technological revolution. One can no longer think of Africa as simply the home of black men. There are Kenya, Ghana, Nigeria, and so on. We now must think of particular Africans with real economic and political challenges.

Huggins, *Harlem Renaissance*, 177–78.

101. "I prefer Proletarian to Liberal, Democrat or Conservative . . . because I hate the proletarian spawn of civilization. They are ugly, stupid, unthinking, degraded, full of vicious prejudices, which any demagogue can play upon to turn them into a hell-raising mob at any time. As a black man I have always been up against them, and I became a revolutionist because I have not only suffered with them, but have been victimized by them—just like my race. . . . I should like to see the indecent horde get its chance at the privileged things of life, so that decency might find some place among them." McKay, *Banjo*, 270–71.

102. Ibid., 270.

103. Ibid., 268.

104. Ibid., 272.

105. As Tillery writes, "*Banana Bottom* reflected his [McKay's] desire to prove that he was an artist of many moods and not simply of the primitive-exotic-picaresque." In part, Tillery bases this judgment on McKay's own reflections. In addition to feeling frustrated that he was only known as a writer of the picaresque, McKay wrote to Max Eastman, "I had about written myself dry on the picaresque style." Tillery, *Claude McKay—A Black Poet's Struggle for Identity*, 128, 129.

106. McKay, *Banana Bottom* (Chatham, NJ: The Chatham Bookseller, 1970), 313. Although the critic George Kent thinks *Banana Bottom* a flawed novel, he argues that what makes this novel of interest is the continuing "relevance . . . of the issue of identity, its portrait of early twentieth century rural Jamaica, and its portrait of folkways and folk laughter." Also see Melvin Dixon, "To Wake the Nations Underground: Jean Toomer and Claude McKay," in *Ride Out the Wilderness: Geography and Identity in Afro-American Literature* (Urbana: University Illinois Press, 1987), 31–55.

107. McKay, *A Long Way from Home*, 349. And McKay gave this claim broad anthropological and political meaning, "Yet it is a plain fact that the entire world of humanity is more or less segregated in groups. The family group gave rise to the tribal group, the tribal group to the regional group, and the regional group to the national group. There are groups within groups. Certainly no sane group desires public segregation and discrimination. But it is a clear historical fact that different groups have won their social rights only when they developed a group spirit and strong group organization." McKay, *A Long Way from Home*, 350.

108. See Adam Lively, "Continuity and Radicalism in American Black Nationalist Thought, 1914–1929," *Journal of American Studies* 18 (1984): 207–35.

109. Locke concludes this article, "Spiritual Truancy," using McKay as a warning for the younger generation of writers just coming into their own: "They must purge this flippant exhibitionism, this posy but not too sincere racialism, this care-free and irresponsible individualism. . . . Negro writers must become truer sons of the people, more loyal providers of spiritual bread and less aesthetic wastrels and truants of the streets." Nathan Huggins, *Voices from the Harlem Renaissance*, 406.

110. Michael G. Cooke, "Claude McKay and V. S. Reid: The Simple Way to 'Magical Form,' " in McLeod, *Claude McKay*, 44.

111. McKay, *Banana Bottom*, 314. W. F. Trotter translates this passage as "true morality makes light of morality, that is to say, the morality of the judgment, which has no rules, makes light of the morality of the intellect." *Pensées: The Provincial Letters by Blaise Pascal*, trans. W. F. Trotter (New York: Random House, 1941) 6.

112. McKay, *Banana Bottom*, 315.

113. Ibid., 314.

114. Ibid. Bita's inspiration is itself inspired by her recollection that "Squire Gensir had once said of it [Pascal's thought] that it was more Pagan and Stoic than Christian. A thought like food. Something to live by from day to day. Unbounded by little national and racial lines, but a cosmic thing of all time for all minds." Ibid.

115. McKay to James Weldon Johnson, 16 May 1935, Claude McKay Papers, James Weldon Johnson Collection, Yale University.

116. McKay to James Weldon Johnson, 31 May 1935, Claude McKay Papers, James Weldon Johnson Collection, Yale University.

117. Ibid.

118. Rhonda Hope [Claude McKay] to W. S. Braithwaite, 11 January 1916, Braithwaite Papers, Harvard University.

119. Ibid.

120. Fifty-six years after Locke's "Spiritual Truancy," Michael North felt it still necessary to respond to these charges. After first calling attention to Locke's criticisms, North writes that, "Language itself is in a condition of spiritual truancy, a condition that has been most apparent, in this century at least, to those [expatriates] who have been truants themselves." In shifting his focus from McKay to the problematics of language, North explores to what degree the space McKay sought to occupy had been preempted by the aesthetic concerns of white modernists: "The real struggle of writers like McKay . . . was often not to preach or inform but rather to free a language from domination." North, however, doesn't leave this a closed space but a field of conflict shaped as well as reshaped by white and black alike. In so doing, he places McKay in a universe of writers, allowing us to see him as neither victim nor truant. We should not, however, lose sight of McKay's insistence on personal independence. If language served to configure his search for autonomy, it did not prefigure this search. North, *The Dialect of Modernism: Race, Language and Twentieth Century Literature* (New York: Oxford University Press, 1994), vi.

Chapter 6

"Worlds of Shadow-Planes and Solids Silently Moving": Jean Toomer, Alfred Stieglitz, Georgia O'Keeffe, and Waldo Frank

In 1969 Arna Bontemps wrote a short introduction to Jean Toomer's "wholly extraordinary" *Cane*, a novel that had been out of print for nearly forty years.[1] In these few pages, Bontemps situated *Cane* historically, suggested its importance as a work of art, and introduced the public to its all-but-unknown author. In so doing, Bontemps informs us that *Cane* preceded Countee Cullen's "Color" by two years; Langston Hughes's "The Weary Blues" and Eric Walrond's *Tropic Death* by three years; James Weldon Johnson's "God's Trombones" by four years; and Zora Neale Hurston's first novel, *Jonah's Gourd Vine*, by eight years. Not only, Bontemps suggested, did *Cane* initiate the "Negro Renaissance," but it continued to have some influence on writing by "Negroes in the United States as well as in the West Indies and Africa."[2] Clearly, *Cane* was a masterpiece that had vanished too quickly, and Jean Toomer was an individual who deserved more than obscurity and neglect.

Just as *Cane* preceded the "Negro Renaissance," Bontemps's introduction preceded by two years Nathan Huggins's *Harlem Renaissance* (1971), a work that was itself a catalyst for a surge of scholarly interest in the 1920s and a flood of dissertations and articles on Toomer, *Cane,* and the renaissance in general. Major studies of Toomer soon appeared as well: Brian Benson and Mabel Dillard's *Jean Toomer* (1980); Nellie McKay's, *Jean Toomer, Artist: A Study of His Literary Life and Work, 1894–1936* (1984); and Cynthia Earl Kerman and Richard Eldridge's, *The Lives of Jean Toomer: A Hunger for Wholeness* (1987). Biographical interest was supplemented by Henry Louis Gates's *Jean Toomer and Literary Criticism* (1987), Therman B. O'Daniel's gathering of forty-six essays in *Jean Toomer: A Critical Evaluation* (1988), and more recently Robert B. Jones's *Jean Toomer and the Prison House of Thought: A Phenomenology of the Spirit* (1993). And Darwin Turner has made several of Toomer's writings available in *The Wayward and the*

Seeking (1980) as has Frederik L. Rusch, *A Jean Toomer Reader: Selected Unpublished Writings* (1994).

Not only did Toomer represent an important voice of the past, but this long-delayed recognition has itself served to link the cultural and racial consciousness of the 1920s with that of the last three decades. Nevertheless, Toomer doesn't easily fit into efforts to construct bridges between past and present, bridges built, that is, on foundations of race. As Bontemps reveals, Toomer preferred to argue that "on the basis of fact" he was "neither white nor black, but simply an American."[3] Not only did Toomer decline to identify himself with a specific racial identity, but he angrily resented those who spoke of *Cane* as a "Negro novel." Toomer, for example, was furious with Horace Liveright, who suggested that the best way to publicize *Cane* was to sound "at the very start . . . a definite note about your colored blood."[4] Thus, upon reading Waldo Frank's introduction to *Cane,* Toomer was plunged into deep anguish as to the motives of his close friend and confidante: "Waldo wrote the introduction, sent it to me, my heart dropped. What was I to do? How could I take issue with a man who had responded to the art of *Cane* so finely and fully?"[5] For years after its publication, Toomer flared at the way in which *Cane* was received. As Toomer wrote to James Weldon Johnson, for example, "My poems are not Negro poems, nor are they Anglo-Saxon or white or English poems. My prose, likewise. . . . I take this opportunity of noting these things in order to clear up a misunderstanding of my position which has existed to some extent ever since the publishing of *Cane.*[6]

If Toomer was reluctant to sound "a definite note about [his] colored blood," the scholarship that has blossomed since Bontemps raised the issue has been only too eager to address the racial enigma of this important writer. Two years after Bontemps's remarks, Darwin Turner initiated in *In a Minor Chord: Three Afro-American Writers and Their Search for Identity* what has proved to be a major focus of discussion. Here, Turner offered "many possible explanations for Toomer's denials of African ancestry." But his argument turned on why it was "that during the summer of 1923 Toomer suddenly protested vehemently against a racial identification which a few months earlier he had accepted casually as a matter of slight importance."[7] The answer Turner offered was dramatic, Toomer's suddenly falling in love with Margaret Naumberg, Waldo Frank's wife, and her interest in the teachings of the Russian mystic George Ivanovich Gurdjieff. Although Turner subsequently qualified his "surprise" explanation, the message was clear: "what matters is that Jean Toomer's artistic stature diminished after he repudiated his African ancestry and rejected Afro-American subjects."[8] In Turner's hands, Toomer was as much a warning as an inspiration for later generations. However, whether as warning or inspiration, Jean Toomer was special and to this day has remained central to our understanding of the promise that Alain Locke sought to nurture.

Although there is little critical disagreement that *Cane* marks a divide in the quality of Toomer's writing, the exact relationship between the success of *Cane* and his subsequent writings is far from clear.[9] A full year before his "fateful" involvement with Margaret Naumberg, Toomer explained to Frank something of his family history and his attitude toward his diverse genealogy:

My own life has been equally divided between the two racial groups. My grandfather, owing to his emphasis upon a fraction of Negro blood in his veins, attained prominence in Reconstruction politics. And the family, for the most part, ever since has lived between the two worlds, now dipping into the Negro, now into the white. Some few are definitely white; others definitely colored. I alone have stood for a synthesis in the matters of the mind and spirit analogous, perhaps, to the actual fact of at least six blood minglings. The history, traditions, and culture of five of these are available in some approximation to the truth. Of the Negro, what facts are known have too often been perverted for the purposes of propaganda, one way or the other. It has been necessary, therefore, that I spend a dispropor-tionate time in Negro study. Recently, facts and possibilities discovered have led to an interest mainly artistic and interpretive.[10]

Toomer's comments challenge the details of Turner's argument, especially the importance of his relationship with Margaret Naumberg. But most important is the emphasis he gives to his life. In this letter, Toomer plays something of a spectator's role. His interest in "Negro" is described as "disproportionate," an interest gener-ated by others who have emphasized and distorted it at the expense of his other racial identities. Importantly, this interest, which is "mainly artistic and interpre-tive," is central to the writing and the meaning of *Cane*. For in *Cane*, Toomer also plays a spectator's role. Only now, in his role as spectator, Toomer is no less a spectator of the role itself. And this reflexive vision of self is importantly linked with Toomer's search "for a synthesis in the matters of the mind and spirit." Not only in *Cane* but in all of his work Toomer sought to give complex states of human consciousness imaginative form while simultaneously reflecting upon his own inner states of conscious awareness. At the same time, Toomer's efforts to construct a personal identity were part of a larger moral vision that framed as well as sprang from his writing of *Cane*. We must be careful, in other words, in how we distinguish *Cane* from the writing that followed. For *Cane* was not simply a line that divided Toomer's life into two distinct and unrelated parts. Toomer did not understand himself in such a truncated way.

Recently, Henry Louis Gates has addressed the critical response to *Cane* and to Toomer and has questioned the fundamental assumptions that have guided most of this commentary. "Toomer forces us," Gates suggests," to abandon any definition of Afro-American literature that would posit the racial identity of an author as its principal criterion."[11] To understand Toomer and what Toomer sought to achieve requires, in Gates's opinion, understanding that "the critical difference for Toomer was not so much his race . . . as what he sought to represent and how he represented it."[12] And he quotes Toomer to show his [Toomer's] struggle to find the language that would not itself distort or falsify the subject he sought to represent:

The reality of man's life, as I perceive and understand it, is complex beyond the possibility of formulation. How represent in sequence that which exists simultaneously? Where begin, where end? Yet a book about man must be written in sequence, and it must begin and end. Thus a book about human life, in its very structure, is a first-class misrepresentation, no matter what facts and truths it may contain.[13]

Gates suggests, as a consequence, that Toomer is best understood as a "postmodern" in that representation, Toomer's quest for language [and for form], had become both the subject and the object of his inventive as well as troubled imagination.

Gates's comments are important, for he provides a way to see Toomer that challenges the essentialist assumptions of earlier critics. In so doing, Gates's sense of Toomer's "remarkably fluid notion of race" allows one to consider Toomer in more complex, more open, and less dismissing ways. Most pointedly, Gates sides with Darryl Pinckney, who emphatically dismissed those who judged Toomer to have committed treason, racial apostasy. However, as with Leonard Harris's effort to see Alain Locke through the eyes of Jacques Derrida, we must be careful not to imply too much in seeing Toomer as a postmodern contemporary.[14] For Toomer, the effort to represent "the reality of man's life" was premised on the conviction that this reality sprang from the fundamental and irrefutable presence of the self. This self, in turn, was part of a transcendent whole, not simply a web of language, that Toomer passionately sought to realize both in art and in life.

Equally important, Toomer's quest for self, for personal wholeness, and his vision of self as a social and moral prism was also shared by others. We should not, in other words, rush too quickly to see Toomer as a postmodern contemporary without first placing him within the intellectual climate he shared with others of his time and place.[15] A letter Toomer received from Lewis Mumford soon after their first meeting in December 1919 helps to suggest the intellectual and emotional concerns that Toomer would embrace and then seek to convert to his own personal and imaginative ends.

In February 1920 Mumford wrote to Toomer to express concern that he [Mumford] had not made contact since their first meeting two months earlier: As soon as I have climbed back nearer to normal . . . I will keep my promise and we shall meet and (I hope) our friendship will begin."[16] Remarks about friendship, however, were soon placed in historical and cultural perspective. Mumford lamented that Emerson, Thoreau, Whitman, and Lincoln were not really friends, all but strangers with little connection to the larger society—"There's no use planting men of genius into a community which lets them die off in fruitless isolation: we must find a way of bringing them together so that they may work upon each other and upon the community itself, effectively."[17] The message was clear: "Today we are as negligent as ever about the necessity of bringing people together, and as a result we are all lame and partial and half-witted, and we miss half our opportunities and feel perpetually frustrated by the limitations of our lonely egos."[18] Toomer was ecstatic, to think that "Whitman and Lincoln and Emerson are probably living today within an hour's ride of each other, and their isolation is as deep and unbridgeable as ever."[19] Mumford's words had a special meaning for Toomer who was then living with his aging grandparents in Washington, DC and feeling very much isolated from kindred souls. Mumford provided not only a vision of community but a vision of purpose, one in which the individual genius flowered in the companionship of others.[20]

Mumford's friendship quickly broadened to include a circle of friends that Toomer avidly embraced—Gorham Munsom, Hart Crane, Paul Rosenfeld and Sherwood Anderson. Years later, Toomer joyfully recalled the exhilaration he experienced when he first found himself amongst this "beloved community" of writers and intellectuals:

To "arrive" meant a great deal in those days of the early 20s, and in the modern idiom, to arrive meant that you were welcomed, officially as it were, into the most remarkable up-swing yet to occur in our national culture. It meant that you found yourself not only with name and place in a local movement or "school" but with function in a regenerative life which transcended national boundaries and quickened people in every country of the post-war world. You were part of a living world of great promise. And in this world, if you so felt it, there was not only art but something of religion.[21]

However, one man in particular, Waldo Frank, was of special importance in the writing of *Cane*. Likewise, Alfred Stieglitz, a symbol to all of the "regenerative life," helps to reveal what Toomer meant by the term "modern idiom."

Alfred Stieglitz played a role and had an influence in America similar to the influence his contemporary Roger Fry had in England.[22] In 1905 Stieglitz opened his Photo Secession Gallery at 291 Fifth Avenue in New York City and immediately "291" became the "storm center" and "mecca" of the avant-garde in America. Here, and in the pages of *Camera Work*, Stieglitz brought from Paris the shocking canvasses, strange pronouncements, and singular personalities that were revolutionizing the meaning of art in the twentieth century. One notes, then, that several years before the Armory Show of 1913 (the International Exhibition of Modern Art) shocked the American public, Stieglitz had already shown the work of Matisse (1908), Rodin (1908), Cezanne (1910), Renoir (1910), Rousseau (1910), Picasso (1911), and Picabia (1913), as well as the American avant-garde—John Marin, Arthur Dove, Marsden Hartley, Max Weber, and Abraham Walkowitz.[23] At the same time, beginning in 1909, Stieglitz began to display African Sculputure at "291."[24] And in 1914 a special exhibition of African sculpture (featured as "the Root of Modern Art") was shown together with the cubist paintings of Picasso and Braque.[25]

Stieglitz's interest in African art sprang from the energy and counsel of the Mexican muralist Marius de Zayas, who, like so many others, had found his way to "291." Alerted by de Zayas as to the influence African sculpture was having on artists in France, Stieglitz began to show African statuary as art and as an art that had awakened European artists to see their work in profoundly new ways. To help make this connection, as well as to instruct those who came to "291," Stieglitz offered in *Camera Work* the following commentary from de Zayas's essay "Modern Art in Connection with Negro Art":

Modern art is not individualistic and esoteric and even less an expression of spontaneous generation. It shows itself more and more frankly an art of discoveries.

Modern art is not based on direct plastic phenomena, but on epiphenomena, on transpositions and on existing evolutions.

It its plastic researches modern art discovered Negro Art.

Picasso was its discoverer.

He introduced into European art, through his own work, the plastic principles of negro art—the point of departure for our abstract representation.

Negro art has had thus a direct influence on our comprehension of form, teaching us to see and feel its purely expressive side and opening our eyes to a new world of plastic sensations.

Negro art has re-awakened in us a sensibility obliterated by an education, which makes us always connect what we see with what we know—our visualization with our knowledge, and makes us, in regard to form, use our intellect more than our senses.[26]

De Zayas's generalizations about Africa and Africans were no less problematic than Roger Fry's.[27] As with Fry, however, both de Zayas and Stieglitz were primarily concerned with breaking with past modes of representation—"direct imitation" or "fanciful symbolism"—and central to their concern was the question of form: "Negro art has made us discover the possibility of giving plastic expression to the sensation produced by the outer life, and consequently, also, the possibility of finding new forms to express our inner life."[28]

De Zayas's distinction between the "outer life" and the "inner life" suggests both the contours and the tensions of Stieglitz's search for a creative as well as cultural aesthetic.[29] In his determined effort to establish photography as art, as a means of expression with qualities uniquely its own, Stieglitz had championed the camera's singular ability to record an object with perfect fidelity. He coupled this recognition with the equally insistent conviction that the "truth" of this objectivity depended upon the emotional, imaginative, and spiritual resources of the individual.[30] However, in coming to terms with Picasso, and the increasingly abstract work of his contemporaries, Stieglitz was forced to examine in the most searching way the meaning that the outer life and the inner life had for him and his own work as a photographer.[31] Central to this search was Stieglitz's deepening commitment to the formal integrity of the work as a whole as well as the philosophical and spiritual significance of form itself. It was within the years of this span of creative development that Stieglitz, his wife, Georgia O'Keeffe, and Jean Toomer became intimate friends.

In commenting on Stieglitz's effort to find the "elusive balance between form and object," Sarah Peters notes that "objectivity and abstraction first came together for Stieglitz during the summer of 1923" in a series of photographs of clouds he called "Songs of the Sky"[32]:

I have found that the use of clouds as subject matter in my photographs has made people less aware of clouds *as clouds* in the pictures, than when I have used trees or houses or wood—or any other objects. In looking at the photographs of clouds, people seem to feel free to think about the actual relationships in the pictures and less about the subject-matter as such, so that what I have been trying to say through my photographs seems most clearly communicated in the series of *Songs of the Sky,* where the true meaning of the *Equivalents* . . . comes through directly without any extraneous or distracting pictorial factors or representational factors coming between the person and the picture.[33]

This series of photographs, begun in the creative presence of Georgia O'Keeffe at their house on Lake George, represents an important milestone in Stieglitz's artistic development.[34] It also represents a threshold in Stieglitz's efforts to channel the intellectual and aesthetic resources of modernism into an American vision, a means to see the American environment, as Paul Rosenfeld expressed it, "on its terms and at the same time on his own."[35]

Years later, Toomer looked back on these years at Lake George to help focus his loving tribute to Stieglitz, "The Hill," which appeared in *America and Alfred Stieglitz* (1934). He notes that he had breakfast with O'Keeffe, Rosenfeld, and Stieglitz and, in the warmth of one another's company, shared a cold winter's day painting and writing.[36] Toomer's remarks, however, are deliberately low-key in that he subordinates his own personal feelings for Stieglitz and O'Keeffe so as to highlight the personal and symbolic qualities that distinguished this man of genius.[37] In truth, Toomer passionately embraced both of them, and this passion helped Toomer to imaginatively chart his own direction and purpose. After viewing Stieglitz's latest cloud photographs, Toomer wrote, "Last night, after leaving you, I walked the streets in a strange deep peace, in a quiet dignity. Had I been unable to find a single word expressive of your art and you, these inward states would have been my sure knowledge. These are my knowledge. And they are yours, for at their height you shared them, and at their source I cannot distinguish the "I" and "You."[38] The next day Stieglitz replied, "I like everything you said-all of your spirit-your clarity-the way you felt the sky. . . . Your letter makes me still more conscious of a great responsibility-and I like the sense of a great responsibility—for it pushes one further into the skies and downward deeper into the Earth itself-contacts becoming clearer-ever clearer."[39]

In addition to a correspondence that ranged over philosophical and aesthetic issues as well as the everyday greetings of friends, Toomer shared his thoughts about his own writing, using Stieglitz as a sympathetic ear to help clarify his own intuitions and intentions. In one remarkable letter to O'Keeffe, Toomer's discussion of his story "Bona and Paul" sounds very much like Stieglitz's discussion of his formal and transcendental concerns in "Song of Clouds":

Have you come to the story "Bona and Paul" in *Cane*? . . . I feel that you and Stieglitz will catch its essential design as no other can. Most people cannot see this story because of the inhibitory baggage they bring with them. When I say "white" they see a certain white man, when I say "black" they see a certain Negro. Just as they miss Stieglitz's intentions, achievements because they see "clouds." So that at the end, when Paul resolves these contrasts to a unity my intelligent commentators wonder what its all about. Someday perhaps with a greater purity and a more perfect art, I'll do the things. And meanwhile the gentlemen with intellect will haggle over the questions as to whether or not I have expressed the "South."[40]

Toomer's concerns and expectations help to clarify our understanding of *Cane*. However, the full significance of these comments is best understood when placed in the context of Toomer's relationship with Waldo Frank. Even more than Toomer, Frank saw Stieglitz as the "true Apostle of self-liberation," one for whom "art [was] the directest conduit to human consciousness-to self and to the world."[41] And it was with Frank that Toomer saw himself united in "the dual task of creating an American literature."[42]

Waldo Frank died in the same year as Toomer (1967) and in even deeper obscurity. When they first met, however, in 1919 Frank was a newly risen star in American cultural life, one that first came to view in the pages of *The Seven Arts*. Here, in language that would later echo in Locke's *The New Negro*, Frank proclaimed a renaissance in American life, a renaissance of the imagination in which the arts would help create a new sense of "national self-consciousness." This self-consciousness, rooted in the diversity of American life and the individual's awakening to his or her deepest potential and desires, promised to unify as well as energize the nation as a whole. Two years after *The Seven Arts* came to an end, Frank gathered his thoughts in *Our America* (1919) to provide a mirror for Americans to see who they were and what they might aspire to become as a people.

Our America is premised on the idea that "America is a turmoiled giant who cannot speak." Much like a child that had grown too fast, it lacked the insight and the vocabulary to know, let alone express, what it most desperately needed—an awareness that life was more than the pursuit of wealth and the consumption of the goods of society. In the past, Frank argues, Native Americans, a people rooted in the land, possess[ed] an "inner harmony with the living world."[43] But theirs was a way of life that was doomed and dying. Only in retrospect could one see what Americans had yet to achieve—a richly subjective, spiritual existence.[44] As a consequence it was Frank's task and others of his generation to "[reach] down to the hidden vitals, and [to bring] these up—their energy and truth—into the play of articulate life . . . to lift America into self-knowledge."[45] Already, Frank noted, a shift in consciousness was taking place: "The vast horizontal Stream that fertilized a continent strains now to become vertical, in order to fertilize a heaven."[46] For evidence to support his claim, Frank pointed to New York City, that "frontier" city lying "between invading Europe and America," and individuals such as Alfred Stieglitz who was helping "to generate within our selves the energy which is love of life."[47]

Toomer was dazzled by Frank. As he later recalled in one of his several autobiographical sketches, "One man stood out. He [Frank] had a fine animated face and a pair of lively active eyes. I felt there could be something between him and himself. I didn't know his name, but I marked him."[48] In Frank, Toomer found the critical intelligence and resonance of imagination he felt so lacking in others:

All along I have felt the inadequacy and shallowness of people in general and critics in particular in their relation to a work of art. The former will naively give out a pat approval or disapproval, while the latter exhaust themselves in a series of intellectual shams to arrive at the same end. Both of them ignore the essential fact of creation. It seems to me that your "Major Issue" is a much needed shaft in the right direction. . . . Your treatment of "Receptivity to Material" and "Program" has helped me quite a bit. I have always felt that "every artist that has lived in the world is a realist insofar as he himself is real and as his material, determined by himself [sic] and the world, must be real also." A dream is real; a dray is real. Program-making . . . assimilates . . . etc. Surely. Programs form "schools." The very implication of the term sustains your position. "For the intellect possesses what was created before." That is a fine and timely distinction.[49]

Their correspondence soon began to end with such endearments as "you are wonderfully dear to me, my brother." As Toomer's confidence increased, he tentatively wondered if "you [Frank] wouldn't mind reading of few of my things?"[50] One month later (April 25, 1922), Frank sent to Toomer a detailed critical reading of Toomer's plays, *Natalie Mann* and *Kabnis*.

Clearly, Frank indicated, Toomer had enormous potential. It was simply a question of "work and fidelity to the wondrously pure vision in you, and the *knowing* that if you nourish it with the best of your self, like the mystery of all life, you will achieve your form."[51] As of yet, however, Toomer had "not quite reached that ultimate where you know you are wholly articulately organically yourself." As a consequence, *Natalie Mann* had not yet achieved formal clarity, "life is not permeated into the whole thing." Likewise, *Kabnis* had not yet fused into a final art, though it possessed "the embryon of an expression" that America desperately needed: "Color, spiritual penetration, counterpoint of human wills, the intuition that they are harmmonics [sic] of a Unit, the power to convey line and volume in words, intellectual cleansing-capacity."[52] Toomer was profoundly encouraged: "What shall I say to you, dear Friend? You have definitely linked me to the purpose and vision of what is best in creative America. You have touched me, you have held me; you have released me to myself. You have brought solidarity and comradeship within handshake, within love of the eternal solitude."[53] Thus, in the year between Toomer's first stay in Sparta, Georgia (1921) and the writing of several stories that would be included in *Cane* and his return to the South (Spartanburg, South Carolina) in 1922, Frank offered important critical encouragement that touched as well as helped to clarify the deepest levels of Toomer's spiritual and aesthetic imagination.

Frank's presence was more than that of a sympathetic, yet distant correspondent. They toured the South together, criticized and celebrated one another's work, and became, in fact, something like spiritual brothers.[54] In the months following their return from Spartanburg, Toomer and Frank eagerly sought one another's advice as to questions of form:

Here's the problem I face in the new "Box Seat." The old one was under-written for many reasons, first of all I think because I consciously shut down on Dan Moore. I wanted him to be sensitive, but weak. The minute I started to rewrite, Dan expanded. I could leave him blurred in the second half of the first *Box Seat*. In the second, he had to live during the boxing scene. The question is, can this new energy, this greater strength slough off up the alley? Would the ego and the consciousness of the New Dan permit such an ending? I didn't feel that they would. A less balanced Jean Toomer, for instance, would raise all sorts of hell. Well, Dan sees Muriel is going to accept the rose from Mr. Barry. She didn't accept it from Dan. To save himself, both in terms of his ego and in terms of his energy, Dan reads wisdom and godliness into the dwarf's face, and shouts him into a possible Jesus. This new energy is ragged, dynamic, perhaps vicious. I don't see how I can channel it into the first rounded form. (I could do this, perhaps: after letting him shout, I could then lead him up the alley. Is this necessary? What do you think?) But I'll weigh the whole thing carefully by your criticism?[55]

Frank was never completely satisfied with "Box Seat," or with "Bona and Paul," finding "a looseness here . . . and in much of the imagery a certain loss of intensity—a certain amount of 'mere writing.' "[56] At least "Box Seat" and "Bona and Paul" were passable (though "not up to the level of your best"), but Frank was emphatic that the poems "Something Is Melting Down in Washington," "Tell Me," "Glaciers of Dusk," and "Prayer" were failures and not to be included in "so beautiful a book." In contrast, he now found the rewritten "Kabnis" "quite perfect as an expression of the man who wrote it" Finally, Frank asked if Toomer couldn't write a better introduction to the Washington cycle ("if not do leave it out") and included a general assessment of Toomer's strengths and weaknesses as a writer."[57]

In reply, Toomer thought that Frank's "marginal notes throughout the mss. are splendid," acknowledged that he did use the word curious loosely, and felt that Frank's "sensitivity to muddy, ragged lines and passages is unerring." Toomer also agreed that the poems Frank disliked would be excluded, although he felt that the idea of "Prayer" was "essential to the spiritual phase of *Cane*," and since it was the only companion piece to "Harvest Song" he was "almost willing to sacrifice the artistic to the spiritual curve." Hopefully, Frank would reconsider his opinion of the poem. In the meantime, Toomer had sent two new poems for Frank's approval and a revised arrangement of the Washington cycle.[58] He also promised to continue working on "Box Seat" and "Bona and Paul" before returning the manuscripts to Frank.[59]

In the same month that Toomer completed the writing of *Cane* (December 1922), he explained to Sherwood Anderson his thoughts on art and the role of the artist: "It seems to me that art in our day, other than in its purely aesthetic phase has a sort of religious function. It is a religion, a spiritualization of the immediate."[60] As such it was the specific responsibility of the artist to unify into a whole the evanescent as well as the eternal, "And I, together with all other I's am the reconciler." Ironically, Frank had championed Anderson in *The Seven Arts* in these very terms but now saw Toomer, not Anderson, as the one who possessed "the spiritual power to hoist himself wholly into a more essential plane: the plane in which the materials of the phenomenal world are recreated into pure aesthetic forms."[61] Toomer's emphasis on the individual and the inner essence of human consciousness together with his sense of a transcendent completeness suggests the demands he would place on his art. In these terms, *Cane* fully met Frank's expectations—"there is no one writing in America today that impresses me with such vast possibilities." But *Cane* also represents the limitations of these expectations and the disillusionment Toomer ultimately experienced.

In responding to Frank's critique of his poem "Prayer," Toomer, as noted, was "almost willing to sacrifice the artistic and the spiritual curve." However, once *Cane* was finished (with "Prayer" securely in place) Toomer assured Frank that the "artistic and the spiritual" had not been sacrificed:

From three angles, *"Cane's"* design is a circle. Aesthetically, from simple forms to complex ones, and back to simple forms. Regionally, from the South up to the North, and back into the South again. Or, from North down into the South and then a return North. From the point of view of the spiritual entity behind the work, the curve really starts with "Bona and Paul" (awakening), plunges into "Kabnis," emerges in "Karintha," etc., swings upward into "Theatre" and "Box Seat" and ends (pauses) in "Harvest Song."[62]

Although Toomer's comments were privately addressed to Frank, they have anticipated and even been the focus of much of the critical commentary that has subsequently been made. As Rudolph P. Byrd has indicated in *Jean Toomer's Years with Gurdjieff*, the aesthetic and regional approaches have been well explored by numerous critics. Likewise, Byrd and Charles Scruggs have made splendid though different use of Toomer's remarks to puzzle out the form of *Cane* and to link this discussion with deciphering the meaning of Toomer's masterpiece.[63]

Given Toomer's relationship with Frank and with Stieglitz, Byrd's comments are especially suggestive in that Toomer's remarks, he argues, "establish in this particular instance the interdependency of theme and structure."[64] Suggestive as this approach is to understanding *Cane*, it is important to emphasize that the quest for form (not simply the form achieved) had itself thematic and structural significance. Although this level of awareness was not fully within the grasp or even the consciousness of each character, it served to frame them individually and collectively and to link them to the form of the work itself. Frank's advice to Toomer, to "achieve your form" and become "organically yourself," was simultaneously personal and aesthetic. At the same time, form and Toomer's formal concerns served to link as well as distance him from the work he struggled to achieve. Much like a mirror, *Cane* allowed Toomer to reflect upon his own reflection in the glass of his imagination. Two pieces in particular, "Bona and Paul" and "Kabnis"—which initiate, according to Toomer, the spiritual curve of *Cane*—help to reveal not only Toomer's complex vision but also his equally complex relationship to those he chose to write about.

"Bona and Paul" centers on the attraction of Bona Hale, a beautiful white Southern woman, for Paul Johnson, a handsome student, rumored to be black, who had also come to Chicago from the South. Her attraction, however, conflicts with deep racial feelings that undercut the passion she spontaneously feels. As Byrd writes, "Bona can neither admit, even to herself, that she is attracted to Paul because he is black, nor is she able to transcend a tradition that defines and limits an individual on the basis of race."[65] Unable to resolve these contradictory feelings, Bona simply steps away at story's end. Paul is no less constrained by the racial consciousness that thickens the emotional atmosphere. Bona's ambivalence, the attitudes of others, and Paul's own ambivalence as to his racial identity contribute to the tensions he experiences. Paul, however, responds to, rather than avoids, the racial emotions that Bona chooses to deny. In so doing, he achieves a degree of personal wholeness based on the acceptance that his own self-history includes images of "the slanting roofs of gray unpainted cabins . . . [and] a negress chant[ing] a lullaby beneath the mate-eyes of a southern planter."[66]

The racial tensions that link as well as divide Bona and Paul thematically unify the story and also serve to initiate the reader into a world "grown from a goat path in Africa." However, the social as well as psychological constraints that Paul and Bona experience are complemented by Toomer's effort to create an aesthetic context that symbolizes as well as fuses with the emotional content of the story. Just as Paul achieves "his form," Toomer seeks to objectify this inward curve of self-reflection in the outward curve of the narrative form itself. One notes, as a consequence, the use of geometrical and architectural images to structure the story and the blending of these images with those of color and organic shapes.[67] In so doing, Toomer not only seeks to fuse the content and the form of "Bona and Paul" but suggests, as well, the transcendent spiritual potential of art itself.

Beginning with Paul's thrilling "blue trousered limbs," Toomer uses color to intensify as well as dramatize the emotional states of his various characters. Paul's roommate Art, for example, is described as a "healthy pink the blue of evening turns a purple pallor." While Paul, in contrast, "is a floating shade in evening shadow," and he thinks of Art as "a purple fluid, carbon-charged, that effervesces beside him." In his mind, Paul contrasts this "pale purple facsimile" with a red-blooded Norwegian friend of his and then wonders if "white skins are not supposed to live at night." It pales their "red passion." Finally, in this one paragraph, Paul's thoughts carry to Bona, wondering if she too might pale in the night. Although he thinks this unlikely—"not that red glow"—his conclusion does not "set his emotions flowing." Thus, Toomer uses color to delineate as well as fuse thought and emotion while he simultaneously strives to achieve, through art, the fluidity and emotion of consciousness itself.

At the same time, the tensions that Bona and Paul experience are manifest in the geometric and spatial forms that contrast with the emotional intensity of color. When Bona is thrilled by the sight of Paul's dancing figure, he is out of step. While she thinks of him as "a candle that dances in a grove swung with pale balloons," the other dancers drill in columns and in rows—"Columns of the drillers thud towards her . . . columns thud away from her. Come to a halt in line formation. Rigid." Similar images of constraint and containment appear in the form of rooms, train tracks, windows, and doors. All of these images are reflective of what lies above, "worlds of shadow-planes and solids, silently moving." Thus, just as Paul achieves a degree of self acceptance—"like green blades sprouting in his consciousness"—Toomer seeks to achieve thematically and aesthetically a similar synthesis.

Paul's moment of psychic wholeness takes place in the Crimson Gardens, a nightclub patronized by stock brokers and students from the University of Chicago. Afterward, in the night outside the club, away from the tensions and hostilities experienced within, that Paul shares with the leering black doorman his apparition that the Gardens "are purple like a bed of roses would be at dusk" and that "white faces [are] petals of roses and dark faces [are] petals of dusk." Now aware that his "thoughts were matches thrown into a dark window" Paul is ready "[to go] out and gather petals." Unframed and without a frame, his vision comes from within and expands to become, as well as conclude, the story. Beyond the boundaries of Paul's imagination, however, the doorman remains within the threshold of the door, and Bona disappears into the night.

In his letter to O'Keeffe, Toomer was convinced that few would catch the story's essential design. Most would, he despaired, focus on specific racial and/or regional meanings. Subsequent interpretations have generally proved Toomer correct.[68] Perhaps Toomer felt that his art, in addressing what Paul would have called a-priori questions of race, had, itself, failed to transcend the very elements of its construction. Thus, whereas Toomer singled out the "inhibitory baggage" of most of his readers, he understood that the challenge and the responsibility was essentially his own—"someday perhaps with a greater purity and a more perfect art, I'll do the thing." Toomer's thoughts, here, help to prepare us for the future direction his writing would take. At the same time, the attention he calls to his own critical reflections importantly relates to a dimension of his art, his own self-conscious presence in the work itself, that also presages his future writings but that he addresses most directly in "Kabnis," the story which concludes *Cane*.

In many respects Paul resembles Toomer himself. Not only does he mirror Toomer physically and intellectually, but the psychological resolution he achieves is grounded in Toomer's own personal and philosophical concerns. But no matter how strong the resemblance, it is a mistake to read *Cane* too biographically. As Susan Blake writes, "Between Jean Toomer and these characters [in *Cane*] is a creative persona—represented sometimes by a narrator, sometimes simply by the narrative voice—who shares his characters goals and whose story unifies the book."[69] Read too narrowly or too specifically, one misses not only the narrative complexity of Toomer's writing, but equally important Toomer's conception of the self as itself a persona that is simultaneously one's intimate self and something of a stranger as well. This ambiguity not only links character and story but also fuses with Toomer's aesthetic and spiritual conception of form. And these considerations are further complicated when Toomer introduces an aspiring poet such as Kabnis into the story. For in creating the persona of the self-conscious artist, Toomer is no less self-reflective about his writing than is Kabnis himself. As Toomer wrote to Frank, "Kabnis is Me."[70]

Ralph Kabnis is a black school teacher from the North who has come to teach in the small Southern town of Sempter, Georgia. Aroused by night winds that filter through cracks in his cabin floor ("These cracks are the lips the night winds use for whispering. Night winds in Georgia are vagrant poets, whispering.") he reflects upon his own hopes and fears and his acute awareness that who he is, who he thinks he is, and the "uncomprehending" thoughts of others exist on separate and conflicting planes. For a moment, this awareness itself becomes inspiration for the poetry he wants to write: "God, if I could develop that in words. . . . If I, the dream (not what is weak and afraid in me) could become the face of the South. How my lips would sing for it, my songs being the lips of its soul." However, Kabnis immediately qualifies his sudden enthusiasm—"Soul. Soul hell, There aint no such thing." Denial is his refuge, and throughout the story Kabnis is never able to accept his situation, others, the South, or himself. The story we read is about a poet, a black poet, locked within his private fears and his inability to achieve the inner strength needed to become the poet he imagines himself to be.

Throughout the story, Kabnis is tested and challenged by a variety of characters who all reveal the deep inner tensions that Kabnis cannot face. Rudolph Byrd, for example, refers to Lewis, Carrie K., and Father John as "restoratives" who might bring about his spiritual healing but are scorned and rejected.[71] Thus, Lewis mocks Kabnis's denial ("An besides he aint my past. My ancestors were southern blue bloods") that he has any relationship to the old man, a former slave, who sits in Halsey's work shop:

Can't hold them, can you? Master: slave. Soil; and the overarching heavens. Dusk, dawn. They fight and bastardize you. The suntint of your cheeks, flame of the great seasons multi-colored leaves, tarnished, burned. Split, shredded; easily burned. No use.[72]

Importantly, Lewis focuses on the racial and historic elements of Kabnis's alienation and the connections he refuses to acknowledge, let alone embrace. But Lewis is something more and something less than a "restorative" figure. He is also something more and something less than what Robert Bone calls "almost a T. S. Eliot creation . . . [whose] function is to shock others into moral awareness."[73]

As the narrator suggests, "He is what a stronger Kabnis might have been, and in an odd faint way resembles him." Although this resemblance is generally interpreted to favor Lewis and to highlight Kabnis's limitations, there is also the implication that what Lewis shares with Kabnis is not to be read only in Lewis's favor.

Like Kabnis, Lewis is a Northern black intellectual who has come South. But unlike Kabnis, he manifests a strength and an inner resolve precisely because he has confronted the pain and suffering of the past. In so doing, he has forged a strengthened sense of his own identity. Upon confronting the figure of the enigmatic old man whom Kabnis scorned ("that black cockroach over yonder") Lewis understands him to be " a mute John the Baptist of a new religion" and willingly sits at his feet, "merg[ing] with his source and lett[ing] the pain and beauty of the

South meet in there." And yet, Lewis remains a somewhat enigmatic and elusive figure. Intellectually remote, he intimidates and cannot fully relate to those about him. As a redemptive figure, Lewis is singularly lacking in human warmth and affection. When caught up in the slowly evolving orgy in Halsey's cellar, he flees into the night. His disappearance qualifies his appearance. He remains, as we first meet him, "on a sort of contract with himself." As a consequence, the focus shifts back to Kabnis.

Once in the Hole, the cellar that holds Father John, now drunk with corn "licker," Kabnis releases a torrent of words that spring from the darkness of his emotions. His words, however, only mirror the chaos he is unable to control:

Those words I was tellin y about, they wont fit int th mold thats branded on m soul. Rhyme, y see? Poet, too. Bad rhyme. Bad poet. Somethin else youve learned tnight. Lewis dont know it all, an I'm atellin y. Ugh. Th form thats burned int my soul is some twisted awful thing that crept in from a dream, a godam nightmare, an wont stay still unless I feed it. An it lives on words. Not beautiful words. God Almighty no. Misshapen, split-gut, tortured, twisted words. Layman was feedin it back there that day you thought I ran out fearin things. White folks feed it cause their looks are words. Niggers, black niggers feed it cause theyre evil an their looks are words. Yallar niggers feed it. This whole damn bloated purple country feeds it cause its goin down t hell in a holy avalanche of words. I want t feed the soul—I know what that is; th preachers dont—but I've got t feed it.[74]

We last see him with "lips curl[ed] bitterly," but he is now silent and has nothing to say. As Susan Blake suggests, "in separating himself from his character, the artist has created from his own struggle with that character's conflicts the work of art that frees him from the character's failure and consequent fragmentation."[75] But Toomer's success also mirrors the torment that silenced Kabnis. As Toomer writes,

Life had tied me in a knot, hard and fast. Even in Georgia I was horribly conflicted, strained and tense—more so here. The deep releases caused by my experience there could not liberate and harmonize the sum of me. *Cane* was a lyric essence forced out with great effort despite my knotted state. People have remarked its simple easy-flowing lyricism, its rich natural poetry; and they may assume that it came to bloom as easily as a flower. In truth, it was born in an agony of internal tightness, conflict, and chaos. It is true that some portions, after I had cleared the way, came forth fluently. Thus "Fern" came out, not without effort, but with comparative ease soon after I labored to write "Kabnis." But the book as a whole was somehow distilled from the most terrible strain I have ever known. I had to use my very blood and nerves to project it. The feelings were in me, deep and mobile enough. But the creations of the forms were very difficult. During its writing, and after it, I felt that I had by sheer force emptied myself and given to that book my last blood. I felt drained and dry, with no immediate or prospective source of recreation. "Harvest Song," better than any other of the book's content, gives an idea of my state at that time. After finishing *Cane*, I swore that I would never again write a book at that price. Thus when people truly moved by *Cane* and valuing it have suggested that I write another book like it, I have smiled my appreciation of their response, but have firmly shaken my head. When they, in all good faith, have advised me, as Sherwood Anderson did, to keep close to the conditions which produced *Cane*, I have denied them. Never again in life do I want a repetition of those conditions. And of equal importance is the fact that *Cane* is a swan song.[76]

Kabnis and Toomer both shared an "internal tightness, conflict, and chaos." However, whereas Kabnis became silent, Toomer was reflective. Clearly another *Cane* was out of the question. But to continue writing was not. Three months after *Cane's* publication, Toomer wrote to Joel Spingarn, noting that he wanted "his next expression to be more perfectly *myself*."[77] In part, Toomer wanted to separate himself from Frank's influence. The self that Toomer now evoked was not confined to the individual who went South to pursue "the opportunity for a vivid symbolism."

The controversy that has continued into the present as to Toomer's racial identification, began, as seen, even before *Cane's* publication. Soon after its appearance, for example, his relationship with various contemporaries—Du Bois, Locke, James Weldon Johnson, Sherwood Anderson, and others—was strained because of their insistence that, as Anderson phrased it, Toomer should remain true to his "Negro self" and that such "selfhood" was his true strength as a writer.[78] Not unlike O'Keeffe, who raged at the strictly sexual readings of her paintings, Toomer also believed "that [he] was exploring [his] whole psyche"—and not just a part of it.[79] That others failed to see this was, for Toomer, a measure of the distance that he as well as they had to go. At the same time, Toomer's repeated insistence that *Cane* was a "swansong" was not just a frustration with the limiting view of others.[80] Before and after *Cane*, the boundary of Toomer's imagination was America itself. Prior to their journey south, for example, Toomer wrote to Frank—"How our mother, this America of ours, needs us, dear brother."[81] Later, Toomer noted in his Notebook (1923–24) that while most American writers had treated the South as a rather "exotic and unrelated fragment" of the larger whole of America, he visualized *Cane* as a seed that would help to initiate "the adjustment, the health, and art and joy and beauty that, expanding, will determine the tone and content of the entire country."[82]

Cynthia Kerman and Richard Eldridge have argued that *Cane* "reflects one stage in his [Toomer's] developing a picture of self that attempted to universalize the individual's experience. While others may have read *Cane* to see how a man could fit his human view into his blackness, Jean was trying to fit the blackness that was a part of him into a more comprehensive human view."[83] As these two scholars suggest, *Cane* was a stage in Toomer's personal and intellectual concerns, one that initiated as well as sprang from the writing of *Cane*. However, Toomer's thoughts regarding identity and his "developing a picture of self" were not limited to his artistic ambitions, aesthetic concerns, or his experience in Sparta, Georgia.

Between the summer of 1920 and the spring of 1922, Toomer read many books on race and the racial problem in America. Disenchanted by what he read, he began to write his own thoughts on the subject both in essay form and in a poem titled, "The First American," wherein he elaborated the idea that "here in America we are in process of forming a new race, [and] that I was one of the first conscious members of this race"[84] These germinal thoughts, which later took form in Toomer's lyrical poem "The Blue Meridian," were further sketched out in his Notebook in which he saw the year 1923 as a turning point in the "spiritual unification of America." One major element of this fusion was the latent energy, yet creative exhaustion, of movements that had discovered "American and modern materials." Here, Toomer had in mind the work of Frank, Van Wyck Brooks, Sherwood Anderson, and those who were open "in a native and organic way" to European art and literature. The other source of transformation that Toomer identified was to be found in the synthesis of the elements of racial consciousness (negative and positive) that was "satisfied with nothing less than essentialized MAN, man as consciousness." This, as of yet unrealized renaissance of being, Toomer observed, would take place in New York City, "the center and apex of the country's quantitative energy . . . the factory of internationalism, but not yet the school of universal man."[85] Toomer further elaborated the racial focus of these thoughts in his unpublished essay "The Negro Emergent."

Beginning on a note of incompleteness, as did Locke in *The New Negro*, Toomer presented black Americans as "emerg[ing] from a crust, a false personality, a compound of beliefs, habits, attitudes, and emotional reactions superimposed upon him by external circumstances."[86] He accounted for this crust of inauthenticity as the result of (1) being black in a white world and (2) the grain, itself, of American civilization common to all Americans.[87] To link these two considerations, Toomer first detailed, historically, racial oppression in America and then folded into this discussion various efforts by blacks to counter, psychologically and culturally, the efforts of white Americans "to plaster a white image on a black reality."[88] Necessary and legitimate as these responses were, however, Toomer argued that these responses ultimately became barriers themselves to an awakened sense of one's essential self.[89] To make his point, Toomer turned his attention to present-day Harlem. There, and in America in general, he saw important signs of black Americans being moved by "the vital determinants of racial heritage." Ideally, however, these movements were but the first step of a larger awareness that black Americans shared with others. Unlike Locke who felt it necessary to qualify the argument Herskovits's had made in "The Dilemma of Social Pattern," Toomer echoed Herskovits, proposing that there was "truth in the statement that Harlem differs from other communities in shade merely, but not in patterns." In addition, he added, "it should be remembered that this shade appeals to something more than the eye of the Negro. He wishes to generously partake of it; he wishes to press beyond its boundaries, for he knows that neither his nor any similar group provides the range to satisfy a large capacity and keen appetite for experience."[90] Thus, whereas Locke argued that Harlem eluded the myopic visions of the sociologist, the philanthropist, and the race-leader, Toomer saw Harlem as itself a transitory phenomenon. Whereas Locke argued philosophically and culturally for patterns of racial consciousness, Toomer opted for patterns of consciousness that ultimately transcended a racial content.

In "Race Problems and Modern Society" (1928) and in "Race and Race Problems" (1928), Toomer made the, by then, somewhat commonplace distinction between race as a biological phenomenon and race as a social and psychological phenomenon. Biologically, Toomer noted, man was without boundaries—"The human organism is locomotive." Universality was mankind's natural biological condition and racial mixture was the norm. To help substantiate this claim, Toomer drew upon Herskovits's *The American Negro* (1928) to discuss race in its "strictly biological sense" and to elaborate the "racial intermixture all over America."[91] Thus grounded, Toomer developed the social and cultural implications of his argument. To do this he paid particular attention to Alfred Kroeber's *Anthropology* (the first five chapters) and Louis Wirth's review of Herskovits's *The American Negro:*

What sort of criteria enable us to tell what constitutes a race and who belongs to it? If the present study shows anything, it indicates that the word race has been used in a great many contradictory ways, and that the physical anthropologists with their anthropometric measurements reduce a race to a highly variable statistical concept. A race, it may turn out, is after all not so much a clearly delimitable homogenous biological group, as a cultural group, whose self and group consciousness is more or less attached to some clearly visible biological trait. Perhaps the old naive notion of classifying races by skin color has, in the final analysis, more practical value than the minute and complex measurements of cephalic index, nostrility, hair shape, etc. If Dr. Herskovits' data and interpretations are correct, a race is something social rather than biological. A race, it turns out, is a group of people that we treat as if they were one. You belong to a certain race, if you feel yourself to be a member, and if others treat you as if you were.[92]

Given Toomer's emphasis on the artificiality of race (he preferred the term "type" to prevailing "notions of stocks and races") and the universality of the human organism, Toomer argued that all social distinctions were essentially arbitrary and artificial. As a consequence, Toomer thought that all groups, those that were exploited and/or those that claimed a separate and intrinsic identity, only reflected the maladjustments of society. His answer was to encourage the individual to discover "what is real within him[self] . . . and by that act at once create himself and contribute his value to America."[93]

Throughout the decade and into the next, Toomer continued to struggle with the disparate elements of his life, the life he imagined in his writings, and the life he imagined for himself and others. Four years after the publication of *Cane*, for example, Toomer failed to find a publisher for his novel *Transatlantic*. His reflections upon this disappointment help to reveal the ongoing concerns he struggled with before and after *Cane*. Form remains his central concern, but form embodies a complex range of meanings, aesthetic and personal, that make it impossible to separate the language of art from the language of self. For this reason, Toomer continually equates the achievement of a "compelling literary form" with the realization of "my individual forms and ways of life." As a consequence, Toomer confides to his notes the need to "continue the forming of myself." At the same time, questions of form and the fate of *Transatlantic* were also linked with questions of racial identity and the role that *Cane* continued to play in this identity.[94] And yet, Toomer's quest for form, however defined and however vexatious, ultimately turned on his reflexive turn of mind, his awareness that differences in awareness as well as self-awareness were central to the challenge he sought to address. For this reason Toomer addressed the question of writing autobiography and the demands of a form that were simultaneously the apprehension as well as the construction of things "dear to me—or to Toomer." Five years later, in his poem "Blue Meridian," Toomer managed to integrate what was dear to himself and to Toomer.

The "Blue Meridian" is an extended evocation and invocation of the meaning of America. The first two lines—"It is a new America, / To be spiritualized by each new American"—initiate both a vision and a quest as nation, and the poem itself, evolve toward the higher level of order (The Blue Meridian) implicit within the dynamic yet inchoate origins of its historic beginnings (The Black and White Meridian). The unity achieved is dialectical and evolutionary, the synthesis of antithetical elements into a greater whole.[95] At the same time, the whole reflects as well as transcends the separate elements of its evolving transformation.

Central to this movement from fragmentation to wholeness is the transformation of America's ethnically diverse and divided peoples into a people whose primary identity is what they share as Americans and as human beings.[96] This transformation, however, though organically related to more fundamental changes shaping America, is neither inevitable nor possible without human imagination. Thus, the "Radiant Incorporeal, The I of earth and mankind," which the poet/narrator evokes to achieve this transformation simultaneously inspires his own imagination and consciousness. When we first read of the "Great African races" coming into America, for example, we encounter a people both enslaved and self-enslaving— "But we must keep keep keep the watermelon." As a consequence, the poet flees their pain and truncated self-awareness. At poem's end, however, the poet, who earlier fled "the shining ground," now understands that,

Earth is earth, ground is ground,
All shining if loved.
Love does not brand as slave or peon
Any man, but feels his hands,
His touch upon his work,
And welcomes death that liberates
The poet, American among Americans,
Man at large among men.[97]

Thus, the integrations that take place within the poem are deeply rooted in the persona of the poet. The poet, in turn, has opened himself to the presence and experience of others. Through others one discovers one's self. Through self one discovers others. The boundaries of one's true identity are not impossible to imagine so long as imagination itself is not limited to the constructs that society seeks to impose.

As Nellie McKay and Rudolph Byrd have made clear, "Blue Meridian," as did most of Toomer's writing after *Cane*, bore the philosophical and spiritual imprint of the Russian mystic George Ivanovich Gurdjieff.[98] But the poem's racial and cultural themes, its formal concerns, and its spiritual reach were rooted in the first drafts Toomer wrote in 1920. At the same time, Alfred Stieglitz and Georgia O'Keeffe were no less present in the imaginative sweep of Toomer's vision. And just as Ezra Pound evoked Walt Whitman to inspire his generation,[99] so too did Toomer in "Blue Meridian" make his pact with America's protean poetic visionary, though for Toomer it was not so much a time for cutting as a time for grafting.[100] Linking all, however, providing sinew, inspiration and direction was Toomer's conviction that in modern society mankind had lost his cultural bearings. *Cane* had been an important beginning, but only a beginning. As a consequence, in the years to follow, Toomer would extend his search for forms and language that allowed for the contingencies of modern life (race being no more divisive than other aspects of the social order) yet also provided the vision of wholeness that was presently missing.

In 1950, years after Toomer had essentially vanished from view, Alain Locke offered in "Self-Criticism: The Third Dimension in Culture" a critical reading of eight recent essays that were themselves critical assessments of black "literary output." In Locke's opinion, these essays marked "a considerable step forward toward objective-criticism." This meant, according to him, the shared understanding that when "racial themes are imposed upon the Negro author either from within or without, they become an intolerable and limiting artistic ghetto."[101] In other words, what was needed was a critical and imaginative literature that was simultaneously objective or particular and universal. In this way, black writers would avoid racial provincialism, and black literature would take its place along side all great literature—"for in universalized particularity there has always resided the world's greatest and most enduring art."[102] Although achieving this "cultural maturity," as Locke phrased it, had been the promise of the "Negro Renaissance," it was a promise that few had realized. Jean Toomer was an exception, and Locke was surprised that no one contributing to *Phylon* had recognized his importance:

I am personally surprised that no one referred to the phenomenal early appearance of such "universal particularity" in Jean Toomer's *Cane* in 1923. Here was something admirably removed from what Mr. Chandler calls very aptly "promotional literature," but it is Negro through and through as well as deeply and movingly human. It was also exempt from any limitation of provincialism although it gave local color convincingly. To wish for more of this is to ask for the transmuting quality of expert craftsmanship combined with broad perspective or intuitive insight, one or the other.[103]

Thus, in his ongoing role as a cultural midwife, Locke reminded his contemporaries that Toomer and Toomer's *Cane* were an important intellectual resource. In so doing, Locke not only celebrated Toomer but also called attention to the Harlem Renaissance and the cultural and aesthetic principles ("the releasing forumla") that held and still held so much promise for the present generation. And yet, in thinking back over the path that Toomer had taken, we should be careful about the focus of Locke's retrospective vision.

Although Locke somewhat casually joined the "particular and the universal" in this article, they existed in dynamic tension in his own thinking throughout the 1920s. To maintain this tension, Locke embraced relativism, philosophically and culturally, so as to distinguish as well as unify the parts and the whole. At the same time, Locke's philosophical conception of form served to yoke the individual and the group as well as consciousness and experience.[104] For Toomer, however, relativism was not the answer. Form was both a glimpse of some transcendent unity and simultaneously a reproach to himself and others who had yet to achieve, in art and in life, this level of psychic integration. The challenge of modern life was to transcend the fragmentation of modernity itself. Relativism, for Toomer, was simply the acceptance of the disorder of the status quo. For this reason, Toomer's vision of wholeness transcended the very tensions between self and others that Locke embraced in his celebration and calibration of a new black consciousness. In exploring the contingencies of his historical and racial identity, Toomer reached for a level of awareness independent of context and circumstance itself. As a result, his writing became increasingly abstract, located in no particular time or place. The price of this abstraction, as many have noted, was the loss of the voice that sang the "swan song" *Cane.* And yet, it was in the singing itself that Toomer recognized another voice still to be heard.

NOTES

1. Published in 1923 and reprinted in 1927, *Cane* was reissued in 1967 and 1969. As Darwin Turner writes, "In 1923, twenty-eight-year-old Jean Toomer . . . was one of the brightest stars in this galaxy [of writers who distinguish the 1920s]. . . . Twenty-five years later, however, when I first read selections from *Cane* in *The Negro Caravan,* Toomer was not being discussed or studied. . . . Within another generation, the memory of Toomer had become so dim that when he died in 1967 in a nursing home near Philadelphia, some admirers of *Cane* were startled because they presumed that he had died many years earlier. Ironically, as Toomer was dying, *Cane* was being discovered by a new generation of readers." Darwin Turner ed., *The Wayward and the Seeking: A Collection of Writings by Jean Toomer* (Washington, DC: Howard University Press, 1980), 1.

2. Arna Bontemps, "Introduction," in Jean Toomer, *Cane* (New York: Harper and Row, 1969), x. Also, Nellie McKay, "The Man—the Artist: An Evaluation" in *Jean Toomer, Artist* (Chapel Hill: University of North Carolina Press, 1984), 225–46.

3. Bontemps, *"Introduction," Cane,* xv.

4. Toomer wrote,

First, I want to make a general statement from which detailed statements will follow. My racial composition and my position in the world are realities which I alone may determine. Just what these are, I sketched in for you the day I had lunch with you. As a unit in the social milieu, I expect and demand acceptance of myself on their basis. I do not expect to be told what I should consider myself to be. Nor do I expect you as my publisher, and I hope as my friend, to either directly or indirectly state that this basis contains any element of dodging. In fact, if my relationship with you is to be what I'd like it to be, I must insist that you never use such a word, such a thought, again. As a B[oni] and L[iveright] author,

I make the distinction between my fundamental position and the position which your publicity department may wish to establish for me in order that *Cane* reach as large a public as possible. In this connection I have told you . . . to make use of what ever racial factors you wish. Feature Negro if you wish, but do not expect me to feature it in advertisements for you. For myself, I sufficiently featured Negro in *Cane*. Whatever statements I give will inevitably come from a synthetic human and art point of view, not from a racial one.

Jean Toomer to Horace Liveright, 5 September 1923, Beinecke Library, Yale University.

5. Toomer, "Outline of an Autobiography," 61. Beinecke Library, Yale University.

6. In a letter to James Weldon Johnson, for example, Toomer wrote, "My poems are not Negro poems, nor are they Anglo-Saxon or white or English poems. My prose, likewise. . . . I take this opportunity of noting these things in order to clear up a misunderstanding of my position which has existed to some extent ever since the publishing of *Cane*." Jean Toomer to James Weldon Johnson, 11 July 1930, Beinecke Library, Yale University.

7. Darwin Turner, *In a Minor Chord* (Carbondale, IL: Southern Illinois University Press, 1971), 35.

8. Ibid., 37.

9. Henry Louis Gates cautions that "Toomer's so-called loss of voice we too easily attribute to his loss of face, to his self-willed effacement of his 'dark' past.' Such judgments, Gates argues, are not only premature ("once the definitive edition of the *Complete Works* is published, we shall be able to begin to consider that received, wishful opinion") but "seem to reflect something we want to be true." Gates, "The Same Difference: Reading Jean Toomer, 1923–1982," in *Figures in Black—Words, Signs, and the "Racial" Self* (New York: Oxford University Press, 1987), 206.

10. Jean Toomer to Waldo Frank, 24 March 1922, Beinecke Library, Yale University.

11. Gates goes even further to suggest that "Toomer teaches us the limitations of biographical criticism and also its implicit fascination as a text of its own, as a parallel text, as it were, to literary structures as *Cane*." Gates, "Black Structures of Feeling," in *Figures in Black*, 206. Alice Walker makes a similar distinction when she concludes "I think Jean Toomer would want us to keep its beauty [his novel *Cane*], but let him go." Walker, "The Divided Life of Jean Toomer," in *In Search of Our Mothers' Gardens* (New York: Harcourt Brace Jovanovich, 1983), 65.

12. Gates, "Black Structures of Feeling," 209.

13. Ibid.

14. It is to be noted that Gates is deliberately cautious in making this claim and awaits the definitive edition of the *Complete Works* before making further judgment.

15. As Casey Nelson Blake writes, "For Brooks and Frank the loss of culture as a mediating language had more tragic consequences. It was not just their criticism that lacked a frame, in tradition, morality, or collective experience, but, increasingly, their very selves . . . Brooks's breakdown in the mid-1920s and Frank's anguished quest for mystical 'wholeness' during the same period are testimony to the psychic costs of the crisis in the Young Americans' critical project." Blake, *Beloved Community: The Cultural Criticism of Randolph Bourne, Van Wyck Brooks, Waldo Frank, and Lewis Mumford* (Chapel Hill: University of North Carolina Press, 1990), 231–32.

16. Lewis Mumford to Jean Toomer, 27 February 1920, Beinecke Library, Yale University.

17. Ibid.

18. Ibid.

19. Ibid.

20. In a letter to Waldo Frank, Toomer despaired,

During the past months I have been through many deaths and many births. These have given me fractions of knowledge, and a great fatigue. No inclusive vision, no synthesis has come. But I have a sense which inhibits the communication of parts. And since my personality dissolved, I seem to have nothing to say on this plane. Both Gorham and Hart must have felt all this in me. For, with no lessening of the inner force that bound us, it was necessary during my last weeks in New York that I withdraw from them, externally. Perhaps they haven't written you of this. For those who are themselves somehow struggling for a base, the implications of my state may not have been joyful. I have heard that this has been a time of deep search and discovery for you. Search and discovery bind us in the spirit, though no words break through the flesh.

Jean Toomer to Waldo Frank, undated letter, Beinecke Library, Yale University.

21. Cynthia Earl Kerman and Richard Eldridge, *The Lives of Jean Toomer: A Hunger for Wholeness* (Baton Rouge: Louisiana State University Press, 1987), 107. Quoted from Toomer's "The Second River," (JTP 66:8), 3.

22. Abigail Solomon-Godeau claims that "the 'lineage of 291's' Anglo-American photographic formalism started in the early 1920s with the writings of Roger Fry and Clive Bell." Solomon-Godeau, "Formalism and Its Discontents," *Print Collector's Newsletter* (May–June 1982): 44. However, Sarah Whitaker Peters argues that "even if Stieglitz had read Fry's "An Essay in Aesthetics" when it was first published in the *New Quarterly* (1909) his own formalist leanings were already apparent, and functioning." She goes on to add that, "How much Stieglitz's repression of subject matter in the 1915–16 photographs from 291 stemmed from Picabia or de Zayas's theory of 'pure objectivity' in *Photography and Artistic Photography* (1913), and how much from his readings in, or awareness of, Fry and Bell, is a topic for further investigation." Influence aside, however, Peters adds that "Certainly the meanings of Fry's and Bell's special terms plasticity, significant form, and musicality were well known to Stieglitz, as was their joint insistence that the originality of a work of art lay not in its subject but in its formal expression of a vision (or idea)." Sarah Whitaker Peters, *Becoming O'Keeffe* (New York: Abbeville Press, 1991), 335.

23. William Innes Homer, *Alfred Stieglitz and the American Avant-Garde* (Boston: New York Graphic Society, 1977).

24. In some respects, the initial response to Stieglitz's showing of African art was more alarming than the response to the Armory Show:

The rank savor of savagery attacks the visitor the instant he enters the diminutive room. This rude carving belongs to the black recesses of the jungle. Some examples are hardly human, and are so powerfully expressive of gross brutality that the flesh quails. The origin of these works is somewhat obscure. The gallery describes them as "the root of modern art," and this might be admitted in the same sense that the family of apes may be called the root of modern man. But to whatever period they belong, and whoever created them , there can be no doubt that they convey a sense of a race of beings infinitely alien to us. . . . But the most striking piece is a mask which lies on a table in a corner, coarse, black, indescribably African. It recalls the haunting sense which broods over Joseph Conrad's story of suffocation, dank and barbaric. It is a nightmare not soon to be forgotten. When the outer door is reached again no insistent signs are necessary to inform you that you have seen savage art. The good, familiar daylight, the friendly white faces on the street, come as a relief after this blackness.

Camera Work 48 (October 1916): 7.

25. "This morning I had a letter from Paul Guillaume in which he tells me that you had told him to write to me. He says that he would be glad to let us have a show of Negro art. Has he really good things and what do you think about it? Of course I would like to have a

show of Negro art as you know. I want to make the next season at '291' a very live one."
Alfred Stieglitz to Marius de Zayas, 3 June 1914, Beinecke Library, Yale University.

26. Marius de Zayas, "Modern Art," *Camera Work* 48 (October 1916): 7.

27. Africans were described as victims of nature in a "Land of Fright."

28. De Zayas, "Modern Art," 7.

29. Writing more generally of this generation, Casey Nelson Blake writes, "As a result of their own youthful mysticism and concerns for spirituality, the Young Americans emphasized an ideal of organic experience uniting inner and outer life that remained at the core of their mature conceptions of personality, culture, and community," Blake, "Organic Community," in *Beloved Community: The Cultural Criticism of Randolph Bourne, Van Wyck Brooks, Waldo Frank, and Lewis Mumford*, 268.

30. "What takes form within oneself will be felt outside oneself. But the subconscious pushing through the conscious, driven by an urge coming from beyond its own knowing, its own control; trying to live in the light, like the seed pushing up through the earth—will alone have roots, can alone be fertile. . . . All idealism that does not have such roots must be sterile; must defeat itself." Dorothy Norman ed., "From the Writings and Conversations of Alfred Stieglitz," in *Twice A Year*, I (fall–winter, 1938), 77.

31. "Now I find that contemporary art consists of the abstract (without subject) like Picasso etc., and the photographic. . . . Just as we stand before the door of a new social era, so we stand in art too before a new medium of expression—the true medium (abstraction)." Peters, *Becoming O'Keeffe*, 127.

32. Peters, *Becoming O'Keeffe*, 142.

33. Bram Dijkstra, *the hieroglyphics of a new speech: Cubism, Stieglitz, and the Early Poetry of William Carlos Williams* (Princeton: Princeton University Press, 1969), 101–2.

34. Paul Rosenfeld, "Alfred Stieglitz," in *America and Alfred Stieglitz: A Collective Portrait*, ed. Waldo Frank, Lewis Mumford, Dorothy Norman, Paul Rosenfeld, Harold Rugg (Garden City: Doubleday, Doran, 1934), 126.

35. As Sara Peters writes, "O'Keeffe may have been a major catalyst for Stieglitz's interest in photographing the Lake George landscape, the place of their first lyrical happiness. It is also highly probable that she was directly responsible for his burgeoning fascination with nature per-se. Compositions based on trees, hillsides, clouds, and water had hardly ever appeared in his photography before late 1918. . . . The earth, water, and sky of the Lake George surroundings thus became fresh artistic territory for Stieglitz and O'Keeffe at almost the same time." Peters, *Becoming O'Keeffe*, 231.

36. "But I felt warmth and a most amazing sense that life was coming into us, that the wide world was immediate out there, that we were in the midst of happenings in America, that Stieglitz had an interior connectedness with life, that through him I also felt connected." Jean Toomer, "The Hill," in *America and Alfred Stieglitz: A Collective Portrait*, 298.

37. Toomer wrote,

A man in his world. A world which he has made, not found already made. No one, no group, no race, no nation could have built it for him. His function in life was not to fit into something that already existed but to create a new form by the force of his growth. Now he calls this form, "An American Place"—which it is, authentically. Whoever goes to room 1710 of 509 Madison Avenue or to The Hill at Lake George will find certain American essences in the paintings, in the photographs, in the very life and atmosphere too. Yet deeper than the national reality is the human reality. He himself and his form are of the great body and spirit of mankind.

An individual who is himself, who is for those of the wide world that claim him by similarity of spirit and of values. Toomer, "The Hill," in *America and Alfred Stieglitz*, 302.

38. Toomer to Alfred Stieglitz, 10 January 1924, Beinecke Library, Yale University. Nine days later, Toomer greatly expanded his earlier remarks,

When I became conscious of that relationship: the sky, the camera, and you, a profound and searching movement started. Revelation seemed immanent, and I knew that some stark clarity must result from it. At first it seemed as though all my previous conceptions of art-relations must be re-valued, for an element of passivity, a new element so I thought, had entered. This element challenged, and was about to dissolve everything. . . . You then were active *through the medium that you controlled.* The camera became significant because you touched it. The sky, because you saw it. But first of all you saw yourself. Secondly, you knew the medium. And then the sky revealed itself as it only could unfold to you, and the *camera.* The relationship is thus mutual and inevitable: one term could not exist without the other. Given a pure conscious content, I know of no higher test for great art. Your photographs are great art. As such, the elements and processes which fused in their achievement, are consonant with those that enter into any pure product, whatever the medium. Hence, while a searching of that relationship did not lead to a general re-valuing by means of it I won my way to fundamentals. And this is revelation.

I want to state these fundamentals, particularly as they are manifest in your art. In doing so, I do not take it to myself that I have measured your reality. Only, that I have clarified my own.

Jean Toomer to Alfred Stieglitz, 19 January 1924, Beinecke Library, Yale University.

39. Alfred Stieglitz to Jean Toomer, 11 January 1924, Beinecke Library, Yale University.
40. Toomer to Georgia O'Keeffe, 13 January 1924, Beinecke Library, Yale University.
41. Waldo Frank, *Our America* (New York: Boni and Liveright, 1923), 186.
42. Toomer wrote to Waldo Frank,

I wrote that letter, and then considered what I had written. And my mind sanctioned my impulse by concluding that it was much better (under the more or less personal conditions) to say exactly and truly what I felt rather than skimp to the strictly commercial. I cannot think of myself as being separated from you in the dual task of creating an American literature, and of developing a public, however large or small, capable of responding to our creations. Those who read and know me, should read and know you. So far as the people here [Washington, DC] are concerned, the path to both of us is blocked somewhat by a rigid moral conventionalism (this, in reaction against the excesses of the slave regime, and found most acute in the otherwise most advanced minds.) And, of course, as yet they are some distance from your art perceptions. But, underneath, the soil is good rich brown, and should yield splendidly to our plowing.

Jean Toomer to Waldo Frank, 2 August 1922, Beinecke Library, Yale University.

43. "The uncorrupted Indian knows no individual poverty or wealth. All of his tribe is either rich or poor. He has no politics. He has not dynastic or industrial intrigue. . . . His physical world is fixed. And in consequence all his energies beyond the measure of his daily toil rise ineluctably to spiritual consciousness: flow to consideration of his place and part in Nature, into the business of beauty." Frank, *Our America,* 114.

44. Frank's thoughts perhaps trace to a recent trip he took in New Mexico As he wrote to Sherwood Anderson,

It was all a revelation to me, Sherwood. It is uncanny how thoroughly one has to unlearn all one has learned in the schools and in the forums of life, and how hard it is, and how the old lies cling one by one. I am certainly no gullible ass when it comes to false doctrines of our so-called civilization. Yet unconsciously, I had to this extent accepted the official ruling about the Indians, that I had given them no thought. And here, all of a sudden, all of a deep great gentle culture swam into vision—a culture whose spiritual superiority to ours no intelligent man would question, who once understood. Behind the sneers in the worse sentimentality of the White about the *noble red man*—God what hypocrisy and sullen complacency in that term—the real Indian . . . has hidden away and kept his soul marvelous pure. . . . But here was a nation with a great religious consciousness—no anthropomorphisms and crucifixions—with a common and great art—with a social system under which poverty and crime were unknown. And we have not had the sense to turn to this fading beauty in our land: nor to preserve it.

Waldo Frank to Sherwood Anderson, 6 August 1918 University of Pennsylvania.

Frank's point of view, however, was widely shared in the 1910s and 1920s. See F. H. Matthews, "The Revolt against Americanism: Culturalism, Pluralism and Cultural Relativism as an Ideology," *The Canadian Review of American Studies* 1 (spring 1970); and George Stocking, "The Ethnographic Sensibility of the 1920s and the Dualism of the Anthropological Tradition," in *Romantic Motives: Essays on Anthropological Sensibility* (Madison: University of Wisconsin Press, 1989), 208–76.

45. Frank to Anderson, 6 August 1918, University of Pennsylvania.

46. Ibid.

47. Frank, *Our America*, 232.

48. Jean Toomer, *"Outline of the Story of the Autobiography,"* 48, Beinecke Library, Yale University.

49. Jean Toomer to Waldo Frank, 10 April 1922, Beinecke Library, Yale University.

50. Jean Toomer to Waldo Frank, 24 March 1922, Beinecke Library, Yale University.

51. Waldo Frank to Jean Toomer, 25 April 1922, Beinecke Library, Yale University.

52. NATALIE MANN "What is clear is: that you have a vision . . . mothered and fathered of true temperament, passion, intellectually well-midwifed . . . the start of a true Form, but that the Form is not yet there. . . . Form out of chaos, as must all true American artists, takes time time time."

KABNIS "You have already left far behind you the imitative stage, the stage of acceptance of even the best near to you. You are already on your *own*. You are in that stage most difficult to navigate through when, being ahead of yourself you are temporarily in chaos . . . have left home planets and not reached your individual star. In this stage, only the deeply intuitive person can sense where your true form is hardening out of the mists. You have left behind the monkey crowd who, thinking they can appreciate literature, really love only its stinking afterbirths . . . and you have not quite reached that ultimate where you know you are wholly articulately organically yourself. Kabnis has in it the embryon of an expression which America has not had even the faintest inkling of, and which America demands if it is to become a real part of the human adventure. Color, spiritual penetration, counterpoint of human wills, the intuition that they are harmonics of a Unit, the power to convey line and volume in words, intellectual cleansing-capacity . . . all here, but not yet fused into the final art." Ibid.

53. Jean Toomer to Waldo Frank, 26 April 1922, University of Pennsylvania.

54. See my "Jean Toomer and Waldo Frank," *Phylon* 41 (June, 1980): 167–78.

55. Jean Toomer to Waldo Frank, 20 September 1922, University of Pennsylvania.

56. Waldo Frank to Jean Toomer, undated, Beinecke Library, Yale University.

57. "At best your lyrics are your weakest ones. You are a poet in prose. You are shackled and thwarted in the verse forms. The circles and spheres of drama and story alone can house your dimensioned song: pure lyricism . . . you." Waldo Frank to Jean Toomer, undated, Beinecke Library, Yale University.

58. "Seventh Street"; "Rhobert"; "Calling Jesus"; " Avey"; " Bee-hive"; "Storm Ending"; "Theatre"; "Her lips Are Copper Wire"; "3 in 1"; "Box Seat"; "Prayer"; "Harvest Song"; and "Bona and Paul." In the final version of *Cane*, "3 in 1" was not included.

59. Throughout this period of time, Toomer was offering Frank advice. Even after the publication of *Holiday*, Frank continued to consult Toomer regarding the validity of the

critical comments being made. Upon reassurance that *"Holiday* is quite perfect as it stands," Frank was content to be satisfied with his achievement: "Your response to T. R. Smith's criticism of *Holiday* is so amazingly in tune with my own intuition that I am strengthened. The line you quote accurately from memory 'It is your wound John' appears to me the fulcrum and climax of the entire work: and that you should so light on it corroborates my feeling of success. Smith's reaction is merely valuable as an indication of what other 'intelligent' persons will say. . . . The point is simply that the vile current realistic novel has spoiled all minds for the essential and pure lines of aesthetic form: they can't see anything except smudges: a true fine pencil stroke or brush-stroke makes no mark upon their retinas." Waldo Frank to Jean Toomer, Summer, 1923, Beinecke Library, Yale University.

60. Jean Toomer to Sherwood Anderson, 18 December 1922, Beinecke Library, Yale University.

61. "[Anderson] lacked the spiritual power to hoist himself wholly into a more essential plane: the plane in which the materials of the phenomenal world are recreated into pure aesthetic forms. He is indeed more of a transitional artist than Dreiser. His work doesn't belong to the category of powerful reflective artists, nor yet does it win a place among the creators of sheer dynamic form. . . . His writing remains still a harbinger, rather than an experience of Emerging Greatness." Waldo Frank, "Emerging Greatness," in *Salvos: An Informal Book about Books and Plays* (New York: Boni and Liveright, 1924), 40.

62. Jean Toomer to Waldo Frank, 12 December 1922, Beinecke Library, Yale University.

63. See Charles Scruggs, "The Mark of Cain and the Redemption of Art: A Study in Theme and Structure of Jean Toomer's *Cane,"* *American Literature* 44 (May, 1972): 276–91.

64. Rudolph P. Byrd, *Jean Toomer's Years with Gurdjieff: Portrait of an Artist, 1923–36* (Athens: University of Georgia Press, 1990), 17.

65. Ibid., 19.

66. Toomer, *Cane,* 137–38.

67. Peters calls attention to the fact that *"Camera Work* critics, and Stieglitz himself, often stressed geometry as a means to attain universal truth in modern art—whether through objectivity or abstraction." To illustrate the point, Peters provides a representative, yet extensive list of articles that appeared in *Camera Work.* As she concludes, "What all these citations suggest is that objectivity as a methodology came to mean geometric forms in composition and, quite frequently, in subject matter as well." Peters, *Becoming O'Keeffe,* 132.

68. Rudolph Byrd concludes, for example, "Why does Bona leave? It seems that she is more at home with ambiguity than with the truth. Paul's exchange with the doorman provides Bona with indisputable truth of his mixed ancestry, of his blackness, and, equally important, proof of his refusal to deny it. Paul's uncompromising stance changes everything. Bona abandons him because she is bound completely to a tradition that forbids a white woman to feel anything but revulsion and superiority for black men and that scornfully terms intimacy between blacks and whites as miscegenation." Byrd, *Jean Toomer's Years with Gurdjieff,* 22.

69. Susan Blake, "The Spectatorial Artist and the Structure of *Cane,"* *CLA Journal* 17 (June 1974): 516.

70. Jean Toomer to Waldo Frank, c. 11 November 1922, Beinecke Library, Yale University.

71. Byrd, *Jean Toomer's Year's with Gurdjieff,* 23–24.

72. Toomer, *Cane,* 218.

73. Robert Bone, *The Negro Novel in America* (New Haven: Yale University Press), 87.

74. Toomer, *Cane,* 224.

75. Blake, "The Spectatorial Artist," 533.

76. Jean Toomer, undated commentary, Beinecke Library, Yale University. As Toomer would later write, "The modern world was uprooted, the modern world was breaking down, but we couldn't go back. There was nothing to go back to . . . such peasantry as America had—and I sang one of its swan songs in Cain [*sic*] was swiftly disappearing, swiftly being industrialized and urbanized by machines, motor cars, phonographs, movies. . . . Back to nature, even if desirable, was no longer possible, because industry had taken nature unto itself. Even if he wanted to, a city person could not become a soil person by changing his locale and living on a farm or in the woods. . . . Those who sought to cure themselves by a return to more primitive conditions were either romantics or escapists." Jean Toomer, *On Being an American-Autobiography* (unpublished ms.), 19 November 1934, Beinecke Library, Yale University, 45.

77. Jean Toomer to Joel Spingarn, 2 November 1923, Spingarn Collection, New York Public Library.

78. As Toomer wrote to Frank,

Sherwood Anderson has doubtless had a very deep and beautiful emotion by way of the Negro. Here and there he has succeeded in expressing this. But he is not satisfied. He wants more. He is hungry for it. I come along. I express it. It is natural for him to see me in terms of this expression. I see myself that way. But also I see myself expressing myself, expressing Life. I expect artists to recognize the circle of expression. When they don't, I'm not disappointed, I simply know that in this respect they are second-rate. That in this respect they differ but little from the mass which must narrow and caricature if it is to grasp the thing at all. . . . The range of his sensitivity, curiosity, and intelligence is not very wide. One's admiration suffers, but one's personal liking need not be affected by this.

Jean Toomer to Waldo Frank, undated, Beinecke Library, Yale University.

79. Peters, *Becoming O'Keeffe*, 45.

80. As Toomer wrote to Frank:

There is one thing about the Negro in America which most thoughtful persons seem to ignore: the Negro is in solution, in the process of solution. As an entity, the race is losing its body, and its soul is approaching a common soul. If one hold his eyes to individuals and sections, race is starkly evident, and racial continuity seems assured. One is even led to believe that the thing we call Negro beauty will always be attributable to a clearly defined physical source. But the fact is that if anything comes up now pure Negro, it will be a swan-song. Don't let us fool ourselves brother: the Negro of the folksong has all but passed away: the Negro of the emotional church is fading. A hundred years from now these Negroes, if they exist at all, will live in art. And I believe that a vague sense of this fact is the driving force behind the art movements directed towards them today (likewise the Indian). America needs these elements. They are passing. Let us grab and hold them while there still is time.

Jean Toomer to Waldo Frank, undated, Beinecke Library, Yale University.

81. Jean Toomer to Waldo Frank, undated letter, Beinecke Library, Yale University, 4–5.

82. Jean Toomer, "Notebook" (1923–24), 6, Beinecke Library, Yale University.

83. Kerman and Eldridge, *The Lives of Jean Toomer*, 115.

84. Jean Toomer, *Outline of the Story of the Autobiography In Eight Books or Chapters*, Beinecke Library, Yale University, 55.

85. Jean Toomer, *Notebook*, (Book 1), Beinecke Library, Yale University, 8–9.

86. Toomer, "The Negro Emergent," (Unpublished Manuscript), Beinecke Library, Yale University, 2.

87. "Nor is it necessary to give a detailed account of those forms and forces which arise from the nature of our civilization and are common to Americans, for these have received

extended treatment: their features and effects are familiar to everyone. The chaos and strain of these times, the lack of a functioning religion, religious pretense and charlatanism, the reaction from these to materialism, industrialism, the ideal of material success, a devitalizing puritanism, herd psychology, the premium placed on individuality, the stupidities, lies, and superstitions . . . in general, all these elements be grouped under the head of environmental influences as opposed to essential nature." Ibid, 5–6.

88. Ibid., 4.

89. "Precisely what, however, do I mean by emergent? Do I mean that the Negro is escaping or trying to escape from these things, that he denies their existence in him and is seeking to forget them? On the contrary, for the first time the Negro is fully recognizing that they do exist in him: this constitutes one aspect of his discovery . . . but, in both cases detachment is possible. The Negro is emerging to a place where he can see just what these factors are, the extent to which he has merely reacted to their stimuli, the extent to which he has been controlled by them. In a sense, he is adjusting to this feature of his reality. Further, he is discovering a self, an essence, interior to this crust-compound." Ibid., 6.

90. Ibid., 7.

91. In *The American Negro* Herskovits argued that the amalgamation "of the principal racial elements of which humanity is composed—White, Negro and Mongoloid" is forming a distinct race in America. This race is "a definite physical type which may be called the American Negro. It is not like any type from which it has come; it is not White; it is not Negro; it is not Mongoloid. It is all of them, and none of them." Herskovits, *The American Negro*, 19.

92. Jean Toomer, "Race Problems and Modern Society," c. 1928, Beinecke Library, Yale University, 9.

93. Toomer, "The Negro Emergent" Beinecke Library, Yale University, 10.

94. His initial remarks suggested that the reason *Transatlantic* was turned down for publication hinged upon a recent review of *Cane* in *"Les Nouvelles Litteraires"* that "called me a black poet, grouping me with [Eric] Walrond and [Claude] McKay." These thoughts, in turn, brought to mind "the difficulty caused by my being associated with Negro." As a result he cursed "the men at the French Line, *Cane*, Waldo Frank, [and] myself." Jean Toomer, Notebook, entry for (September 20, 1929), Beinecke Library, Yale University.

95. As Toomer wrote,

> A strong yes, a strong no,
> With these we move and make a drama,
> Yet may say nothing of the goal.
> Black is black, white is white,
> East is east, west is west,
> Is truth for the mind of contrasts;
> But here the high way of the third,
> The man of blue or purple,
> Beyond the little tags and small marks,
> Foretold by ancient seers who knew,
> Not the place, not the name, not the time,
> But the aim of life in men,
> The resultant of yes and no
> Struggling for birth through ages.

Jean Toomer, "Blue Meridian," in *The Collected Poems of Jean Toomer*, ed. Robert B. Jones and Margery Toomer Latimer (Chapel Hill: University of North Carolina Press, 1988), 72.

96. From "Blue Meridian":

> Unlock the races, Open this pod by outgrowing it,
> Free men from this prison and this shrinkage,
> Not from the reality itself
> But from our prejudices and preferences
> And the enslaving behavior caused by them,
> Eliminate these—
> I am, we are, simply of the human race.

Ibid., 64.

97. Ibid., 71.

98. "On the stage of Leslie Hall [1924] he [Toomer] had witnessed, to his amazement and satisfaction, the choreographed expression of a philosophical system [the Gurdjieff system] whose theories and methods would extend, clarify, and give greater authority to the themes and concerns first propounded in *Cane*." Byrd, *Jean Toomer's Years with Gurdjieff*, 70.

99. As Pound wrote in his poem, "A Pact," it was Whitman who had broken "the new wood" and now it was time "for carving"—time for Pound to acknowledge this debt. Ezra Pound, *12 American Poets*, ed. Stephen Whicher and Lars Ahnebrink (New York: Oxford University Press, 1961), 135.

100. To help show the influence of Toomer on later writers, Byrd notes that Alice Walker's novel *Meridian* and her heroine, Meridian Hill, relate in name and spirit to Meridian Hill Park where Toomer often went to look out over Washington, DC and the hills of Virginia. It was also from this vantage point that Toomer wrote to Frank regarding America's need for their work, and in this letter Toomer imagined a statue of Whitman occupying a commanding view of the panorama below: "I am on Meridian Hill. The city lies beneath me. As the sun peels off its haze, the capitol dome, Washington's monuments, and the wireless towers of Arlington become distinct. . . . Really a wonderful place for Walt Whitman. I'd love to see him here, rising out of some great granite block." Jean Toomer to Waldo Frank, undated letter, University of Pennsylvania, 1, 3. George Hutchinson more generally observes that, "Whitman's legacy to the African American literary tradition remains a largely unexplored topic." Hutchinson, "The Whitman Legacy and the Harlem Renaissance," in *Walt Whitman*, ed. Ed Folsom (Iowa City: University of Iowa Press, 1994), 201–16.

101. Locke, "Self-Criticism: The Third Dimension in Culture," *Phylon* 2 (1950): 392.

102. Ibid.

103. Ibid., 392–93.

104. Nathan Huggins, "The Alain L. Locke Symposium," *Harvard Advocate* (December 1973): 11.

Chapter 7

"My Soul Was with the Gods and My Body in the Village": Zora Neale Hurston, Franz Boas, Melville Herskovits, and Ruth Benedict

In August 1927, Zora Neale Hurston posed with Langston Hughes and Jessie Fauset at the foot of the statue of Booker T. Washington on the campus of Tuskegee Normal and Industrial Institute in Tuskegee, Alabama. Now, after six months of collecting African American folklore—customs, games, jokes, lies, songs, superstitions, and tales—Hurston was ready to return to New York City and to finish her Bachelor of Arts in anthropology at Barnard. She had left New York City the previous February and had spent most of her time in and around her home town of Eatonville and Tallahassee, Florida before driving across the Florida panhandle to Mobile, Alabama. There she interviewed Cudjo Lewis, reputed to be the only living survivor of the last ship to bring slaves from Africa to America.[1] By chance, Hurston also met Hughes, who had just arrived in Mobile by train from New Orleans. Soon after, she and Hughes drove up to Tuskegee, joined Fauset to lecture to summer students, then continued on their way to New York City.[2]

If Washington had been able to peer over the veil of ignorance he was lifting from the young man kneeled before him, he would have looked with mixed emotions upon the three Harlem literati grouped below. Not only did all three represent, intellectually and aesthetically, a consciousness he had little use for, but they brought to Tuskegee traces of a past Washington had long struggled to come to terms with. In 1906, for example, Washington informed J. C. Hamilton [the Canadian anthropologist] that he would not be able to write an introduction to his book:

Frankly, I do not believe there is much interest in speculation as to the future of the Negro based upon anthropology and ethnology, and my experience has led me to believe that such discussions are neither valuable nor helpful in the solution of the practical problems in which we in the South are engaged. . . . What is needed now, I believe, is first hand information which will let us a little deeper into the secret of what these people have thought and felt and done, in short not speculation, but history.[3]

Now here was Hurston, a student of anthropology under the guidance of Franz Boas, the most famous anthropologist in America, speaking of her work to the students of Tuskegee. Hughes, as well, in part because of Hurston's encouragement, had also come South to research folk material.[4]

Perhaps Washington would have been less dismissing of anthropology if he had been more aware of the broad attack Boas and his students were making on (1) the scientific racism that served to legitimize discrimination in America and (2) the emphasis on history to challenge evolutionary theories used to argue for the biological inferiority of African Americans. To complicate matters, however, Boas was also closely linked with Washington's formidable rival, W.E.B. Du Bois, who had already invited Boas to Atlanta University to give the commencement address at the spring graduation (May 31, 1906).[5] As a consequence, so as to undermine Du Bois's growing prestige, Washington made every effort to suppress the reporting of Boas's speech in the black press.[6] And now, not only was Jessie Fauset, Du Bois's personal secretary and literary editor of the *Crisis*, in Hurston's company, but Hughes had just given the commencement address the previous month at Fisk, Du Bois's alma mater.

Despite Washington's best efforts to suppress Boas's speech, it began to have a life of its own, circulating in wider and wider circles, and no one was more diligent in promoting this speech than Boas himself. In particular, he sought to gain the attention and the favor of Northern white philanthropists.[7] His motive was money: "I am endeavoring to organize certain scientific work on the Negro race which I believe will be of great practical value in regard to the Negro problem."[8] With this money, Boas was hopeful that "some students of . . . anthropology would become interested in the importance of these problems."[9] Although little money was immediately forthcoming, these efforts represent the genesis of support that led to Hurston's work with Melville Herskovits in Harlem in the summer of 1926, her presence at Tuskegee in 1927, and her return to the South in December of that same year.[10]

Hurston's return to the South began in Mobile, another interview with Cudjo Lewis, and then turned east to Eatonville and, soon after, Longhman in Polk County, Florida. By the time she returned to New York City and "Papa Franz" two years and three months later (March 1930), Hurston had also traveled to New Orleans, Miami, and the Bahamas. These years of collecting were a great success, culminating in two articles that appeared in the *Journal of American Folklore:* "Dance Songs and Tales from the Bahamas" in the July-September, 1930 issue and "Hoodoo in America" in the October-December 1931 issue. Later she revised and expanded this latter article into her first book, *Mules and Men*, the first collection of African American folklore published by an African American. Boas was so impressed with Hurston's collecting that he strongly urged her to begin study with him for a doctorate in anthropology.[11]

In his fine biography, *Zora Neale Hurston: A Literary Biography* (1977), Robert E. Hemenway has carefully documented this formative period of Hurston's scholarly life. As he writes, "[The] five months between August and December of 1928 was a dramatic time for Hurston, transforming her from an enthusiastic artist-folklorist into a mature, thoughtful scholar."[12] At the same time, Hemenway has also marked the creative turn that marks these years:

As she organized her field notes during 1930-32, she conceptualized black folklore, exploring the ways black history affected folk narratives, hypothesizing about racial characteristics in traditional communication. This mature conception of folklore changed only slightly over the years, and it antedates her best work as an artist. Even though her first novel [*Jonah's Gourd Vine* (1934)] was published prior to *Mules and Men* (1935), it was written after she had completed the folklore research. In a sense her career as a folklorist ended when she finished with her field notes, and after the fall of 1932 she usually conceived of herself as a creative writer—even when writing about folklore.[13]

To help explain this transitional period, Hurston's emergence as a major literary and dramatic talent, Hemenway situates Hurston within two competing intellectual and imaginative approaches to the apprehension and rendering of experience: anthropology and art.[14] As a consequence, Hemenway argues, Hurston felt constrained as well as stimulated by Boas:

Hurston's ambivalence about folklore study grew from her dual identity between 1925 and 1927 as a serious academic and active creative artist. Before going to the field in 1927, she had relatively little difficulty in maintaining both identities. Once removed from the abstractions of the anthropology books, confronted with the reality of a Cudjo Lewis, she had to make choices. The type of reportorial precision required of the scientific folklorist bored Hurston; she was used to assimilating the aura of a place and letting that stimulus provoke her imagination. Neither Boas nor Carter Woodson was that interested in her impressions; they wanted the facts as she had collected them.[15]

Although it was Hurston's genius ultimately to find her own voice, the tensions with which she struggled between impressions and facts were themselves built into the paradigm of culture that Boas himself presented to his students. As Margaret Mead has written, "We lived, in a sense, lives in which the arts and sciences fought uneven battles for pre-eminence."[16] Whether anthropology is best understood as a science, an art, or both remains an ongoing question. Of Boas's students, however, it is Ruth Benedict who most successfully brought this tension to creative fruition. As Barbara A. Babcock writes, "Much too much has been written both pro and con about *Patterns of Culture* in relation to culture and personality; many scholars regard the book as little more than a rendering of those ideas with regrettable generalization and over-statement into readable and accessible terms—'Psychological Types' and 'Configurations of Culture' writ large. Much less has been said about the literary and philosophical pre-texts of *Patterns of Culture* or about the fact that this is the book of a poet, a philosopher, and a feminist as well as an anthropologist."[17] Years later, Boas would remark admiringly of Benedict's supple prose that "he wished he could write as well."

Important and inspiring as Boas was for Hurston, there were others who were also important, influenced her work, and with whom she confided. In addition to Boas, Hemenway gave considerable attention to Hurston's relationship with Locke and Hughes.[18] But with Benedict, Boas's colleague at Columbia University, Hemenway merely noted that "as [Hurston] came under the influence of Ruth Benedict, Gladys Reichard, and Franz Boas of Columbia's anthropology department, her image of herself as a writer dimmed."[19] Hemenway then quickly went on to document Hurston's deep respect for the man whom she called "the greatest anthropologist alive" and "king of kings." The following two letters written during Hurston's first trip south, however, help to suggest that, for Hurston, Benedict was a figure of considerable importance in her own right.

In the first letter, Hurston wrote to Boas about her arrival in Jacksonville (March 29, 1927) and her meeting with Carter G. Woodson, who was there for a conference for Negro History Week. Nothing is said of Woodson himself or the conference, but Hurston did inform Boas as to what she had thus far collected. In particular, Hurston noted that she had discovered some objects used in conjuring as well as a former slave who was a master carver. What gave these discoveries special significance was her concern that these skills, which linked her people with their African past, and even their appreciation as cultural artifacts were rapidly fading from cultural memory. In contrast with African Americans, Hurston ventured that American Indians had less contact with white culture and for this reason continued to lead a more authentic life. As a consequence, their past remained an ongoing part of their living present.[20]

In the second letter, Hurston offered to Benedict a more personal account of her efforts to explore the past of African Americans and the problems she met and sought to overcome. Above all, she encountered the resistance of local black folk who suspected her motives and claimed that the information she sought only perpetuated the stigma of slavery. Motivated by what Hurston thought to be their false sense of race consciousness and race pride, she was confronted by individuals who wanted her to write about local success stories, the school principal for example, and not about issues they claimed only served to confirm the stereotypes whites had of blacks.[21] Discouraging as this was, Hurston reserved her greatest frustration, even scorn, for Carter G. Woodson, who had just given a formal address to the Negro Historical Society. If a false sense of race consciousness served to make blacks ashamed of their past, the answer was not to invent a glorious past simply to assuage or massage popular opinion but to educate people to appreciate what had actually taken place. For this reason, Hurston valued so highly the work of Boas and felt disgusted with Woodson who "dish[ed] up the old race superiority stuff . . . dragging emperors, queens, statesmen, wholesale into the colored race."[22] Although Hurston was not likely to criticize Woodson to Boas—Woodson had financed her research trip in great part because of Boas's strong endorsement—it is clear that Hurston felt that she could confide in Benedict and that Benedict was an authority whom Hurston respected. In closing, Hurston alerted Benedict to some snapshots she had included so that Benedict could visualize the stories that Hurston had to tell. If questions still needed to be answered, Hurston noted that she had written on the back of each photo so as to provide direction.[23]

Hurston's letters to Benedict extend to the year prior to Benedict's death in 1948. In June 1945, Hurston wrote to Benedict from her houseboat, *Sun Tan,* in Daytona Beach, Florida, indicating her desire to go Honduras. She wondered whether Benedict herself, or Dr. [Otto] Klinberg, might not soon follow, and she concluded with an observation that Benedict would richly appreciate—her conviction that men were less interested in the facts than in what they wanted to believe.[24] Two years later, and now in Honduras, Hurston detailed three areas of interest that she hoped might entice Benedict and/or Dr. [Gladys] Reichard, to "see your way to come down": (1) the Black Caribs, (2) the Zamboes, and (3) the Icagues. The Caribs were especially interesting in that they were "a stable ethnic unit," comprised of Carib, Arawak, and Negro, and they lived "in their own crude pueblos."[25] Clearly, Ruth Benedict played a role in Hurston's life that has been overshadowed by the profound influence, and the attention to this influence, that Boas had on Hurston and on all of his students.

Any assessment of Benedict's importance must first take note of the more general status of women in anthropology in the early decades of the twentieth century. As Nancy J. Parezo has argued in *Hidden Scholars: Women Anthropologists and the Native American Southwest* (1993), "of all the sciences anthropology has the reputation for being most open to women scholars."[26] But this reputation, though not without some basis in fact, did not deny the more general fact that, since its inception, anthropology, like the other social sciences, had been "male-dominated and male-oriented."[27] As a consequence, though generally understood to be "one of this century's truly outstanding anthropologists," Benedict confronted problems that others faced as well. However, given these obstacles and the limited number of women then teaching, indeed for these very reasons, Benedict's presence and accomplishments were all the more impressive.[28] To some extent, then, Benedict's significance for Hurston was as much symbolic as it was the result of specific moments of personal and professional contact. It was a symbolism, however, whose meanings ranged from pursuing a career in anthropology (a career that surpassed marriage in personal fulfillment), the use of language that, in the words of Margaret Mead, made anthropology "available to the man on the street,"[29] and the crafting of a style of writing that bridged what Hemenway called Hurston's "dual identity between 1925 and 1927 as serious academic and active creative artist."

When Hurston first encountered Benedict, she was a lecturer in anthropology at Columbia University, a colleague of Boas, and a teacher of a course at Barnard together with Margaret Mead. Already she had written a series of articles in various magazines (*American Mercury, Century, Harpers, Nation, New Republic,* and *Scribner's*) to help popularize the meaning and significance of culture. She was also editor of the prestigious *Journal of American Folklore* and a newly elected member of the Council of the American Anthropological Association. Most important, though, is that Benedict had begun to explore the seminal ideas that would ultimately find their fullest expression in her immensely popular and influential *Patterns of Culture.*

In 1928, Benedict presented her ground-breaking article, "Psychological Types in the Culture of the Southwest," to the International Congress of Americanists, in which she addressed the question of mental phenomena and conceptualized this phenomena as patterned constructs of emotion specific to a people's way of life:

All our efforts to trace out the influences from other areas [in the Southwest] are impressive for the fragmentariness of the detail; we find bits of the weft or woof of the culture, we do not find any very significant clues to its pattern. From the point of view of the present paper this clue is to be found in a fundamental psychological set which has undoubtedly been established for centuries in the culture of this region, and which has bent to its own uses any details it imitated from surrounding peoples and has created an intricate cultural pattern to express its own preferences. It is not only that the understanding of this psychological set is necessary for a descriptive statement of this culture; without it the cultural dynamics of this region are unintelligible.[30]

Benedict's conceptual breakthrough centered on the understanding that these mental or psychological patterns were themselves rooted in visionary or spiritual experiences. Thus, beginning with her article "The Vision in Plains Culture" (March 1922) and continuing throughout the 1920s with her studies of folklore and mythology, Benedict had initiated a line of thinking wherein culture was ultimately understood to be the outward expression of a deeply imagined core of values unique to a people's collective existence. At the same time, as Margaret Caffrey has argued, Benedict's study of the "vision quest and the guardian spirit complex in which the vision was fundamental" also served to stimulate thoughts as to her own identity and the tension she felt between her deepest intellectual and emotional nature and the values of her culture. As a consequence, Benedict's anthropological writings, stimulated as well by her writings as a poet, are a complex mix of cultural observation and self-discovery. Finally, Benedict, as did Boas, turned her attention to the racism that marked her own discipline as well as the larger society.[31] In "The Science of Custom: The Bearing of Anthropology on Contemporary Thought," for example, she linked her theoretical formulations of culture with an attack on racial prejudice and the prejudice that race was scientifically meaningful.[32]

Hurston did not need Benedict's arguments to convince her that "black people [were] complete, complex, undiminished human beings," though she would certainly have been pleased with her use of anthropology to critique biological explanations of cultural identity.[33] But in making her case, in what was to become the first chapter of *Patterns of Culture*, Benedict raised challenging theoretical questions that would distinguish her own work as well as that of Hurston. Again, images of vision are conceptually important, but now they serve to call attention to the very conceptions that inform one's understanding. Thus, to critique race as an explanatory concept as well as to validate the diversity and integrity of various cultures, Benedict emphasizes the limits of human perception—no man ever looks at the world with pristine eyes" and "[he] sees it edited by a definite set of customs and institutions and ways of thinking." In effect, we are all culture bound, blind to the ways of others as well as the boundaries of our own ways of thinking. But to complicate the matter, the very boundaries that shape one's vision are themselves the means to see others. Custom, Benedict writes, is "the lens without which [social theorists] could not see at all" but which, because it is so fundamental, "had its existence outside the field of conscious attention." As a consequence, there is a need for individuals "who can see objectively the socially conditioned behaviour of other peoples." There is no less a need for individuals to question themselves, to confront the blindness that conditioned one's own way of seeing.

Benedict's attention to the indispensability, yet invisibility, of one's own cultural grounding as well as the self-reflexivity of the observer echoed in Hurston's introduction to *Mules and Men*. Thus, Hurston notes that with "the spy-glass of Anthropology" she was now able not only to see herself "like somebody else" but also her native surroundings that previously had fit "like a tight chemise" and thus "I couldn't see it for wearing it." Like Benedict, Hurston attempted to use this awareness and self awareness to advantage, to help provide the distance that would allow her to see up close the "capers of Brer Rabbit" and "the Squinch Owl" atop the house. At the same time, Hurston also called attention to her own presence in her work as she began to discover not only those she observed but herself as well. For if anthropology was to provide insight into those out of sight, clearly one had to look at least in two directions: to discover the "other," it was no less necessary to uncover one's presence as well. In so doing, it was also necessary to discover the "other" within. To do this, Hurston, no less than Benedict, employed images of vision and seeing.

In the critical awakening in our own time to the Harlem Renaissance, Hurston herself has moved from the margins of invisibility to the focus of critical attention. Thus, whereas Darwin Turner placed Hurston in a book titled *In a Minor Chord*, Henry Louis Gates has more recently observed,

Of the various signs that the study of literature in America has been transformed, none is more salient than the resurrection and canonization of Zora Neale Hurston. Twenty years ago, Hurston's work was largely out of print, her literary legacy alive only to a tiny, devoted band of readers who were often forced to photocopy her works if they were to be taught. . . . Today her works are central to the canon of African-American, American, and Women's literatures. Last year at Yale alone, seventeen courses taught *Their Eyes Were Watching God*![34]

Central to the centrality of this canonization has been the discovery of Hurston's spellbinding use of language and her ear for the language of a "loquacious" and "bodacious" people.[35]

No one, perhaps, has been more brilliant than Gates himself in locating Hurston within an African American oral/narrative tradition and providing a close reading of Hurston's rhetorical strategies (what Gates calls the "Speakerly Text") "designed to represent an oral literary tradition" that "produce[s] the illusion of oral narration."[36] Other important readings of Hurston that amplify Gates's essential point include Houston A. Baker, Jr.'s *Blues, Ideology and Afro-American Literature: A Vernacular Theory* (1984), and Eric J. Sundquist's more recent *The Hammers of Creation: Folk Culture in Modern African-American Fiction* (1993).

At the same time, Hurston's work has been immensely important to a wide range of feminist readers who have also made language central to their exploration of Hurston's historical and cultural importance. Cynthia Bond, for example, emphatically states in "Language, Speech, and Difference in *Their Eyes Were Watching God*" the general consensus that "Hurston's expertise at dialect writing is indisputable, and her recognition of the cultural significance of the black oral tradition is central to her work."[37] Little wonder that critical readings of Hurston's work have primarily focused on her gift for language and her ear for what others said and how they said it. Thus, beginning with Alice Walker's early need for "Hurston's work sometime before I knew Her work existed," and extending through the more recent critical work of Hazel Carby, Nellie McKay, Mary Helen Washington, and Deborah McDowell (to name but a few of her critical readers), Zora Neale Hurston now speaks to an audience throughout the world.

By privileging language, recent critical interpretation has itself not only recognized this "Genius of the South" but affirmed through Hurston a distinctive African American cultural identity. At the same time, in giving attention to Hurston's attention to the art and artifice of telling "lies" (hers as well as those of others), critical opinion has both discovered and celebrated in her prose cultural webs first spun in the storied landscapes of West Africa. Thus, in contrast with the privileging of vision in Western culture as the superior or the primary of the senses, Hurston is understood to represent a counter tradition whose vernacular origins trace back to the conjurers of Nigeria (the Yoruba) and the praise singers of Benin and Dahomey.[38] As Houston A. Baker, Jr., writes of *Mules and Men,* "The work [a *locus classicus* for black women's creativity] assumes this status through its *instantiation* (a word that marks time and suggests place) of the conjure woman as a peculiar imagistic, Afro-American space. Hurston's collection constitutes a locational moment of perception and half-creation within the space comprised by the voodoo doctor, the hoodoo fixer, the two headed bearer of wisdom in Afro-America."[39] Although Hurston has indeed been "a *locus classicus* of black women's creativity," not all women have discovered in her language quite the same resources Baker has revealed. At the same time, there is a tension in Hurston's writings between language and vision wherein images of vision have served to configure as well as challenge the cultural space she inherited at birth.

In Cynthia Bond's reading of Hurston, the linguistic self-reflexivity that Gates as well as Baker broadly celebrate as African American is more narrowly seen as "an essentially male signifying tradition." As a consequence, Bond discerns in

Hurston's work a distinction between a textual tradition and a speakerly tradition so as to establish a context that now includes the voice of women. Even more critically, Mary Helen Washington argues that Hurston's ambivalence about the freedom possible within the traditions and narrative boundaries of the community extended to an ambivalence about language itself.[40] Thus, Washington points out that Janie's advice to Phoeby in *Their Eyes Were Watching God*—"Talkin' don't amunt tuh uh hill uh beans when you can't do nothin else . . . Phoeby you got tuh *go* there tuh *know* there."—challenges the assumption that language per se translates into meaningful inclusion and self-fulfillment.[41]

At the same time, the emphasis on language has obscured visual strategies that Hurston, as well as others before her, both appealed to and employed. Hurston, after all, did arm herself with the "spy glass of Anthropology."[42] Seven years earlier, Alain Locke argued in *The New Negro* that, for one to understand the changes taking place among African Americans, it was necessary "that the Negro of to-day be seen through other than the dusty spectacles of past controversy."[43] And at the turn of the century, in *The Souls of Black Folk*, W.E.B. Du Bois framed the problematic of an African American identity as the result of the "peculiar sensation...of always looking at one's self through the eyes of others."[44] Clearly, Hurston's spy-glass was a novel and appropriate metaphor, but it was not without precedent. As with Locke's and Du Bois's visual concerns, it gathered light from the vision of Franz Boas to help illuminate new ways to see and present African Americans. But more than methodology is involved. For with Hurston, as with Benedict, vision both opened onto and drew upon cultural worlds beyond the horizons of those who, as Hurston phrased it, were "parched up from not knowin' things."[45]

Upon returning to Eatonville, Hurston imagined herself returning to the world of her childhood, a time when tales were told of "Brer Fox, Brer Deer . . . Ole Massa and his wife . . . walking the earth." Little had changed, "same love and talk of song." Before she could get out of her car, Calvin Daniels rushed to tell her "a tale 'bout John and de frog." Not only were tales of the past exchanged in the present but the telling of "lies" was itself a tradition that continued to voice as well as shape the ongoing life of the community. Thus, language fused the everyday with all the days, the factual with the fabulous. Language itself, the music of imagination and myth, linked the present not only with the past but with the time when God walked the earth and talked with men. As Hurston reveals, however, those who voiced the collective memory as well as the collective present were predominately the "men folks" who gathered on the porch of Joe Clarke's store. Although "the women folks" would occasionally enter in, they were to be more seen than heard. As a consequence, in her efforts to record the tales and language of her people, Hurston gave special attention to the responses of women to the "lies" they, at least, were allowed to hear.[46]

In effect, Hurston could see that in her own status as a woman and as an outsider she shared common experiences and common feelings. At the same time, in her recording as well as her observing, Hurston became increasingly conscious that her own identity was both a reflection upon as well as a reflection of those she had come south to hear and see. For these reasons, Cheryl A. Wall has argued that the persona of the narrator, first introduced as "Lucy Hurston's daughter, Zora," becomes throughout the text more an individual in her own right, more the active participant and less the outside observer until in the final section of *Mules and Men*, "Hoodoo," she "is completely transformed."[47] Although the extent and nature of this transformation is somewhat unclear, Wall suggests an important perspective to help unify the work as a whole.

In an effort to focus dramatically the thematic concerns of the text and "Zora's" relationship to these concerns, as well as to legitimate their embodiment in the strong figure of "the hard-living, knife-toting" Big Sweet, Hurston brilliantly constructed a sermon, 'Behold de Rib,' to argue for female equality. As Wall concludes, "The purposeful selection of "Behold de Rib" allows her both to celebrate a verbal art she greatly admired and to register a protest against the tradition that shaped it, a tradition that for the most part neither welcomed women's participation nor fostered their equality."[48] Although Wall makes a persuasive case for the centrality and significance of this sermon, she only quotes the last third, beginning with the line "So God put Adam into a deep sleep." But Hurston's protest is initially developed in terms of images of vision and sight in the first two-thirds of the sermon. In other words, Wall fails to address Hurston's ocular emphasis that prepares the reader as well as the listeners for the emergence of "wo-man" from the side of Adam.

The sermon begins with an explanation of its title, "Behold means to look and see." For us to "Look at this woman God done made," though, it is first necessary, we are told, "to gaze upon God's previous works." And gaze we do, as the preacher lays before us the wonders that God has created. Not only do we see his works but, "Wid de eye of Faith," we see him at work:

I can see him
Standing out on de eaves of ether
Breathing clouds from out his nostrils,
Blowing storms from 'tween his lips
I can see!![49]

After a panoramic view of the physical universe, we are once again inspired to "Behold, and look and see!" before proceeding to see the forms of life God also created. Once surveyed, we are now ready for the entrance of man, the one creature made in the image of God himself. At this point, the refrain "I can see" now gives way to "Behold de rib" which carries to the end of the sermon.

Although the sermon draws upon religious and vernacular traditions familiar to people in the audience, its message, the equality of women, is delivered by a traveling preacher (a "stump-knocker") who leaves the community as soon as the collection plate has been passed. In other words, the message of equality, an unorthodox reading of Genesis 2:21, could only be voiced by someone who lived outside the boundaries of Polk County.[50]

Likewise, the emphasis on vision carries the audience beyond the horizons of their immediate verbal world to glimpse a principle that transcends the reach and weight of their voices. This transcending of boundaries helps to prepare us for the world of Hoodoo, part two of *Mules and Men*, in which vision itself spiritually grounds this underground system of belief. In leaving the visible world of Christian faith for the invisible world of Afrocentric illumination, we pass from the rhetorical domain of men to the spiritual legacy of Marie Leveau, the dead priestess of New Orleans.

In her introductory comments on Hoodoo, Hurston notes that "belief in magic is older than writing. So nobody knows how it started."[51] This assertion allows her to fill in the gaps, to link New Orleans, the "hoodoo capital [*sic*] of America," with Haiti and Africa as well as to suggest root connections with the Judeo-Christian tradition. As she writes, "Moses never would have stood before the Burning Bush, if he had not married Jethro's daughter. Jethro was a great hoodoo man.[52] It also suggests that the most authentic way to possess the inner essence of spiritual belief—magic—is neither through reading nor in listening to another individual give voice to the written word.

In New Orleans, Hurston made her way to the French Quarter (the Vieux Carre), where Marie Leveau had lived and died. Here, under the tutelage of Luke Turner, a self-proclaimed nephew of Leveau's who sought to continue her work, she was initiated into Hoodoo. After fasting for three days and nights while lying naked on a snake skin, her own spirit successfully passed into the spirit world. Once accomplished, she was symbolically marked—a lightening symbol was drawn down her back, a sun on her forehead, and a pair of eyes painted on her cheeks "as a sign that I could see in more ways than one."[53] Now ready to assume control of her newly acquired power, Turner lifted her veil and lit "my candle" so that "from then on [she] might be a candle-lighter [her]self."[54] Only at his point in the narrative did Hurston call attention to the ceremonial use of language:

He stood there dazedly while the chant of strange syllables rose. I asked Turner the words, but he replied that in good time I would know what to say. It was not to be taught. If nothing came, to be silent.[55]

In effect, Hurston had entered a world wherein language, while important, was subordinate to vision, was grounded in vision itself, and inspiration, not tradition, prompted what one had to say. The individual, not the community, sanctioned the impulse to speak, and silence was a moral principle as well as a personal choice, not a subordinate status.

Subsequent chapters detail Hurston's deepening immersion in Hoodoo under the tutelage of various mentors. Throughout the remaining pages, ritual ceremonies and symbols of visibility represent thresholds of spiritual enlightenment and empowerment. Under the guidance of Father Watson (the Frizzly Rooster), for example, Hurston became "Boss of Candles," which gave her "the power to light candles and put out candles, and to work with the spirits anywhere on earth."[56]

Simultaneously, however, the text increasingly returns to the more familiar world of language. Not only does Hurston detail the lives and problems of people whom she meets as they seek the healing counsel of master conjurers, but she also interpolates into the text from "Hoodoo," her *Journal of American Folklore* article, the measured voice of the professional anthropologist: "All over the South and in the Bahamas the spirits of the dead have great power which is used chiefly to harm. It will be noted how frequently graveyard dust is required in the practice of hoodoo, goofer dust as it is often called."[57] *Mules and Men* concludes with a final "lie" that returns us to the porch of Joe Clarke's store in Eatonville. The line, "I'm sitting here like Sis Cat washing my face and usin' my manners," links with her comments that introduce the work: "The white man is always trying to know into somebody else's business. All right, I'll set something outside the door of my mind for him to play with and handle. He can read my writing but he sho' can't read my mind."[58] Whether anyone can read Hurston's mind, at least in concluding as she does with the story of Sis Cat, has been the subject of considerable speculation. Houston Baker, for example, argues that Hurston has not only quite consciously challenged the ethnographic authority of Franz Boas, but in so doing has reclaimed this world for those for whom it is a "soul-piece" and not simply the intellectual property of a "dominant, scholarly elite."[59] Barbara Johnson argues more generally, however, that the effort and/or the difficulty to come to terms with this "strange, unglossed final story" is, in fact, the very point Hurston is making—"Hurston suspends the certainty of reference not by erasing these differences [black and white, inside and outside] but by foregrounding the complex dynamism of their interaction."[60] For this reason, Johnson wonders, given the particular story posed, "Who, in the final analysis, has swallowed what?" The reader? Mrs. Mason? Franz Boas? Hurston herself?"[61] Both scholars, however, see Hurston as a master of language, one now confident enough to participate in the language community of Eatonville. This participation, however, would be later. Already, Hurston had set her eyes on a larger world, an extension of the spiritual legacy of Marie Leveau.[62]

While still working on *Mules and Men*, Hurston wrote to Benedict to tell her of thoughts that she had to expand her folkloric research beyond the boundaries of the United States. She had recently met a Mr. Workus who was known as the king of one of the Haitian islands, La Gonave. Given his interest in conjure ceremonies and his skill as a photographer, Hurston noted that they had agreed to collaborate on a comparative study of conjure in the United States and the West Indies.[63] In a handwritten postscript, Hurston added that she was applying for a Guggenheim Fellowship in order to do work in the Bahamas, St. Martinique, the West Indies, and Haiti.[64] In a follow-up letter, Hurston wondered if there was any chance of getting a Rosenwald Fellowship, something that Boas had once suggested to her.[65] Sixteen months later, Hurston again informed Benedict that she had applied for a Guggenheim Fellowship, although she now singled out the West Coast of Africa as her objective and combined this information with the impending publication of *Jonah's Gourd Vine* (1934) for which she wondered if Benedict and Boas might write an advanced review.[66]

Although Hurston would eventually receive a Guggenheim Fellowship, it was not with Benedict's help. In the month prior to her December letter, Benedict wrote in embarrassment to Dr. Henry Allen Moe, director of the Guggenheim Fund: "I am shocked to find Zora Hurston's application in my desk. It had been slipped into the wrong file and overlooked. As you will see from my report on the application I don't think she is Guggenheim material and I hope some of her patrons will provide the money for this trip and that she'll write up her expenses when she returns in collaboration with some anthropologist."[67] Before the award of the Guggenheim Fellowship, however, Hurston was first granted a Rosenwald Fellowship (December 19, 1934) to study anthropology at Columbia University.[68] Anticipating the award, Hurston wrote to Boas with the "Great news!" and coupled this information with an assessment of her commitment to the work that now lay ahead:

Now I realize that this is going to call for rigorous routine and discipline, which every body seems to feel that I need. So be it. I want to do it. I have always wanted to do it and nobody will have any trouble about my applying myself. I wonder if it ought not to be taken into consideration that I have been on my own since fourteen years old and went to high school, college . . . because I wanted to, and not because I was being pushed? All of these things have been done under most trying circumstances and I stuck. . . . But oh, Dr. Boas, you dont know how I have longed for a chance to stay at Columbia and study. Otherwise there would be no point to my using every thing possible to get this scholarship.[69]

Within two weeks, however, these plans began to unravel. Hurston still expressed to Boas that she would prefer to study at Columbia, but if Boas thought it best she would be willing to go to Northwestern University to study with Herskovits.[70]

Since Hurston had helped Herskovits with his anthropological measuring in Harlem in 1926, they had not seen each other for over ten years.[71] Recently, however, Herskovits had reentered her life and, now that Boas suggested she study in Evanston, Hurston wrote to Herskovits, who had just returned from Haiti, to tell him of her newly formulated plans.[72] After first explaining why Columbia would not be the best place for her to train for Haiti, Hurston joyfully proposed that they collaborate as well as travel together. Given her two-year fellowship, which allowed her a summer in Haiti and a following summer in Martinique, Hurston saw the two of them providing in their writing information that was desperately needed in America.[73] Herskovits replied, expressing his great pleasure that she would be studying at Northwestern, informed her of class times and offerings, but suggested that without a knowledge of French her work in Haiti and Martinique would not likely be successful.[74]

Herskovits's pleasure and Hurston's plans, however, quickly evaporated. Not only did graduate study prove to be impossible but the Rosenwald Fellowship itself was soon lost as well, restructured to end in June 1935. Worried, and feeling ill, Hurston wrote to Benedict from Benedict's desk that the strain of the Rosenwald Fund was especially worrisome.[75] Three months later, however, Hurston was in Belle Glade, Florida, helping Alan Lomax collect materials in the Everglades. In a letter to Benedict, Hurston detailed the various kinds of folk expressions she and Lomax were collecting with his newly acquired tape recorder.[76] Marginal notes to Benedict suggested how she could trace their steps, and Hurston concluded with speculation as to how to provide Boas with much of this valuable collecting.

After abruptly leaving Lomax and returning to New York City, Hurston continued to think of ways to pursue her understanding of Hoodoo and the implications Hoodoo had for the spread and reformulation of African culture in the Carribean and North America. Once again, she proposed to the Guggenheim Foundation to study Obeah practices (magic) in Jamaica and Haiti. This time she was successful. On March 18, she accepted their offer of a fellowship and soon after set sail for Jamaica. Now, her letters are primarily exchanged with Herskovits, their correspondence linking past concerns with the unfolding circumstances of her research and her daily experiences.

Once in Jamaica, Hurston wrote to Herskovits, immediately returning to thoughts of their possible collaboration. Again she stressed the fact that there was virtually no valid anthropological data for those who wished to study black Americans. Only this time, she supported her argument by contrasting the work Boas was doing at Columbia on the American Indian with the work on the American Negro Herskovits had begun at Northwestern. Important as Columbia was under the important leadership of Boas, it was Hurston's experience that Columbia had little to offer in the study of African Americans. Why shouldn't Northwestern become a comparable intellectual center?[77] In the rest of the letter, she indicated that she would soon leave for Haiti and spoke enthusiastically of Jules Faine, who was working on a book that Hurston thought would be a coup for Herskovits if it were to be published by Northwestern University Press.

Herskovits, however, was less than enthusiastic with Hurston's decision to go to Haiti. In part, he stressed that "we must realize that the time has gone when significant work can derive from anything but intensive study in a restricted locality."[78] Thus, he encouraged her to go to the Bahamas, "where you already have a good start." At the same time, he elaborated upon his earlier caution that Haiti presented special problems that might prove insurmountable:

As for work in Haiti, I doubt very much whether you ought to spend much time there. The language presents a considerable hurdle, for to master Creole enough to carry on field work, and by that I mean to be able to converse fluently in it, one must have a very good initial command of French. In addition to this, Haitian culture presents many technical field problems. Since it presents a bewildering amalgam of European and African elements, unless one is thoroughly versed in West African cultures, it is very easy to misinterpret what one sees.[79]

To illustrate the problems that he had raised, Herskovits offered a searching critique of the book by Jules Faine that Hurston had so enthusiastically brought to his attention:

No better illustration of this could be had than the outline of the book of Jules Faine which you sent me. I have read the parts of his work which have been published in *La Releve*. I quite agree with you concerning the scholarly nature of his approach and the careful way in which he has worked. But where he falls seriously short is in his inability to evaluate the African elements in Creole. Thus to attempt to derive principles of Creole phonetics from Norman French alone is the exact parallel of the work of Guy Johnson in his attempt to derive Gulla Island speech from Elizabethan English, which you and I both, I believe, feel to be not tenable. So not only would I not be interested in seeing this work published, but I should deeply regret its publication, as I believe M. Faine himself would were he to take two or three years and study the languages of West Africa as carefully as he has studied Norman French.[80]

Although he warmly offered to help her and to have her come to Northwestern, he ended with the admonition to go to the Bahamas "as soon as you can and eventually produce as fine a job describing Bahama Negro life as you did for the Florida and New Orleans folk you studied a few years ago."[81]

Unpersuaded by Herskovits's objections, Hurston wrote in late July to say that she would soon leave for Haiti after the big Maroon ceremony of the first of August. She coupled this information with a brief review of what she had learned in Jamaica. In particular, she emphasized that there existed a vital underground world of magic invisible to the authorities and the uninitiated. Questions that had long puzzled her, especially those that had to do with the widespread fear of poisoning, now made sense.[82] In reply, Herskovits wished her well, now resigned to her determination to go to Haiti, and expressed interest in learning more of the Maroon ceremony that had taken place in August. Most of the letter was devoted to addressing Hurston's concern that the Rosenwald Fund had decided to support Katherine Dunham, who was carrying out, Hurston claimed, the very proposal she herself had proposed. By implication, at least, Herskovits had some responsibility in Dunham's selection.[83]

Back in New York City, having already written *Their Eyes Were Watching God* and having learned that she had received a second Guggenheim Fellowship to continue her work in Haiti, Hurston wrote a long letter to Herskovits. Her letter ranged from "amazement" at the duplication of "American Negroes Tales" with tales from Jamaica and Haiti, a detailed review of the machinations of the Rosenwald Foundation, a new perspective on Katherine Dunham, and a critique of the role that the Maroons had now come to play in the political and commercial life of Jamaican society. As she had written earlier, Hurston distinguished between the official or public world of Maroon culture and the dancing that took place in the distant mountains far from public eye. For the most part, what one was allowed to see and what was officially celebrated as authentic was essentailly a government effort to provide entertainment for tourists. In Hurston's eyes only the use of primitive medicines was of genuine interest since it continued to be used beyond the control of the government.[84]

In reply, Herskovits made another effort to clarify the Rosenwald-Katherine Dunham connection and somewhat defensively conceded Hurston's criticisms of the Maroons.

I was glad to hear about the Maroons. Of course I was there only a part of the day, and wanted to get an impression of their physical type as much as anything else. It is perfectly possible that there is more of interest in other parts of Jamaica, though I suppose it depends again on what you are looking for as to how you will evaluate the significance of a given fulture [*sic*] for your work.[85]

He closed, affirming Hurston's comments regarding the essential unity of folkloric stories while taking the opportunity to assert his own authoritative voice: "Of course the unity of Negro folklore all over the World is well recognized, and one need only compare the large collection of tales from Jamaica, Haiti, the Bahamas, and other parts of the West Indies, with American Negro stories and West African ones to recognize the existence of this unity."[86]

Robert Hemenway has directed detailed attention to what he calls "the Rosen-wald-Columbia fiasco" and Hurston's whereabouts prior to her arrival in Haiti, but nothing is said of her contact with Benedict or with Herskovits. Others, however, have suggested that Benedict should not be entirely ignored. Given his reading of *Mules and Men* as a "kind of cultural autobiographical pharmaceutics," Houston Baker, for example, argues that Hurston's text, much like the arts of Hoodoo itself, functions to kill "the kingly script of a mentor's ['King Boas'] and a patron's ['Queen R. Osgood Mason'] power."[87] Baker links this challenge with the more general challenge of feminist anthropological discourse in the 1920s: "The pharmakon, as poison, may well be deemed Hurston's contamination of the formal discourse and terms of the anthropology of her own era—an era in which womanist concerns such as those of Ruth Benedict, Margaret Mead, and Elsie Clews Parson were proliferating."[88] Baker, however, claims too much (Benedict remained close to Boas and Boasian anthropology) and too little (Benedict's "womanist concerns," as did Hurston's, encompassed much more than the "formal discourse and terms" of anthropology). Also, Gwendoly Mikell, in "When Horses Talk: Reflections on Zora Neale Hurston's Haitian Anthropology," argues that Benedict's impact on Hurston was most evident in her Caribbean fieldwork (possible traces of "Haitian personality as violent and cruel . . . characterizations of Jamaica as the rooster's egg") but that Hurston's sensitivity to the historical experience of colonial peoples distinguished her work from that of Benedict's:

Hurston saw colonial domination as a major causal factor in shaping the cultural forces within Haiti's history. She pinpointed Haiti's difficult racial history and the struggles for liberation and against mulatto/black domination as causal factors in accounting for the personality configuration that she observed in rich and poor alike. This nascent element of causation . . . separates Hurston's approach from the straight cultural configurationism of Benedict.[89]

Mikell importantly notes that Hurston's formal concerns as a professional anthropologist (an "inside" personalized and subjective view combined with an "outside," scholarly and analytical view) were joined with "the fact of her blackness," her own complex identification with the history of peoples brought from Africa as slaves. It is important to ask, however, whether Hurston's historical framework fully distinguishes her vision from that of Benedict's or whether the history Hurston presents is itself rooted in concerns both women shared.

Clearly, as Hurston's letters suggest, her interests in the African diaspora, African American culture, and Jamaica/Haiti were most directly shared with Melville Herskovits. And in *Tell My Horse*, she praised him as the one person who had written about voodoo (his *Life in a Haitian Village*) and actually knew something about it.[90] As Mikell suggests, however, "Benedict's impact on Hurston . . . was most evident in the Caribbean fieldwork."[91] I would also suggest that two aspects of *Patterns of Culture*, in particular, were important to Hurston and she used them to her own advantage. First, *Tell My Horse* serves to reveal something of Jamaican and Haitian culture, its African roots, and the efflorescence of these roots in American soil. At the same time, and unlike Benedict, Hurston also drew sharp contrasts that decidedly privileged aspects of the American experience as well as the American experience itself. Thus, whereas Claude McKay had celebrated Touissant L'Ouverture, Hurston marked his triumph as the beginning of a long period of stagnation that contrasted with the phenomenal growth of the United States.[92] Secondly, this "we" but "they/not they" dichotomy, to paraphrase Clifford Gertz, simultaneously served to frame Hurston's role as an outsider and to establish and comment on her marginal status as a woman in a society dominated by men.

Tell My Horse is both anthropology and history. The one, anthropology, documents as well as interprets the complex spiritual world Hurston first glimpsed in New Orleans. The other, history, frames Jamaica and Haiti externally and chronicles, to some degree, political and social life internally. Although it is impossible to separate the two completely, Hurston, for the most part, treated the sacred and the secular as separate realms of experience. Where they did merge, primarily, was in Hurston's own complex response to what she learned and experienced in her dual roles as anthropologist and historian and in her dual perspectives as insider and outsider. As Gwendoly Mikell writes,

Hurston's ethnography is thus a delicate balance between the calm insider's and the agitated outsider's perspectives. Literature and a flair for the cloaking of reality in "etherial garb" became the medium by which the two perspectives were brought together. Often Hurston was outraged by color discrimination, male chauvinism and class oppression. At such points she made no pretense of being a value-free analyst, but transformed her rage into a worded-blade which sliced through deceptive layers of culture.[93]

However, if Hurston's rage was transformed "into a worded-blade," she did not simply address the history and culture of a colonized people but the language and politics of those who now made history. Thus, Hurston thrust her "word-blade" deepest into those whose politics was little more than rhetoric. Although she drew a parallel with a "tongue-and-lung era" in the American past, it was clear that "Race Men" continued to orate in the American present.

These talking patriots, who have tried to move the wheels of Haiti on wind from their lungs, are blood brothers to the empty wind bags who have done so much to nullify opportunity among the American Negroes. The Negroes of the United States have passed through a tongue-and-lung era that is three generations long. These "Race Men's" claim to greatness being the ability to mount any platform at short notice and rattle the bones of Crispus Attucks.[94]

And the language of these "talking patriots" was grounded in the more general language of a culture that conditioned women to be silent but adoring appendages of men:

If you try to talk sense, they [a lot of darkish men] look at you right pitifully as if to say, "What a pity! That mouth that was made to supply some man (and why not me) with kisses, is spoiling itself asking stupidities about banana production and wages!" It is not that they try to put you in your place, no. They consider that you never had any. If they think about it at all, they think that they are removing you from MAN's place and then granting you the privilege of receiving his caresses and otherwise ministering to his comfort when he has time to give you for such matters.[95]

As a consequence, doers, not talkers, were Hurston's prescription for the social needs of the country. However, whether a core of brilliant young Haitian intellectuals could overcome the one factor ("that habit of lying") that Hurston singled out as "responsible for Haiti's tragic history" remained to be seen. The stakes were high, for "gazing across the Frontier with a steely eye" was the dynamic and forceful president of Santo Domingo, "Trujillo, the Ever-Ready."

Trujillo's imperial gaze serves, in fact, to divide the book. From this point on, subsequent chapters move deeper and deeper into the spirit world of voodoo.[96] The previous emphasis on history, politics, and class and color consciousness was now subordinated to the dynamics and passions of a world divided between good Rada gods (headed by *Damballah*) and evil Petro gods (headed by one spirit with three names—Baron *Samedi*, Baron *Cimeterre*, and Baron *Crois*). Hurston, however, was not one to leave unqualified the pivotal role she herself gave to Trujillo. Trujillo was clearly and only a warning, contrasting with those who "indulge[d] in the national pastime of blowing up a hurricane with his tongue." Trujillo was an outsider, though, and a political figure with a "steely eye" lacked the stature of one whose vision was both moral and intellectual. As a consequence, except for the short three-page final chapter "God and the Pintards" (a trickster tale), *Tell My Horse* concludes with the chapter "Doctor Reser."

Dr. Reser, the director of the state insane asylum at Pont Beudet, is a curious figure with which to conclude this book. Born in the Ozarks, "where Missouri laps over on Arkansas," he was a former navy man, a brilliant conversationalist (his subjects included "philosophy, esoterics, erotica, travel, physics, psychology, chemistry, geology, religions, and folk lore"), a teller of folk tales with a "hill-billy brogue," and a voodoo priest. And yet this white American "is better known than any other living character in Haiti."[97] More than just known, he is adored. Hurston, too, is clearly fascinated, visiting many times so as to enjoy the company of this exceedingly kind and brilliant man.

In Hurston's dramatic concluding paragraph, an apotheosis to Dr. Reser's mind and spirit, he is physically as well as psychically transformed into the very soul of Haiti itself:

Dr. Reser began to tell of his experiences while in the psychological state known as possession. Incident piled on incident. A new personality burned up the one that had eaten supper with us. His blue-grey eyes glowed, but at the same time they drew far back into his head as if they went inside to gaze on things kept in a secret place. After awhile he began to speak. He told of marvelous revelations of the Brave Guede cult. And as he spoke, he moved farther and farther from known land and into the territory of myths and mists. Before our very eyes, he walked out of his Nordic body and changed. Whatever the stuff of which the soul of Haiti is made, he was that. You could see the snake god of Dahomey hovering about him. Africa was in his tones. He throbbed and glowed. He used English words but he talked to me from another continent. He was dancing before his gods and the fires of Shango played about him. Then I knew how Moses felt when he beheld the burning bush with a fiery ego and I had never seen a man who dwelt in flame, who was coldly afire in the pores. Perhaps some day I shall visit his roomy porch again and drink his orangeade and listen to him discourse on Aristotle, but even in the midst of it, I shall remember his hour of fire.[98]

Perhaps Hurston saw in Dr. Reser the perfect Boasian, this "well-read man of science [and this] credulous man of emotions." Though an outsider, he was simultaneously an insider, a man who found "his soul and his peace in the African rituals of Haiti." However much she identified with him (at least became self-conscious enough of her own professional stature while in his presence to tell the reader of her anthropological skills), Hurston was unable to cross the spiritual threshold he had crossed.[99] Haiti was not her home. Her soul was to be found in the more familiar landscape of Florida. Although written in Haiti, *Their Eyes Were Watching God* takes us back to Eatonville and the "tongueless, earless, eyeless conveniences" who crowded the porch of Joe Clarke's store.

John D. Kalb, in "The Anthropological Narrator of Hurston's *Their Eyes Were Watching God*," and Hazel Carby, in "The Politics of Fiction, Anthropology and the Folk: Zora Neale Hurston," not only provide provocative interpretations of Hurston's novel but explore, as well, her debt to Boasian anthropology. Kalb argues, for example, that Hurston's complex use of various narrative voices, the voice of the narrator (the outside observer) and the voice of the spectator (the inside participant), are rooted in the methodological concerns she first learned at Barnard. As a consequence, not only does *Their Eyes Were Watching God* function on several narrative levels, but the story Janie has to tell mirrors Hurston's own effort to record as well as represent the very same people she and Janie grew up with. Carby, too, argues that anthropology provided "a professional point of view," but she is as interested in Hurston's existential relationship as an intellectual to this point of view as she is in the tensions within the novel's narrative structure:

Hurston, like Benedict, was concerned with the relationships among the lives and cultures that she reconstructed and her own search for a construction of the self. She lived the contradictions of the various constructions of her social identity and rewrote them in *Their Eyes Were Watching God*. Her anthropological "spyglass" which she trained on the society that produced her, allowed her to return to that society in the guise of being a listener and a reporter. In her fictional return, Hurston represents the tensions inherent in her position as an intellectual—in particular as a writer—in antagonistic relation to her construction of the folk as community. It is in this sense that I think Hurston is as concerned with the production of a sense of self as she is with the representation of a folk consciousness through its cultural forms.[100]

Although both Carby and Kalb distinguish their point of view from earlier approaches, they, too, focus on the question of voice and the language used to create that voice. As the title of Hurston's novel suggests, however, the act of watching (a question of vision) is the first thing that strikes the reader's eye.

The novel opens panoramically, with "the biggest thing God ever made, the horizon." But the horizon, though of divine origin, is also a social construct. As a consequence, there is a tension throughout the novel between the divine and the social as well as a tension within the social world, for it is the men who are the Watcher[s] who scan the horizon. At the same time, as Hurston suggests, there is a close link between sight and language: "There is a basin in the mind where words float around on thought and thought on sound and sight . . . there is a depth of thought untouched by words . . . deeper still a gulf of formless feelings untouched by thoughts."[101] As a consequence, the tensions within the social world are also reflected in the language of that world—the "thought pictures" that people pass around for others to see. Thus, as Janie returns to Eatonville and walks past Joe Clarke's store she immediately falls under the gaze of the men and women censorious yet jealous of her behavior. These sitters, who have been "tongueless, earless, eyeless conveniences" now have something to look at. And, in looking, the words begin to flow: "They made burning statements with questions. . . . Words walking without masters."[102]

Janie's dramatic entrance, however, is also a return, for she has been to the horizon and discovered not only something about the world but, most importantly, something about herself. Her return, then, complicates the opening frame of the novel, for Janie has fused both horizon and dream, something that neither the men nor the other women could ever imagine. In so doing, it is her eyes that have seen the God without as well as the God within.[103] To achieve this understanding, though, she first has to confront a world that separates both dream and horizon in thought and behavior. Marriage is the social form in which Janie's quest takes place, marriage first to Logan Killicks, next to Joe (Jody) Starks, and third to Tea Cake Woods.

Janie's first experience of self-awareness (her sexual awakening) is in the form of a vision while lying beneath a pear tree, a vision that becomes her measure of what marriage is to provide: "Ah wants things sweet wid mah marriage lak when you sit under a pear tree and think."[104] Her first marriage, at least to Mr. Killicks, reveals that "marriage did not make love." Although Joe Starks, when he first makes his appearance, "did not represent sun-up and pollen and blooming trees," he did speak for "far horizon." In running away with Starks, however, Janie learns he is little different from "Nanny who had taken the biggest thing God ever made, the horizon . . . and pinched it in to such a little bit of a thing that she could tie it about [Janie's] neck tight enough to choke her."[105] Janie's relationship with Starks, however, is especially important, for here the tension between vision and language is not only most acute but opens onto the moral center of Hurston's own vision.

Starks's unconscious way of initiating conversation, "I god," represents not only his powerful and ambitious ways but elides his quest "tuh be uh big voice" with the panoramic perspective that opens the novel. As a consequence, Starks's first act as newly elected mayor is to bring light to Eatonville. However, while Starks basks in the light of his own light, Janie realizes for the first time how much she stands in his shadow. From this point, on their relationship begins to deteriorate, until his death ends their escalating war of words.

Jody's death serves to liberate Janie not only from his domineering ways but from her own sense of limits and limitations. Looking down upon his still warm body, Janie "thought back and forth about what had happened in the making of a voice out of a man." Her empathy, however, also leads her to take a good look at herself in the mirror. Although Janie immediately feels the joy of liberation, "she had found a jewel down inside herself and she had wanted to walk where people could see her and gleam it around," Hurston consecrates her joy and moment of self-reflection. Not unlike her use of the sermon "Behold da Rib" in *Mules and Men*, Hurston reconstructs God's divine plan for humankind and interprets Janie's history within its moral radiance:

When God had made The Man, he made him out of stuff that sung all the time and glittered all over. Then after that some angels got jealous and . . . covered each one over with mud. Like all the other tumbling mud-balls, Janie had tried to show her shine.[106]

Thus, Hurston links her earlier naturalistic explanation—"There is a basin in the mind where words float around on thought and thought on sound and sight"—with the account of humankind's divine constitution—"stuff that sung all the time and glittered all over." The horizons of self are deep within, and deep within one can glimpse "the biggest thing God ever made." Between self and God, however, is the mud of life.

Janie's third husband, Tea Cake, is a vision of love itself: "He could be a bee to a blossom—a pear tree blossom in the spring." With Tea Cake's death, however, Janie is destined to live alone and return to Eatonville. When we last see her, she is climbing the stairs to her bedroom, bathed in the light of the lamp she carries: "The light in her hand was like a spark of sun-stuff washing her face in fire." Once in her room, though, she is lit from deep within:

The kiss of his memory made pictures of love and light against the wall. . . . She pulled in her horizon like a great fish-net. . . . So much of life in its meshes! She called in her soul to come and see.[107]

Seeing, an invitation to see, is the final line of the novel. Words, even if they do amount to more than "uh hill uh beans," are only "moonshine" unless everyone has done two things for one's self: "They got tuh go tuh god, and they got tuh find out about livin' fuh theyselves." Once done, however, words can be sunshine, for now they come from within and are not the pale reflection of another's light.

In her autobiography, *Dust Tracks on a Road*, Hurston writes, "My soul was with the gods and my body in the village."[108] It is a suggestive way to frame her life and her writings. Other perspectives she offers, however, are no less suggestive: "Light came to me when I realized that I did not have to consider any racial group as a whole. God made them duck by duck and that was the only way I could see them. I learned that skins were no measure of what was inside people"[109] How to sort out these and other self-representations is not always clear. However, as Judith Robey and Elizabeth Fox-Genovese both suggest, what these representations do have in common is Hurston's "struggle to evade categorization . . . and to erect an independent, authoritative self."[110] Perhaps, as Hurston suggests, this tension between self and "the constraints of group identification" dates from childhood, when "I was always asking and making myself a crow in a pigeons nest."[111] But, once she flew the nest and "the pigeon hole way of life," these unconscious promptings became conscious reflections, for with the "telescope of Anthropology" Hurston learned "to see herself like somebody else."

NOTES

1. Robert E. Hemenway, *Zora Neale Hurston: A Literary Biography* (Urbana: University of Illinois Press, 1977), 96. Hurston's interview with Cudjo Lewis, "Cudjo's Own Story of the Last African Slaver," appeared in the *Journal of Negro History* (October 1927): 648–63.
    2. As Robert Hemenway writes, "the Harlem literati had much to tell the Alabama students about the Renaissance in New York." Hemenway, *Zora Neale Hurston*, 105.
    3. Booker T. Washington to Dr. J. C. Hamilton, 22 March 1906, American Philosophical Society Library, Philadelphia, Pennsylvania.
    4. Arnold Rampersad, *The Life of Langston Hughes* (New York: Oxford University Press, 1986), 149.
    5. Initially, W.E.B. Du Bois had invited Franz Boas to speak at the Eleventh Conference for the Study of Negro Problems at Atlanta University (October 1905). Boas was unable to appear, but this invitation led to his going to Atlanta the following year.
    6. As William S. Willis has written,

Although Washington did not object to what Boas said, he did object to where Boas said it. Boas at Atlanta University was a coup for Du Bois, a coup Washington tried to minimize. In 1906, the enmity between Washington and Du Bois was at its peak, and Washington was doing everything possible to discredit and isolate Du Bois. . . . At this time, Washington's influence with the black press was considerable. This influence, based on long-standing friendships with editors, advertisements, subscriptions, and even secret ownership, permitted Washington to censor news coverage as well as editorial policy.

Willis also makes the interesting point that the only notice of Boas's address that did appear was in the *Southern Workman*, a journal published by Hampton Institute. Although Hampton was Washington's alma mater, Boas was a close friend of Hampton's president, Hollis B. Frissell (he once attempted to help Boas gain a large research grant from Andrew Carnegie), and Boas had helped Alice B. Bacon (a Hampton teacher) and the Hampton Folk-Lore Society in collecting African American folklore. American Philosophical Society Library. 22–23.

7. Reprints, for example, were sent to Archer M. Huntington (scion of the railroad family), George Foster Peabody (Wall Street), and Robert C. Ogden (director of New York City's Wanamaker's department store). Boas even sent a reprint to Washington himself. Willis, unpublished manuscript, American Philosophical Society Library. 24.

8. Ibid., 24.

9. Ibid., 25.

10. Hurston initially received most of her support from Mrs. Charlotte Osgood Mason.

11. During her first trip to the South, however, Boas expressed dissatisfaction with Hurston's reporting:

What you obtained is very largely repetition of the kind of material that has been collected so much. You remember that when we talked about this matter I asked you particularly to pay attention, not so much to content, but rather to the form of diction, movements, and so on. I would also suggest that it might be a good plan to lay more stress upon current superstitions and to get as many of these as you can. We ought to compare the superstitious beliefs that occur among the English speaking Negroes with those that occur among the Spanish and French speaking Negroes. Also practices that refer to marriage, birth, death, and other important events in life would be important. The methods of dancing, habitual movements in telling tales, or in ordinary conversation; all this is material that would be essentially new. . . . There is a very peculiar problem involved in the question of transmission of European tales, proverbs, riddles, games, and songs because the planters certainly did not bring along much of it and the question is who the Europeans were from whom all this material was obtained.

Boas to Hurston, 3 May, 1927, American Philosophical Society Library.

12. Hemenway, *Zora Neale Hurston*, 123.

13. Ibid., 159–60.

14. As Robert Hemenway writes,

Although anthropology and art are not incompatible vocations, they can imply different uses of personal experience. When Hurston became fascinated with anthropology, she acquired the relatively rare opportunity to confront her culture both emotionally and analytically, both as subject and as object. She had lived Afro-American folklore before she knew that such a thing existed as a scientific concept or had special value as evidence of the adaptive creativity of a unique subculture. . . . The discovery of such scientific "facts" eventually made the imaginative truths of literature pale, and by 1927 her writing had become less interesting to her because of the growing sophistication of her anthropological study.

Ibid, 21–22.

15. Ibid., 101–2.

16. Margaret Mead, *An Anthropologist at Work: Writings of Ruth Benedict* (Boston: Houghton Mifflin, 1959), xviii.

17. Barbara Babcock goes on to explore the structural and imagistic relationships with Virginia Woolf's *The Waves*, a work Benedict was reading while writing *Patterns of Culture*. Babcock, "Not in the Absolute Singular: Rereading Ruth Benedict," in *Hidden Scholars:*

Women Anthropologists and the Native American Southwest, ed. Nancy J. Parezo (Albuquerque: University of New Mexico Press, 1993), 118–19.

18. As Robert Hemenway writes, "Hurston's correspondence with Hughes during the first year of her collecting trip was frequent and conspiratorial. It provides an unintentional documentary of the expedition. She saw the two of them as secret sharers of racial lore and as conspirators for the dramatic vehicle that would make it public. . . . At other times she imagined Locke together with them as a glorious artistic triangle; once she drew such a figure with LH and ZH at the base, AL at the apex." Hemenway, *Zora Neale Hurston*, 115.

19. Ibid., 63.

20. Zora Neale Hurston to Franz Boas, 29 March 1927, American Philosophical Society Library.

21. Zora Neale Hurston to Ruth Benedict, c. March 1927, Special Collections, Vassar College Libraries, Poughkeepsie, NY.

22. Ibid.

23. Ibid.

24. Zora Neale Hurston to Ruth Benedict, 19 June 1945, Special Collections, Vassar College Libraries, Poughkeepsie, NY. Hurston's words bring to mind feelings Benedict had earlier shared with Mead:

After the committee meeting yesterday Sapir came down to the house and spent the evening with me. But it was more trouble jollying him along than it could possibly be worth. I know enough to keep off conversation about you, but I praised Reo's book and talked of Papa Franz some. And he glowered. Oh darling, I'm glad neither you nor I am bound to care what his pleasures and displeasures are. . . . At last by all my wiles I got him to talk about the paper itself [my Configurations article]; "I was too lurid in my description of NWC": "Apollonian and Dionysian were too literary terms for him" "of course I said a great many things in the article that he'd used in his classes for years," etc. By that time I wasn't paying much attention to him any more but just giving thanks to God that there was no man living whose whims and egotisms I had to take seriously.

Ruth Benedict to Margaret Mead, 22 May 1932, Margaret Mead Collection Special Correspondence [1928–37], Manuscript Division, Library of Congress.

25. In her letter to Benedict, Hurston sketched the political and ethnic history of the Black Caribs, a mixture of Carib, Arawak, and Negro. Although initially three separate peoples, they merged due to the penetration of the Spanish and the British into the Carribean. As with the Black Caribs, Hurston noted that the Zamboes were also a distinct culture, a people living in isolation on the border of Guatemala, who continued to speak a complex language of their own. Most isolated were the Icaques who were especially fearful of the diseases that the Spanish had brought from the Old World. Zora Neale Hurston to Ruth Benedict, c. 1947, Special Collections, Vassar College Libraries, Poughkeepsie, NY.

26. Nancy J Parezo, *Hidden Scholars*, 3. Parezo, for example, quotes Margaret Mead's reflection in *The Golden Age of Anthropology* that "Anthropology . . . welcomed the stranger. As a science which accepted the psychic unity of mankind, anthropology was kinder to women, to those who came from distant disciplines, to members of minority groups in general," 3.

27. For this reason, the rationale for this book is based on the following: "The rediscovery of women scholars is a critique of the history of anthropology and a call for a reexamination of anthropology, academia." Ibid., 29.

28. According to Nancy Parezo,

By 1910, 20% of faculty were women: of these, 10% were professors, 5% associate professors, 10% assistant professors, and 73% instructors. Above the ranks of instructor, women were found almost exclusively in the professions of domestic science/home economics, English, music, and modern languages. In 1924, according to an American Association of University Professors survey, 4% of 680 women teachers were professors, 5% associate professors, 19% assistant professors, and 72% instructors. Women were still concentrated in English, home economics, and the Romance languages.

Ibid., 21.

29. Ibid., 118.

30. Ruth Benedict, "Psychological Types in the Cultures of the Southwest," in Mead, *An Anthropologist at Work*, 261.

31. Although Benedict was primarily interested in the Native American cultures of the Southwest, as were all of Boas's students except Herskovits, "The Science of Custom" initiates a concern that led to her important book, *Race: Science and Politics* (1940). Other publications include "We Can't Afford Race Prejudice," "Let's Get Rid of Prejudice," and "Race Prejudice in the United States," Special Collections, Vassar College Libraries, Poughkeepsie, NY.

32. This article, initially published in *Century Magazine* (April 1929), would later appear as the first chapter in *Patterns of Culture*.

33. Because of her work with Herskovits taking cranial and facial measurements in Harlem, Hurston was quite familiar with the scientific critique of race. Also, see Francoise Lionnet-McCumber, "Autoethnography: The An-Archic Style of *Dust Tracks on a Road*," in *Zora Neale Hurston: Critical Perspectives Past and Present*, ed. Henry Louis Gates, Jr., and K. A. Appiah (New York: Amistad, 1993), 241–66.

34. Gates and Appiah, *Zora Neale Hurston*, xi.

35. In the rediscovery and early critical literature on the Harlem Renaissance, Darwin T. Turner's *In a Minor Chord: Three Afro-American Writers and Their Search for Identity* (1971) captures in its title the general opinion of Hurston held by even those who made the effort to discuss her out-of-print writings. For Nathan Huggins, Hurston had created uncomplicated, superficial "types." In 1972, however, Robert Hemenway challenged his readers to discover "one of the most significant unread authors in America, the author of two minor classics and four other major books." Hemenway, "Zora Neale Hurston and the Eatonville Anthropology," in *The Harlem Renaissance Remembered*, ed. Arna Bontemps (New York: Dodd, Mead, 1972), 190–214 . Hemenway's alert, together with Alice Walker's discovery and search for this doubly neglected writer, was a catalyst that ignited what has become a major focus of critical scholarship.

36. Henry Louis Gates, "*Their Eyes Were Watching God*: Hurston and the Speakerly Text," in Gates and Appiah, *Zora Neale Hurston*, 165.

37. Cynthia Bond, "Language, Speech, and Difference in *Their Eyes Were Watching God*," in Gates and Appiah, *Zora Neale Hurston*, 205.

38. As Hans Jonas has argued,

Since the days of Greek philosophy sight has been hailed as the most excellent of the senses. The noblest activity of the mind, theoria, is described in metaphors mostly taken from the visual sphere. Plato, and Western philosophy after him, speaks of the "eye of the soul" and of the "light of reason." . . . Sight, in addition to furnishing the analogues for the intellectual upperstructure, has tended to serve as the model of perception in general and thus as the measure of the other senses.

Hans Jonas, "The Nobility of Sight: A Study in the Phenomenology of the Senses," in *The Phenomenon of Life: Toward a Philosophical Biology* (New York: Dell, 1966), 135.

Not only has vision been privileged but, as Martin Jay notes, it could also lead to the denigration of language in several respects. As Jay writes,

Outside of the often maligned tradition of Sophism, language was deemed inferior to sight as the royal road to the truth. It was the realm, as we have noted, of mere doxa (opinion) instead. Rhetoric was thus banished from genuine philosophy. Even when the Greeks discussed verbal phenomena like metaphors, they tended to reduce them to transparent figures, likenesses that were mimetic resemblances, not the interplay of sameness and difference. "To produce a good metaphor," Aristotle claimed in his *Poetics*, "is to see a likeness."

Jay, *Downcast Eyes: The Denigration of Vision in Twentieth-Century French Thought* (Berkeley: University of California Press, 1994), 33. Also see Stephen A. Tyler, "The Vision Quest in the West, Or What the Mind's Eye Sees," *Journal of Anthropological Research* 40 (spring 1984): 23–39.

39. Houston A. Baker, Jr., "Workings of the Spirit: Conjure and the Space of Black Women's Creativity," in Gates and Appiah, *Zora Neale Hurston*, 282.

40. Mary Helen Washington, "I Love the Way Janie Crawford Left Her Husbands: Emergent Female Hero," in Gates and Appiah, *Zora Neale Hurston*, 98–109.

41. Ibid., 105.

42. In his seminal article "On Alternating Sounds," Franz Boas likened mishearing to "sound blindness." And in "Characteristics of Negro Expression," Hurston not only singled out an African American genius for dramatic action and self-dramatization but celebrated the use of language as "the interpretation of . . . English . . . in terms of pictures." Zora Neale Hurston, *The Sanctified Church* (Berkeley: Turtle Island Foundation, 1981), 49.

43. Locke, *The New Negro* (New York: Antheneum, 1992), 5.

44. W.E.B. Du Bois, "Of Our Spiritual Strivings," in *The Souls of Black Folk* (New York: Penguin Books, 1989), 5.

45. Hurston, *Their Eyes Were Watching God* (Urbana: University Illinois Press, 1980), 285.

46. As Cheryl A. Wall suggests, "the issues of sexual politics . . . soon prove to be the subject of the first section of *Mules and Men*." Wall, "Mules and Men and Women: Zora Neale Hurston's Strategies of Narration and Visions of Female Empowerment," *Black American Literature Forum* 23 (winter 1989): 663.

47. Ibid., 661–80.

48. Ibid., 671.

49. Hurston, *Mules and Men* (New York: Negro University Press, 1969), 180–81.

50. Although *Mules and Men* was created from Hurston's field notes, it is not clear that this sermon was not one of her "in between" inventions. In this respect, Hurston herself plays the role of the outsider, the jackleg preacher who voices thoughts women in the village were unable, or unwilling, to express. "Full of tremors," Hurston wrote to Boas asking if he would write an introduction to *Mules and Men*. Her fear was that Boas would find the book too "unscientific" since her publisher (Lippincott) was fearful that the book was too technical for the average reader. Her strategy, as she explained to Boas, was to insert "the between story conversation and business" that, though true, were for the "sake of the average reader." To strengthen her plea, Hurston argued that no one knew more folklore than Boas and Benedict. For this reason, if Benedict would also read the manuscript and offer editorial suggestions, Hurston was confident that *Mules and Men* would help to teach the public and not simply add to the "enormous amount of loose writing [that] is being done." Boas finally

agreed to Hurston's appeal. Zora Neale Hurston to Franz Boas, 20 August 1934 in Hemenway, *Zora Neale Hurston*, 163–64.

51. Hurston, *Mules and Men*, 229.

52. Ibid., 230. Hurston's comments are rooted in speculations she first tried out on Langston Hughes. In particular, Hurston argued that Christianity was originally a form of nature worship no less rooted than conjure in magic and myth. Thus, Hurston detailed to Hughes her conviction that the Trinity and baptism had evolved from water and fire worship and that cannibalism later took form as the sacrament. Zora Neale Hurston to Langston Hughes, 30 April 1929, Beinecke Rare Book and Manuscript Library, Yale University.

53. Hurston, *Mules and Men*, 249.

54. Ibid., 249–50.

55. Ibid., 250.

56. Ibid., 269.

57. Ibid., 281.

58. Ibid., 18–19.

59. Baker writes:

She knows at the close of her work that she refused to craft a compendium of "negro Folktales and Voodoo Practices" that would satisfy dry, scholarly criteria of anthropology. Hence, she tacitly slips the yoke that even the eminent Franz Boas seems to put on her efforts in a preface that invokes Uncle Remus as the prototype of the Afro-American taleteller. . . . But Zora has not merely slipped the yoke or "turned the trick" on a limited anthropology by the conclusion of *Mules and Men*, for, surely, she has also reclaimed the whole soul of the human enterprise for her conjure. She has rectified the theft of the "soul-piece" and become her own patron's superior through initiation into a world that practices arts different from what she calls "the American pharmacopoeia,"

Baker, "Workings of the Spirit," in Gates and Appiah, *Zora Neale Hurston*, 302.

60. Barbara Johnson, "Thresholds of Difference: Structures of Address in Zora Neale Hurston,"in Gates and Appiah, *Zora Neale Hurston*, 139.

61. Ibid.

62. Zora Neale Hurston to Ruth Benedict, 17 April 1932, Special Collections, Vassar College Libraries, Poughkeepsie, NY.

63. Ibid.

64. Zora Neale Hurston to Ruth Benedict (undated letter) Vassar College Libraries, Poughkeepsie, NY. Hurston also thanked Benedict for the work she had done editing materials Hurston had sent her for her Hoodoo article that appeared in the *Journal of American Folklore*. The correspondence carried into the next year. On February 11, 1933 Benedict acknowledged Hurston's promise to pay for the reprints of her article and inquired about further material Hurston had for the journal:

I've got the manuscript of Tokula, but you took the unedited manuscript that was the result of your first field trip. Have you ever done anything with it, and can I have it back and have it edited here? I'd use it in one of the Journal issues. So send it back just as soon as you can.

Benedict to Hurston, 11 February 1933, Special Collections, Vassar College Libraries, Poughkeepsie, NY.

In a follow-up letter Hurston elaborated upon her financial problems, now that she had been cut off financially by Mrs. Charlotte Osgood Mason, and detailed possibilities of establishing an anthropology department in Rollins College (Florida). Hurston to Benedict, 23 February 1933, Special Collections, Vassar College Libraries, Poughkeepsie, NY.

65. Hurston also inquired if the Museum of Natural History would loan her a sliding caliper and a pair of spreading calipers, hopeful that with these instruments to take head measurements she could do something that would please Boas. Hurston to Benedict, 4 December 1933, Special Collections, Vassar College Libraries, Poughkeepsie, NY.

66. Although Benedict did not write a review of *Jonah's Gourd Vine*, she wrote her congratulations to Hurston and coupled her remarks with further business for the *Journal of American Folklore*:

I wonder where you are these days. Congratulations on your book. I enjoyed it, and was delighted at all the good reviews you got. Aren't you enjoying it? I am getting the Negro Tales from the Gulf States ready for the next number of *JAFL*. The list of informants is not grouped so that the state where you collected the tale can be decided. Send me your address so that I can sned [*sic*] youthe [*sic*] list to identify. Are chickens in the south fed on nux voromica? and why? Do you remember the tale? Is there any point to the story of rabbit's filling the air with dust from the rock when he danced? Or is it supposed to be nonsense?

Benedict to Hurston, 25 June 1934, Special Collections, Vassar College Libraries, Poughkeepsie, NY.

Herskovits also thought highly of Hurston's novel. In a reply to a letter that a Miss Marie C. Joyne had addressed to Hurston, Herskovits writes,

Your letter to Miss Zora Hurston has been sent by her to me with the request that I give you some references. I am afraid what you ask is a little difficult, since there is really no "psychology of the Negro," but actually a vast number of people who have attitudes and opinions, aptitudes and deficiencies much as the individuals of any large aggregate might have. Much has been written on this subject, but I must confess I do not have very great faith in most of it, as in the majority of cases, books and articles by white authors usually contain misinterpretation through misunderstanding, and of Negro authors, a similar misinterpretation through a desire to apologize for real or fancied defects.

Herskovits, however, did recommend Hurston's *Jonah's Gourd Vine*: "You will find much of what your are after in that. But definite books on the subject are either lacking or are not good." Herskovits to Miss Marie C. Joyne, 4 December 1934, Melville Herskovits Papers, Northwestern University Archives, Evanston, IL.

67. Ruth Benedict to Dr. Henry Allen Moe, 15 November 1933, Special Collections, Vassar College Libraries, Poughkeepsie, NY.

68. As the letter from the Rosenwald Fund concludes: "We are glad to cooperate in your further studies in an amount [$3,000] far beyond our normal fellowship awards because we believe you will greatly benefit by a full two years of study and supervised field work, and because we have such great confidence in the contributions which ultimately you may make to anthropology and to an understanding of the special cultural gifts of the Negroes." Julius Rosenwald Fund to Zora Neale Hurston, 19 December 1934, American Philosophical Society Library, 2.

69. Hurston to Franz Boas, 14 December 1934 in Hemenway, *Zora Neale Hurston*, 207–8.

70. Hurston to Franz Boas, 4 January 1935, American Philosophical Society Library.

71. As Herskovits wrote to Boas, "Zora Hurston is in Chicago these days, and she was up here last Sunday. It was the first time in over ten years that I had seen her and it was interesting to see how she has developed in that time. I was very well impressed with the kind of information she has apparently obtained in the Bahamas and in the South, and in hope that she will be able to get this out in somewhat systematic form." Melville Herskovits

to Franz Boas, 24 October 1934, Melville Herskovits Papers, Northwestern University Archives.

72. In her letter to Herskovits, Hurston explained that only he, of those who had studied with Boas, had the kind of interests and experience that could most help her prepare for her trip to Haiti. Even Boas, she reported, was somewhat puzzled by Benedict's suggestion that she [Hurston] should study linguistics, not clear, that is, how Pawnee or more generally the language of the Plains Indians might be of use to her. Hurston to Herskovits, 6 January 1935, Melville Herskovits Papers, Northwestern University Archives.

73. Ibid.

74. Herskovits to Hurston, 9 January 1935, Melville Herskovits Papers, Northwestern University Archives.

75. Hurston to Benedict, 6 March 1935, Special Collections, Vassar College Libraries, Poughkeepsie, NY.

76. Hurston arranged folk expression into five categories: Songs, Sermons, Children's Games, Woofing, and Instrumentation. Hurston to Benedict, 28 June 1935, Special Collections, Vassar College Libraries, Poughkeepsie, NY.

77. Hurston to Herskovits, 15 April 1936, Melville Herskovits Papers, Northwestern University Archives.

78. Hurston to Herskovits, 22 April 1936, Melville Herskovits Papers, Northwestern University Archives.

79. Ibid.

80. Ibid.

81. Ibid.

82. Hurston to Herskovits, 30 July 1936, Melville Herskovits Papers, Northwestern University Archives.

83. As Herskovits wrote to Hurston:

Let me, however, set you straight concerning Katherine Dunham and her program. The Rosenwald Fund is not responsible for her stay in Jamaica, since it is in who planned her program of field work. Needless to say, in had no idea that you were planning to go to Jamaica, though even had in known it, it would not necessarily have made any difference, since there is no reason on earth why two persons should not study the same people. On the contrary, there is every reason why this should be done, and it is for this that in have send students of my own into areas where in myself have studied. Incidentally, since Katherine Dunham is primarily interested in the study of dance, in do not think you will find her material conflicts with yours.

Herskovits to Hurston, 28 September 1936, Melville Herskovits Papers, Northwestern University Archives.

84. Hurston to Herskovits, 6 April 1937, Melville Herskovits Papers, Northwestern University Archives. In a letter to Henry Allen Moe, Hurston detailed the following: "It has occurred to me to make a collection of all the subtle poisons that Negroes know how to locate among the bush and [in] the use of which they are so expert. No one outside the hoodoo or bush doctors know these things. But as in am learning day by day more and more in think that in will be doing medical science a great service to identify these weeds so that antidotes can be prepared. The greatest power of voodoo rests upon this knowledge. Some of these bushes are quite marvelous. One of them in *know* will kill by being placed so that the wind will blow from it to the victim. Another can be rubbed on the clothing and enters thru the pores as soon as the victim sweats." Hurston to Moe, 22 May, 10 June, 1936 in Hemenway, *Zora Neale Hurston*, 229–30.

85. Herskovits to Hurston, 10 April 1937, Melville Herskovits Papers, Northwestern University Archives.

86. Ibid.

87. Baker, "Workings of the Spirit," 303.

88. Ibid.

89. Gwendoly Mikell, "When Horses Talk: Reflections on Zora Neale Hurston's Haitian Anthropology," *Phylon* (September 1982): 221.

90. Hurston, *Tell My Horse: Voodoo and Life in Haiti and Jamaica* (New York: Harper and Row, 1990), 204.

91. Mikell, "When Horses Talk," 221.

92. Hurston, *Tell My Horse,* 22.

93. Mikell, "When Horses Talk," 222.

94. Hurston, *Tell My Horse,* 75.

95. Ibid., 57–58.

96. After passing from the twilight world of the Zombies (the "bodies without souls"; the "living dead"), to the secret societies of human flesh eater variously known as the *Cochon Gris, Secte Rouge,* and the *Vinbrindingue,* Hurston concludes with a chapter on Guede, the one entirely Haitian god that represented as well as voiced the conscious and unconscious concerns of the common people. Ibid., 219–36.

97. Ibid., 246.

98. Ibid., 257.

99. As Robert Hemenway writes,

Zora Hurston was convinced that her illness and her voodoo studies were related. She had learned how horse hair chopped fine and put into one's food could kill, how gleanings from a curry comb were sometimes hidden in vegetables. . . . She backed off from continuing intense research and began to make plans to finish *Tell My Horse* on American soil. She was forced to admit that she could not "pretend to give full account of either voodoo or voodoo gods." She had gone deeply enough into the Caribbean night.

Hemenway, *Zora Neale Hurston,* 248.

100. Hazel Carby, "The Politics of Fiction, Anthropology, and the Folk: Zora Neale Hurston," in *New Essays on Their Eyes Were Watching God,* ed. Michael Awkward (New York: Cambridge University Press, 1990), 80–81. in would only add to Carby's extremely insightful analysis that, as in have argued, the tension she addresses was itself rooted in the Boasian school of anthropology.

101. Hurston, *Their Eyes Were Watching God,* 43. Hurston's conception of thought and feeling reminds one of Alain Locke's similar formulation in his dissertation, "The Problem of Classification in the Theory of Value." Ph.D. diss, Harvard University, 1918.

102. Hurston, *Their Eyes Were Watching God,* 10.

103. As Martin Jay has written, "the eye is not only, as the familiar cliches would have it, a 'window on the world,' but also a 'mirror of the soul.' " Martin Jay, *Downcast Eyes,* 10.

104. Hurston, *Their Eyes Were Watching God,* 43.

105. Ibid., 138.

106. Ibid., 138–39. It is interesting to note that in her personal relationships Hurston also employed images of light to conceptualize a sense of self-identity and personal self-worth. In a long and emotional letter to the anthropologist Jane Belo, for example, Hurston encouraged her to escape her dependency on those too blind to see her real worth. Invisible to others she was also invisible to herself. Only if she dared not to conform to the expectations

of others, Hurston argued, would she discover the "inner light" of her real and valuable self. Hurston to Belo, 3 December 1938, Margaret Mead Papers, Manuscript Division, Library of Congress.

107. Hurston, *Their Eyes Were Watching God*, 286.

108. Hurston, *Dust Tracks on a Road* (Urbana: University of Illinois Press, 1984), 235.

109. Ibid.

110. Judith Robey, "Generic Strategies in Zora Neale Hurston's *Dust Tracks on a Road*," *Black American Literature Forum* 24 (winter 1990): 668–69. And as Elizabeth Fox-Genovese writes, "She [Hurston] aspires, in some way, to transcend the constraints of group identification. By insisting on being a self independent of history, race, and gender, she comes close to insisting on being a self independent of body." Fox-Genovese, "To Write My Self: The Autobiographies of Afro-American Women," in *Feminist Issues in Literary Scholarship*, ed. Shari Benstock (Bloomington: Indiana University Press, 1987), 176.

111. Hurston, *Dust Tracks*, 33–34.

Afterword

In response to the breakdown of political and aesthetic consensus in America ("left and right") and with the American Renaissance as an interpretive touchstone, Sacvan Berkovitch has recently addressed the question of ideology so as to explore new ways to imagine social and cultural coherence. To succeed, he suggests, means "taking the American Renaissance out of the realm of cultural schizophrenia which was the legacy of the old consensus, and relocating it firmly in history."[1] It is understood, however, that ambiguity and the "energizing tensions" to be found in the genius and writings of Herman Melville best represent the history that needs to be reclaimed. Above all, Berkovitch searches for answers more complex than what he sees as the simplifications that mark contemporary discourse:

The American way is to turn potential conflict into a quarrel about fusion or fragmentation; a continual oscillation between harmony-in-diversity and diversity-in-harmony. It is the hermeneutics of laissez-faire. All conflicts are obviated by the continual flow of the one into the many, and the many into the one.[2]

Thus, "with Melville's counter-model in mind," Berkovitch concludes, "let me urge that the option need not be limited to consensus or multiplicity."[3]

Berkovitch's several considerations help to direct our attention to the ambiguous presence that another renaissance, the Negro or Harlem Renaissance, has had in past and recent interpretations. Although "schizophrenia" is too strong a term to frame this scholarship, both Houston A. Baker, Jr. and George Hutchinson reject (1) earlier representations of the renaissance as a "failure" and (2) the use of "failure" as a conceptual key to understand not only the past but also the present. For both men the major failure they see is in the interpretive responses themselves, especially as the critical concerns of "high modernism" inform this judgment. Given this, however, each constructs a past that bears little resemblance to that of the other, grounding their own accounts in a modernism consistent with what they argue to be the intellectual and cultural space of that time and place.[4] Thus, Baker configures the renaissance exclusively within an African American vernacular tradition. What he calls "the mastery of form" and "the deformation of mastery" represents the boundaries of racial consciousness that frame the unique historical and cultural identity of African Americans. Hutchinson, in contrast, constructs a field of discourse broadly American that blacks and whites together brought into existence. In so doing, Hutchinson makes "the forms of uncanonical, 'native' (white) modernism" central to the cultural dynamic known as the Harlem Renaissance.

Recently, Paul Gilroy in *The Black Atlantic: Modernity and Double Consciousness* has also addressed the question of modernity, but his approach, while it shares something with both Baker's and Hutchinson's, points to a very different understanding of its cultural and conceptual importance. Like Baker, Gilroy challenges narratives of modernity and ethnic and national identity that fail to come to terms with slavery: "Defenders and critics of modernity seem to be equally unconcerned that the history and expressive culture of the African diaspora, the practice of slavery, or the narratives of European imperial conquest may require all simple periodisations of the modern and the postmodern to be drastically rethought."[5] However, in contrast with Baker and in close agreement with Hutchinson, Gilroy is especially critical of arguments "where racist, nationalist, or ethnically absolutist discourses orchestrate political relationships so that identities appear to be mutually exclusive."[6] As a result, and here Gilroy's emphasis now bears a close resemblance to that of Berkovitch, Gilroy establishes his goal to be "the theorisation of creolisation, métissage, mestizage, and hybridity . . . ways of naming the processes of cultural mutation and restless (dis)continuity that exceed racial discourse and avoid capture by its agents."[7] In the context of these theoretical considerations, he discusses Du Bois and what Gilroy calls "the genre of modernist writing he [Du Bois] inaugurated in *The Souls of Black Folk.*"

What Gilroy understands to be modern in Du Bois's writings is his ambivalence toward "the antinomies of modernity" together with his effort to construct from these antinomies the historical and cultural identity of African Americans. As a consequence, Gilroy argues, Du Bois's works as a whole "produce a self-consciously polyphonic form" that simultaneously mirror both the complex world Du Bois sought to address and the problematics of his own self-awareness. As a result, *The Souls of Black Folk* is best read as "a narrative of emergence from rather than immersion in racial particularity." Not only are "the boundaries of the racial family/nation [thrown] into question" but "the closing chapters confirm the transformation and fragmentation of the integral racial self."[8] One sees in the tensions that Gilroy locates in Du Bois ("the tensions between the racial self and the racial community") the problematic of the one and the many that not only Du Bois but those soon to follow all struggled to come to terms with in one way or another.[9]

As all four of these scholars suggest, the question of representation is both a cultural as well as epistemological issue. As a consequence, arguments about the past are very much arguments about the present. For this reason, perhaps, it is the question of representation (even the quest for representation) that continues to attract us to the men and women of the Harlem Renaissance as we too confront a crisis of representation, a crisis that marks as well as symbolizes our own problematic times and our own problematic identities. Thus, Helen Carby challenges us in "The Quicksands of Representation: Rethinking Black Cultural Politics," that the Harlem Reniassance is itself a challenge to rethink not only the past but why and how we construct that past.

Carby's concern for the complexities of representation is more than a present-day dispute, an effort to give a new reading to dominant readings of the past. For the question of representation was itself a key issue that unified as well as divided the Harlem intellectuals. No question perhaps was more central yet more ambiguous and symbolically suggestive than the one posed in *Crisis,* "The Negro in Art: How Shall He Be Portrayed?" unless, that is, one considers Locke's later question, "Who and What Is Negro?" For this reason, Carby took the title of her article from a novel of the day, Nella Larsen's *Quicksand* (1928), and used this work to explore the "contradictory impulses of the Harlem intellectuals" in the 1920s. We continue to live with those contradictions, those "energizing tensions," for they represent our continuing effort to come to terms with our individual and collective identities, past and present.

NOTES

1. Sacvan Berkovitch, "The Problem of Ideology in a Time of Dissensus," *The Rites of Assent: Transformations in the Symbolic Construction of America* (New York: Routledge, 1993), 363.

2. Ibid., 373.

3. Ibid.

4. As Baker I writes,

The ready acknowledgement that *The New Negro* is the first fully modern figuration of a nation predicated upon mass energies returns us to the present discussion's exploration of definitions of Afro-American "modernism." Locke's collection is not, however, the clearest instance of a full discursive engagement with such mass energies. Although his work set the stage for such an engagement, the editor left the task itself to a "younger generation."

Baker, *Modernism and the Harlem Renaissance* (Chicago: University Chicago Press, 1987), 91.

In contrast, Hutchinson concludes,

Thus, the Harlem Renaissance achieved only a toehold in mainstream thinking about American national culture and did not make it into the academy—because of racism, and because of the way the institutionalization of the fields of "American literature" and "modernism" took place. . . . The lesson to take away from this is not necessarily that the concept of "American culture" should be abandoned as an outmoded ideological construct. African American modernists were right to make claims on the national identity. It is up to us to reconceive what "American modernism" is.

Hutchinson, *The Harlem Renaissance in Black and White* (Cambridge: the Belknap Press, 1995), 447.

5. Paul Gilroy, *The Black Atlantic: Modernity and Double Consciousness* (Cambridge: The Belknap Press, 1993), 42.

6. Ibid., 1.

7. Ibid., 2.

8. Ibid., 138–39.

9. Given this, the understanding of modernism advanced by Sanford Schwartz deserves attention: As Schwartz writes, "Like the philosophers, the architects of the Modernist tradition explored the dialectic of form and flux, and were attracted to constructs that unify concrete particulars without suppressing the differences between them. Philosophers and poets were thus addressing the same issues in much the same terms, and this coalescence of assumptions and interests makes it possible to construct a framework that unites them." Schwartz, *The Matrix of Modernism: Pound, Eliot, and Early 20th Century Thought* (Princeton: Princeton University Press, 1985), 7.

Select Bibliography

The following bibliography is essentially limited to works that give, or importantly complement, a global reading of the Harlem Renaissance. Because of the widespread scholarly
interest in the Harlem Renaissance in the last thirty years, it is now necessary to limit a
bibliographical work to a particular theme or critical focus.

Baker, Houston A, Jr. *Modernism and the Harlem Renaissance*. Chicago: University of
    Chicago Press, 1987.
———. *Afro-American Poetics: Revisions of Harlem and the Black Aesthetic*. Madison:
    University of Wisconsin Press, 1988.
Bontemps, Arna, ed. *The Harlem Renaissance Remembered*. New York: Dodd, Mead, 1972.
Cooper, Wayne F. *Claude McKay: Rebel Sojourner in the Harlem Renaissance*. Baton
    Rouge: Louisiana State University Press, 1987.
Davis, Thadious M. *Nella Larsen: Novelist of the Harlem Renaissance*. Baton Rouge:
    Louisiana State University Press, 1994.
De Jongh, James. *Vicious Modernism: Black Harlem and the Literary Imagination*. New
    York: Cambridge University Press, 1991.
Douglas, Ann. *Mongrel Manhattan in the 1920s*. New York: Farrar, Straus and Giroux, 1995.
Fabre, Michel. *From Harlem to Paris: Black American Writers in France*. Urbana: University
    of Illinois Press, 1991.
Floyd, Samuel A. *Black Music in the Harlem Renaissance: A Collection of Essays*. Westport,
    CT: Greenwood Press, 1990.
Hemenway, Robert E. *Zora Neale Hurston: A Lilterary Biography*. Urbana: University of
    Illinois Press, 1977.
Huggins, Nathan. *Harlem Renaissance*. New York: Oxford University Press, 1971.
———, ed. *Voices from the Harlem Renaissance*. New York: Oxford University Press, 1976.
Hutchinson, George. *The Harlem Renaissance in Black and White*. Cambridge: Harvard
    University Press, 1995.

Ikonné, Chidi. *From Du Bois to Van Vechten: The Early New Negro Literature, 1903-1926.* Westport, CT: Greenwood Press, 1981.

Kellner, Bruce. *Carl Van Vechten and the Irreverent Decades.* Norman: University of Oklahoma Press, 1968.

————. *The Harlem Renaissance: An Historical Dictionary for the Era.* Westport, CT: Greenwood Press, 1984.

Kerman, Cynthia Earl, and Richard Eldridge. *The Lives of Jean Toomer.* Baton Rouge: Louisiana State University Press, 1987.

Kirschke, Amy Helene. *Aaron Douglas: Art, Race and the Harlem Renaissance.* Jackson: University of Mississippi Press, 1995.

Kramer, Victor A., ed. *The Harlem Renaissance Re-Examined.* New York: AMS Press, 1987.

Levy, Eugene. *James Weldon Johnson: Black Leader, Black Voice.* Chicago: University of Chicago Press, 1973.

Lewis, David Levering. *When Harlem Was in Vogue.* New York: Vintage Books, 1982.

————. *W.E.B. Du Bois: Biography of a Race, 1868-1919.* New York: H. Holt, 1993.

————, ed. *The Portable Harlem Renaissance Reader.* New York: Penguin Books, 1994.

Locke, Alain. *The New Negro.* New York: Anthenum, 1925.

Rampersad, Arnold. *The Life of Langston Hughes 1902-1941.* New York: Oxford University Press, 1986.

Spencer, Jon Michael. *New Negroes and Their Music: The Success of the Harlem Renaissance.* Knoxville: University of Tennessee Press, 1997.

Tillery, Tyrone. *Claude McKay-A Black Poet's Struggle for Identity.* Amherst: University of Massachusetts Press, 1992.

Wagner, Jean. *Black Poets of the United States.* Urbana: University of Illinois Press, 1973.

Wall, Cheryl A. *Women of the Harlem Renaissance.* Bloomington: Indiana University Press, 1995.

Watson, Steven. *The Harlem Renaissance: Hub of African-American Culture.* New York: Pantheon Books, 1995.

Wintz, Cary D. *Black Culture and the Harlem Renaissance.* Houston: Rice University Press, 1988.

Index

About the Author

MARK HELBLING is Associate Professor in the Department of American Studies at the University of Hawaii, Manoa. He has also taught in Africa and Germany. His essays have appeared in such journals as *Prospects: An Annual of American Cultural Studies, Phylon, Negro American Literature Forum, Polish Review, Research Studies,* and *Ethnic Forum.*

ISBN 0-313-31047-5

9 780313 310478

HARDCOVER BAR CODE